PILLOW
OF STONE

OTHER BOOKS BY AL LACY

Angel of Mercy series:
A Promise for Breanna (Book One)
Faithful Heart (Book Two)
Captive Set Free (Book Three)
A Dream Fulfilled (Book Four)
Suffer the Little Children (Book Five)
Whither Thou Goest (Book Six)
Final Justice (Book Seven)

Journeys of the Stranger series:
Legacy (Book One)
Silent Abduction (Book Two)
Blizzard (Book Three)
Tears of the Sun (Book Four)
Circle of Fire (Book Five)
Quiet Thunder (Book Six)
Snow Ghost (Book Seven)

Battles of Destiny (Civil War series):
Beloved Enemy (Battle of First Bull Run)
A Heart Divided (Battle of Mobile Bay)
A Promise Unbroken (Battle of Rich Mountain)
Shadowed Memories (Battle of Shiloh)
Joy From Ashes (Battle of Fredericksburg)
Season of Valor (Battle of Gettysburg)
Wings of the Wind (Battle of Antietam)
Turn of Glory (Battle of Chancellorsville)

Hannah of Fort Bridger series (coauthored with JoAnna Lacy):
Under the Distant Sky (Book One)
Consider the Lilies (Book Two)
No Place for Fear (Book Three)
Pillow of Stone (Book Four)

Mail Order Bride series (coauthored with JoAnna Lacy):
Secrets of the Heart (Book One)
A Time to Love (Book Two)

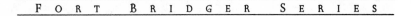

PILLOW OF STONE

BOOK FOUR

AL AND JOANNA LACY

MULTNOMAH PUBLISHERS

PILLOW OF STONE
published by Multnomah Publishers, Inc.

© 1998 by Lew A. and JoAnna Lacy
International Standard Book Number: 1-57673-234-7

Cover illustration by Frank Ordaz
Design by Left Coast Design

Scripture quotations are from:
The Holy Bible, King James Version

Multnomah is a trademark of Multnomah Publishers, Inc.,
and is registered in the U.S. Patent and Trademark Office.
The colophon is a trademark of Multnomah Publishers, Inc.

Printed in the United States of America

For information:
MULTNOMAH PUBLISHERS, INC.•POST OFFICE BOX 1720•SISTERS, OREGON 97759

Library of Congress Cataloging-in-Publication Data
Lacy, Al.
  Pillow of stone / Al and Joanna Lacy.
      p. cm. — (Fort Bridger series ; bk. 4)
    ISBN 1-57673-234-7 (alk. paper) 1. Frontier and pioneer life—Wyoming—Fort
Bridger—Fiction. 2. Women pioneers—Wyoming—Fort Bridger—Fiction. 3. Fort
Bridger (Wyo.)—History—Fiction. I. Lacy, Joanna. II. Title. III. Series: Lacy, Al. Fort
Bridger series ; bk. 4.
PS3562.A256P5   1998   98–29213
813'.54—dc21   CIP

98 99 00 01 02 03 04 — 10 9 8 7 6 5 4 3 2 1

This book is dedicated with much love
to my special friend,
Carolyne Elliott,
who has always been
and always will be
"a friend indeed."

JoAnna
Philippians 1:3

23274

PROLOGUE

T here are more stories about the Old West than will ever be told. The great migration westward in the latter half of the nineteenth century was an exciting time in the life of this young nation. The events that took place from the grassy west bank of the Missouri River to the white-foamed Pacific shore served to shape and mold this great country into what it is today.

With all its faults, the United States of America is still the greatest nation on earth. The authors of this book proudly salute its flag, defend its Constitution, and give honor to those men and women of our armed forces who have served, fought, and died on foreign shores to protect our own shores and to maintain the freedom and liberty that we continue to enjoy.

Stories of the Old West describe the North American Indians (friendly and hostile), forts, cavalry, military families, wagon trains, railroads, stagecoaches, mountain men, fur trappers, explorers, and gold seekers. They deal with cattle ranchers, sheepherders, range wars, boomtowns, lawmen and outlaws, bounty hunters, vigilantes, jails, gallows, hanging trees, churches, and saloons.

They show the contrast in the lives of gunfighters and drifters, preachers and bartenders, doctors and nurses, the courageous and the cowardly; and gallant men, women, and children.

Many who pointed their faces westward across the windswept prairies were looking through rose-colored glasses. They saw only opportunities for riches, excitement, and a new style of life that promised happiness and satisfaction. Few realized the vicissitudes of the journey—sickness and disease, trials and disappointments, graves beside the trail.

Only the hardy withstood it. Many turned back for home. If a person stayed, he either became strong or he died.

Not everyone who went west really wanted to go. Sometimes it was go or be left behind. With others it was a matter of survival. They had to leave the East and follow family members who had already gone west.

Because the West was what it was, and the people who settled it were what they were, stories naturally arose from their hardships, romances, and adventures.

In our continuing saga of Hannah Cooper, gallant woman of the West, another story emerges....

CHAPTER ONE

September 1870

T he morning air was sultry as the sun heated up the hazy New Orleans sky on Friday, September 26. A soft, humid breeze toyed with the moss-covered trees. Sunlight danced on the surface of beautiful Lake Pontchartrain to the north, and on the surface of the wide Mississippi River as it wended its way through the city toward the Gulf of Mexico.

Attorney Clay Haltom walked south along Central Avenue toward the offices of New Orleans's highly respected Knight and Knight law firm, where he had worked for the past year.

Haltom loved his job. He had been hired from a list of over thirty applicants, and if he did his work well, one day the sign over the door would read Knight, Knight, and Haltom, Attorneys at Law.

He entered the outer office where three secretaries' desks were being dusted by janitor Max Wendell.

"Good mornin', Mr. Haltom. You're in a bit early, aren't you?"

Haltom smiled at the old man. "Only a half hour, Max. I have a private meeting with the senior Mr. Knight."

"Mm-hmm. He came in 'bout seven. But I didn't pay any attention, 'cause he usually gets here an hour ahead of everybody else just about every day. His daddy used to do the same thing."

"Maybe that's why they've built such a successful firm, do you suppose?"

"Could be."

Haltom moved down the hall, passed his own office door, and came to that of Jason Knight. The door was slightly ajar. He tapped on it lightly and called, "Mr. Knight…"

"Yes, Clay. Come in."

Jason Knight was tall and handsome. His hair was just starting to gray at the temples. He smiled warmly at Haltom and stood up, then gestured to the chairs facing his desk.

As Clay Haltom took a seat, Jason Knight returned to his plush chair and said, "I asked you to come in early, Clay, because I have something important to talk to you about."

"Yes, sir?"

"As you know, we're scheduled to meet with the executives of the Daguerre Shipyards Company at ten o'clock this morning."

"Yes, sir."

"I'm going to tell you something that I believe will make you a very happy man."

Haltom smiled as he shifted his position on the chair.

"You will recall," Knight said, "that when we hired you last September, Dad and I told you that if you performed the job the way we expected you to, you would become a partner in the firm."

"Yes, sir."

"Well, you've done excellently so far."

"Thank you, Mr. Knight."

"The big test was when Thomas graduated from Harvard Law School last May and we brought him in and made him a partner when we've stipulated you would have to wait three years. Dad and I watched your attitude, Clay. If you had an ego problem, it would have shown up then. You never even blinked an eye."

Haltom grinned. "Mr. Knight, I completely understand the situation. After all, Thomas is your son. He ought to be treated as such, especially when he graduated at the top of his class, and with honors. You and your father have treated me well, and I have no complaints. I'm just thrilled to be a part of this firm, and Beverly is as thrilled as I am about it."

Knight smiled. "That's a lovely wife you have, and all three of your children are fine kids."

"Thank you, Mr. Knight. I only wish your father could have lived to watch Thomas develop as an attorney."

"I do, too."

"Clay," Jason Knight began, "you are aware that our firm has been managing the Jacques Pierre Daguerre estate for many years."

"Yes, sir, although I don't know any of the particulars."

"Let me tell you about the part that will make you a happy man. But first, I want you to know that Thomas is unaware of this information."

"Oh?"

"I'll tell him at the meeting with the Daguerre executives. I want to surprise him with the news. But I felt I should let you in on it before we get there."

Haltom's heart quickened.

"Let me start at the beginning. Jacques Pierre Daguerre established his shipbuilding company in 1839, on the banks of the Mississippi, three blocks from here. He did well from day one. He was a multimillionaire by 1847, the same year his only child, Julianna René, was born."

"Isn't she married to Jean-Claude LeCroix?"

"Yes. It was one of those arranged marriages, and from what I hear, not a very happy one."

"I see. And isn't it true that Jean-Claude is unwell?"

"That's what I understand. Cirrhosis of the liver. He won't be around much longer. Anyway, the Daguerre company built ships for shipping companies and navies from countries all over the world. Jacques grew richer and richer.

"Then the Civil War came along. Jacques and his wife, Collette, were caught in crossfire on the streets during the Battle of New Orleans and killed. Jacques had stated in his will that all of his holdings—the shipyards, the money he had invested in this country and in France, and the huge New Orleans mansion would go to his wife and daughter in the event of his death. Collette would become president of the company in his place. Dad and I drew up the will for him.

"The will further stated that in the event of both parents' deaths, their only child, Julianna René, would inherit the entire estate. If she was at least twenty-three years old when both parents died, Julianna would become president of the company. If she was under twenty-three, Charles Cartier, his faithful and trusted first vice president, would become executive vice president and run the company without Julianna actively involved."

"Do you mean that she would still have control because she would be president of the company?"

"That's right," Jason said. "The entire estate would be put in trust until Julianna turned twenty-three. Then she would become active president of the company, and Cartier would go back to being first vice president. George Barzun, who is now first vice president, would drop to second vice president, and Philip Callot, who is now second vice president, would drop to third."

Jason Knight paused for a moment as he looked at Clay meaningfully. Then he said, "The reason we're meeting with these men today is because Julianna René Daguerre LeCroix will turn twenty-three the day after tomorrow. The entire Daguerre estate will come under her management and be taken from the management of Knight and Knight, attorneys at law."

Clay nodded his understanding and said, "That means losing a large fee we collect each month from the estate."

Jason Knight let a crooked smile capture his lips. "Except that it's not going to happen."

"Excuse me?"

The grin was still there as Jason said, "This is the happy part. Dad and I, along with Cartier, Barzun, and Callot entered into a plan—well, I might as well be honest with you, we entered into a conspiracy—to take the company and all holdings from the heiress. It's perfectly legal. Julianna is about to lose it all, and she doesn't even know it."

"Sir, I—" Haltom's face turned suddenly pale. "Sir, I don't understand the reasoning behind this. Why would you do this to Julianna?"

"It's called money, Clay."

Haltom looked ill. "Mr. Knight, I don't know if I want anything to do with this. I—"

"Just stay with me for a minute, okay? We're looking at a total estate of $30 million, to be split like this: Cartier, Barzun, and Callot will each get $6 million. Our firm, since it has two partners, will get $12 million—$6 million for me, and $6 million for Thomas."

"How do I figure in, sir?"

Jason chuckled. "You're slated to become a partner in two years if you keep up the good work, right?"

"Yes, sir, but I'm not sure I can go along with—"

"With what we're doing to the rich girl?"

Clay nodded.

"Let's say that based on what you've just learned, you decide those three executives and I are bad men, and you go to the police with the story."

"Oh, Mr. Knight, I wouldn't do that. I just don't know if I can have any part in—"

"Let me finish. Now, Clay, you're a good man, and you have great potential in our firm. Just suppose you go to the police and tell them what you know. They could investigate all they wanted, but it's all perfectly legal. They would uncover no criminal act. You'd look like a fool, then, wouldn't you?"

"Well, yes, sir. But like I said, I wouldn't go running to the law. It's just that seeing that young lady lose everything...well, I don't think I could be party to it."

"Not even if it made you a rich man?"

"Excuse me, sir?"

"When I spring this on Thomas at the meeting, I'm going to remind him that you've been a faithful employee in this firm since you came here, and that your work has added considerably to our prestige in this city. And...you've brought a good deal of money to our bank accounts because of your excellent work."

"But you've paid me well, Mr. Knight."

"And you've earned it. Furthermore, I'm going to remind Thomas that you're in line to become a partner, and we can't afford to ever lose you to another firm. So what I'm going to tell Thomas is that we're each going to immediately share with you $250,000 from our $6 million. Could you use a half million dollars, Clay?"

Clay Haltom stared at his boss in open-mouthed astonishment. The color came back to his face, and a broad smile worked its way over his mouth.

"Think of the kind of house you could buy or build for Beverly and those children of yours, Clay. And all the nice things you could buy them...how happy they would be with all that money."

Clay finally found his voice. "Mr. Knight, I'm overwhelmed. I don't know what to say."

"Just say everything's all right, and you're going to stay with this firm and become a partner."

Haltom stood up, extended his hand across the desk, and said, "You've got my word on that, sir!"

The air was getting hotter and the humidity rising as Jason and Thomas Knight and Clay Haltom approached the river.

Thomas Knight, like his father, was tall and handsome. Clay had often noted their similar looks and manner of speaking. Now, as he strode down Central Avenue with them, he decided they even walked alike.

The shipyards came into view, stretching a half mile along the bank of the Mississippi. Giant derricks were silhouetted against the sky close to huge ocean vessels under various stages of construction.

The three attorneys entered the Daguerre Shipyards Company office building and were escorted by a male secretary to the executive offices on the second floor and ushered into the conference room. When they stepped inside, Jason Knight introduced Charles Cartier, George Barzun, and Philip Callot to his son and to Clay Haltom.

As they all took their seats around an expensive oak conference table, Cartier said, "Jason, when you set up this meeting with me, you asked for a few minutes to go over the whole situation. You have the floor."

Jason nodded. "Thank you, Charles. I haven't yet told Thomas what we're here for, gentlemen. I wanted to wait until we were all together."

Jason reviewed the history of the Daguerre shipyards and mentioned that he and his father had drawn up the will for Jacques Pierre Daguerre. He smiled as he said, "Gentlemen, the day is here. On Sunday Julianna turns twenty-three."

Young Thomas looked puzzled at the gloating looks and chuckles all around the table. He scanned the men's faces, then turned to his father and said, "What's so funny?"

Jason took some legal papers from his briefcase and laid

them on the table in front of his son. "Here, Thomas, read these."

The others watched Thomas's eyes as he began to read the papers. After a while, he looked up at Haltom. "Clay, did you know about this?"

Before Haltom could reply, Jason said, "I told him just this morning."

Thomas read on. Soon his eyes lit up. Then he looked at his father and said, "Thirty million?"

Jason laughed. "Well, we know he can read, gentlemen!"

"To be divided up how, Dad?"

"For these three men, and you and me—six million apiece."

Thomas's mouth fell open. "Six m—"

"Well, a little less than six, son. I propose that you and I each give Clay a quarter of a million for his part. After all, he's going to become a partner."

Thomas smiled at Clay. "I'll be glad to do that."

When Thomas had finished a second reading, he said, "Dad, you and Grandpa really did something here. The wording is perfect. It absolutely looks like Jacques Daguerre set it up so Julianna would be cut off from the entire inheritance and any link to the company when she turned twenty-three, and that his trusted law firm and company executives would divide the estate between them. You even left out the amount of the portions to be divided. It's ingenious!"

"Tight as a drum," Jason said.

"But how did you get this past Daguerre?"

"It was really quite simple, son. Jacques's eyesight was going bad when we set up the will. He trusted your grandfather and me. So we had him sign what he thought was the will, after we read it to him. Instead, it was the will you just read. The copy we gave Julianna after her parents were killed had no signature, but she didn't question it.

"We appended the part about the estate being in trust for her until she turned twenty-three. She and Collette read it, and Jacques signed it in front of them. Though Julianna was quite young then, she still understood what was going on. We were going to fix that part when we could get him alone and obtain another signature from him, but the Yankees came, and before the battle was over, Jacques was dead, as well as Collette. So we've had to ride this out until now."

Charles Cartier laughed. "Just wait till Julianna comes to the office on Monday, thinking that she's taking over as president!"

There was laughter all around.

"Yeah!" George Barzun crowed. "And just wait till she finds the sheriff at the mansion with the eviction notice in his hand!" He laughed even harder, and the others joined in.

CHAPTER TWO

At the same time the attorneys and the Daguerre Shipyards executives were meeting, the Daguerre family gardener, Grover Reed, was weeding the flower garden near the broad, sweeping front porch of the mansion.

Sunlight shone down on the huge white pillars supporting the porch, and dew from the previous night dripped from the massive oak and cypress trees that shaded the estate.

Grover Reed, a small, wiry man of sixty-five, had been with the Daguerre family since before Julianna was born. Two of the women servants, Pearl Littlefield and Hattie Vaughn, had been with the family just as long. Pearl was the housekeeper, and Hattie was the cook. The nanny, Sapphire Johnson, had been hired by Julianna just before little Larissa Catherine LeCroix was born nine months ago.

As Grover bent over the flower bed, he heard a horse snort and blow behind him. He turned to see Dr. Dan Mallory in his buggy. Young Mallory had become the LeCroix family physician three months earlier, when Dr. Gordon Winters retired. Mallory had been called in to care for the ailing Jean-Claude LeCroix, who at age twenty-nine was dying from cirrhosis of the liver.

As the doctor reined in at a hitching post near the porch, Grover laid down his small hoe and hastened toward the buggy. "Good morning, Dr. Mallory. Right nice day."

"Good morning, Mr. Reed. Yes, it's a beautiful day."

"Oh, here! Let me tie up the horse for you," Grover said as the doctor alighted.

"Thank you." Mallory reached into the buggy for his black medical bag. He waited for Grover to tie the reins to the hitching post, then said, "How's Mr. LeCroix doing today?"

"I think he's worse than when you saw him last week. Seems like he gets a little weaker each day."

Mallory shook his head sadly. "He's not going to get better, Mr. Reed. It's only a matter of time."

"Yes, sir. I know that. And so does Miss Julianna. This is pretty tough on her."

"But she's stuck by him. Most women would've told him to get off the bottle or get out."

"Miss Julianna's a sweetheart, Doctor. She really is. And she's had more than the liquor to put up with. Mr. Jean-Claude's parents gave him a great deal of money when he married Miss Julianna and told him he would get no more. They hadn't been married a year when Jean-Claude lost every dollar at the gaming tables. They not only live in Miss Julianna's house, but they live on the money she gets from the Daguerre Shipyards."

"Do they ever see his parents?"

"No, sir. They live in Boise, Idaho. Mr. Compton LeCroix is in the lumber business there."

Mallory glanced toward the mansion. "Well, I guess I'd better get in there and take a look at the man. Nice talking to you."

"You too, Doctor."

Mallory mounted the steps, lifted the heavy door knocker and let it fall. He could hear its metallic sound echo inside the huge house. A moment later, the door opened.

"Oh, hello, Dr. Mallory," said Pearl Littlefield, swinging the door open wider. "We been 'spectin' you. Please come in. Mistah Jean-Claude ain't doin' so good."

"That's what Mr. Reed was telling me, Pearl. But there's no way to repair what Mr. Jean-Claude has done to his body with the alcohol."

"Yes, suh. Miss Julianna knows that. But it's hard for her to face it."

"Of course," said Mallory, heading for the wide spiral staircase. At the top of the stairs, he drew up to Jean-Claude's bedroom door, which stood open. Julianna was bending over her husband's bed, trying to make him more comfortable.

"Okay if I come in?" Dr. Mallory said.

Julianna turned, and relief showed on her face. "Hello, Dr. Mallory. We've been expecting you." Her warm smile was missing, and the dimples in her cheeks were hardly noticeable.

"How's our patient doing?" Mallory said softly as he stepped into the room.

He looked down at Jean-Claude and could see that his eye sockets were sunken more deeply into his face than a week ago, and the whites of his eyes were a sickly yellow, almost blending into the color of his skin.

The doctor opened his black bag and said, "Jean-Claude, there's not much I can do for you, but let me see if I can ease your suffering some."

In the nursery down the hall, Sapphire Johnson was bathing chubby little Larissa Catherine in a small tub.

At nine months, Larissa had an infectious giggle, and her dark brown eyes sparkled with happiness. Her black hair was a glistening cap of wet ringlets against her head, and when she giggled—as she was doing now—a deep dimple twinkled in her right cheek.

Sapphire beamed down at the little baby, her teeth shining brightly in her dark face.

Larissa clearly adored her nanny, and the love on Sapphire's face spoke for itself.

As Jean-Claude LeCroix lay quietly while the sedative took effect and eased his tension, Julianna walked down the hall toward the staircase beside Dr. Mallory.

"Miss Julianna," Mallory said, "your husband's time on earth is drawing to a close."

"Yes, Doctor."

"I don't believe he has more than two or three days."

"Oh! That soon?"

"I could miss my guess, of course, but he's close to the edge. I'm sorry. I wish there were a way I could save his life."

"I understand, Doctor, that you've done all you can."

They reached the ground floor and headed for the spacious vestibule.

"I wish I could walk every person in the world past your husband's bed, Miss Julianna," Mallory said. "Let them take a look at what alcohol can do. It's a curse on mankind. But I'm afraid we're fighting a losing battle on that count. People keep drinking, families keep suffering because of it, and the drinkers keep dying before their time." He opened the front door and said, "So long for now, ma'am. Don't hesitate to send for me if he gets worse before the end."

Grover Reed was still working at the flower bed by the porch. When he saw Julianna and the doctor, he made a dash for the hitching post and untied the reins.

"Thank you, Doctor," Julianna said, and forced a smile to her lips. She followed him onto the porch and waited there while Mallory and Reed exchanged friendly words. As soon as the doctor drove away, she said, "Grover, I need you to run an errand for me."

"Yes, ma'am."

"Dr. Mallory just told me that Jean-Claude only has a few more days."

"Yes, ma'am. I'm sorry, ma'am."

"As you know, I've been planning to assume presidency of the shipyard next Monday, since my twenty-third birthday is tomorrow."

"Yes, Miss Julianna."

"I must stay by my husband's side until he goes. I need you to drive over to the office and give Charles Cartier a message for me."

"Certainly, ma'am."

Grover Reed hauled the buggy to a stop in front of the Daguerre Shipyards office building. Three men were just coming out the door, carrying briefcases, and seemed quite happy about something. One of them held the door open as Grover moved inside. He stopped at the receptionist's desk and said, "Good morning, Mrs. Halstead. How are you today?"

"Just fine, Grover," she replied, smiling. "And who do you need to see with a message from Miss Julianna today?"

"Mr. Cartier, please."

She turned about on her chair and spoke to the secretary who sat at a desk a few feet behind her. "Gene, I assume the meeting is over, since the attorneys just left. Do you know for sure?"

"No, but I'll find out. Hello, Grover. Which one?"

"Mr. Cartier."

Gene was gone less than a minute when he reappeared and said, "Mr. Cartier said you could come back, Grover."

When Grover approached the open door of Cartier's office, both George Barzun and Philip Callot were standing by his desk. Cartier was seated. All three set inquisitive eyes on him as Cartier said, "Come in, Grover. What's the message from Miss Julianna?"

Grover removed his hat. "Well, sir, Miss Julianna wanted me to tell you that she won't be able to come to the office to take over as president until Mr. Jean-Claude is gone. She would like for you to carry on as usual."

Cartier glanced at his cohorts, then looked at the gardener. "All right. Tell her we'll do that."

"Thank you, sir. It was good of you to see me right away like this."

"Nothing's too good for Miss Julianna," Cartier said.

Grover hesitated, thinking that all three men would have some message of comfort for Miss Julianna. When no one spoke, he turned and left.

As soon as Grover Reed was out of earshot, Cartier broke into a laugh. "Yes," he said, "nothing's too good for Julianna, and that's exactly what she's going to be left with…nothing!"

When the laughter had subsided, Cartier said, "Well, gentlemen, instead of Julianna finding out she's a pauper at eight o'clock on Monday morning, she'll find it out when she's served her eviction notice by the sheriff two hours later!"

Hattie Vaughn was busy at the cupboard when Julianna entered the kitchen. Tears were pooled in Julianna's eyes as she stopped near the kitchen table.

Hattie turned from the cupboard, took one look at Julianna's face, and said, "What did the doctor, say, honey?"

The tears spilled down Julianna's cheeks. "Jean-Claude won't live more than three days, Hattie."

The cook pulled Julianna into her arms and held her close, whispering words of comfort, much as she had done when Julianna was a little girl.

"Hattie, you know I've never pretended to be in love with Jean-Claude, but it still hurts to see him wasting away a day at a time."

"Sho' it do, honey. I admired you so much fo' bein' so kind an' good to Mistah Jean-Claude when all he has ever done is mistreat you and use yo' money."

There were footsteps in the hall, and Sapphire entered, carrying Larissa. Holding the baby in one arm, Sapphire used the other to hug Julianna's neck and said, "Honey, I was jis' gettin' Larissa up from takin' her nap when Pearl came an' tol' me what the doctor say 'bout yo' husband. I jis' want to tell you that I love you, and I'm prayin' fo' you."

"Thank you, Sapphire. I love you, too."

The baby was still feeling a little sleepy but was reaching for her mother. Sapphire put her in Julianna's arms, and the baby snuggled down close to her mother's breast.

Pearl came in at that moment and said, "We's right here with you, Miz Julianna, an' you can lean on us when... when—"

"Yes, I know," said Julianna. "And I love all three of you for it."

They heard the front door open and close.

Larissa stirred, and Julianna lifted her up to kiss a fat, rosy cheek. The baby gave her a lopsided grin and reached out to play with a brooch on her mother's dress.

Grover appeared at the kitchen door. "I got right in to see Mr. Cartier, Miss Julianna. He said they would carry on as usual until you can come and take over."

Julianna smiled. "I knew he would understand. Thank you, Grover."

The silver-haired man smiled. "My pleasure, ma'am."

Julianna turned to the cook. "Hattie, I think it would be best if you ladies and Grover don't have my birthday party as planned for Sunday. Not with Jean-Claude like he is."

"We understand, Miz Julianna," Hattie said. "Maybe in a week or two we can have a party fo' you."

"We'll see about that."

All day Saturday and all day Sunday, Julianna stayed close to Jean-Claude, though he slept most of the time. The doctor had left sedative powders for Julianna to mix with water and give to him often. From time to time she left Pearl with him to give Larissa some attention.

On Monday morning, Jean-Claude was in much pain. Dr. Mallory had left laudanum after showing Julianna how to administer it, and she had just given Jean-Claude a dose when Pearl appeared at the bedroom door and said, "Miz Julianna, Sheriff Will Bradley is here. He wants to see you."

A frown etched itself on Julianna's brow. "The sheriff wants to see me? Did he say what about?"

"No, ma'am. He's a-waitin' fo' you to come down."

Julianna nodded, then looked down at her husband and said, "I'll be back in a little while, Jean-Claude. You try to get some sleep."

The sick man gave her a pitiful look and closed his eyes.

Sheriff Will Bradley was standing in the vestibule, facing Grover, as Julianna drew up.

He was visibly nervous as she smiled and said, "Sheriff Bradley, I'm Julianna LeCroix. What can I do for you?"

"Mrs. LeCroix," he said with a slight quaver in his voice, "it is my duty to serve you these papers."

Julianna accepted an envelope and took out the official-looking papers. As she read them, the color drained from her face, and by the time she finished, a look of shock and disbelief filled her eyes. "Sheriff, how can this be? How can Jason Knight order me to vacate this property, saying that it no longer belongs to me? How can he say I am no longer the president of the company, and that the only money I now possess is whatever cash I might have in my possession? What is this? How can he say that all the investments my father put in trust for me are no longer mine?"

The servants looked on, wide-eyed.

Bradley cleared his throat. "Ma'am, I have nothing to do with the why of it. It is only my job to deliver the papers and to back up the eviction notice. You have until midnight, October 18. By then, you and your servants must be out of the house. If you are not, it will be the duty of my deputies and me to forcibly put you out. And if you read the notice closely, you know that except for clothing and other such personal items, everything else is to stay here."

Julianna hugged herself, trying to stop her body from trembling and keep control of her emotions. Her eyes were brimming with unshed tears as she said, "All right, Sheriff, you've done your duty. You may leave now."

Sheriff Will Bradley left without another word.

Jason Knight heard Julianna's voice outside his office door and his secretary saying, "Mrs. LeCroix, you can't go in there unless I announce you and Mr. Knight gives permission for you to enter."

Julianna's high-pitched words cut through the door: "I'll announce myself!"

The door flew open, and Jason Knight could see that Julianna's features were a deep red.

The secretary ran up behind her, saying, "Mr. Knight, I'm sorry! I couldn't stop her!"

Knight was on his feet by this time. "It's all right, Velda. I'll talk to Mrs. LeCroix."

Julianna moved close to the desk and shook the eviction notice in his face. "I want to know where you got the gall to send the sheriff to my house with these papers, Jason! What's going on? I want an answer, and I want it now!"

Jason Knight gave her a cool look and said, "The answer is simple, my girl. Your father left a will, and as his attorney, I am here to see that it's carried out to the letter."

"His will didn't say anything about my being thrown out as president of the company, losing all the trust investments and all the bank accounts!"

"Of course it did. I'll show you." He called toward the door, "Velda!"

"Yes, sir?"

"Bring me the Daguerre file. I particularly need Jacques's last will and testament."

Velda returned quickly and handed him the file, then left, closing the door behind her.

Jason opened the folder, pulled out the will, and handed it to Julianna. "Would you like to sit down while you read it?"

"I'll stand."

Puzzlement showed in her dark eyes as she read the will. Looking at Knight again, she snapped, "What's going on? This isn't my father's will!"

"It most certainly is."

"It can't be!"

"Do you know your father's signature?"

"Of course."

"Is that it at the bottom of the last page?"

Julianna flipped to the last page and studied the signature. "Yes, but..."

"But what?"

Fumbling with the other papers in her hands, she came up with her copy of the will and thrust it at him, saying tartly, "This is his will! You gave it to me yourself!"

Jason held her eyes and said, "Apparently you haven't read it."

"Of course I've read it! I reread it before I left the house today!"

"Then you didn't read it closely, or you would have seen that your father's signature isn't on it."

"Well, of course not! It's a copy."

Jason Knight smiled. "A copy that's not worth the paper it's written on. Without his signature, it's null and void."

"You planned this all along, didn't you? You low-down, slimy snakes have stolen my estate!"

"And there's nothing you can do about it. Remember, girl, you're to be out of the house by midnight, October 18. If you're not, the law will back me up and throw you out. And you'd better not take a stick of furniture, or I'll have you behind bars."

A long-bladed letter opener lay on the desktop. Julianna pictured herself snatching it up and plunging it into his chest. Instead, she whirled and headed for the door.

Jason burst into hoarse laughter.

She whipped the door open, and without looking back, entered the outer office. She could still hear Jason Knight's laughter as she passed through the door into the hall.

Back on the street, Grover helped her into the carriage. "We're going down the street to another attorney's office," she said.

Attorney Gerald Bromley handed Julianna her papers. "I'm sorry, Mrs. LeCroix," he said, "but there's nothing you can do. Without your father's signature on this will, it's meaningless."

Julianna was trembling all over. She started to rise from the chair and fell back. Grover was immediately at her side to help her up. He thanked the attorney and guided her out the door.

"Miss Julianna," Grover said, "you don't look so good. I'll take you to Dr. Mallory's office."

"No. Just help me into the carriage. I'll be all right if I can sit down for a few minutes."

Grover helped her up. When he had climbed in beside her, she looked at him with dull eyes and said, "What am I going to do, Grover? My husband is about to die. I have a little girl to raise and provide for. And then there's you and Hattie and Pearl and Sapphire. Where will the four of you go? What will happen to you?"

Grover put a fatherly hand on her shoulder. "It'll work out all right, Miss Julianna. Don't worry about us. We'll be okay. And somehow you and little Larissa will be okay, too."

Julianna bent her head down almost to her knees and shook her clenched fists. She was too angry to cry and too numb to scream.

Grover sat silently, patting her shoulder.

After a few minutes, Julianna sat up, squared her shoulders, and raised her chin. "Grover, you're right. It has to be okay. I'll do all I can to help you and the ladies find jobs, and I'll raise my daughter the best I can, even if we're going to be poor."

CHAPTER THREE

Julianna LeCroix stood before her servants and explained what had happened. She tried to hold on to the optimism she had built up in her mind and told them she would help them find other jobs. Somehow she and Larissa would survive this devastation.

The three women embraced Julianna, saying that even though she couldn't pay them, they would stay with her until the day she moved out. Grover assured her he would do the same. They also told her she had enough to worry about, and not to even think about helping them find jobs.

"So what do you plan to do, Miss Julianna?" Grover asked.

"I don't know. I don't have any plans yet. But I'll have to use what little money I have to rent a room, then try to find a job of some kind…and someone to take care of Larissa while I work."

"Oh, Miss Julianna," Sapphire said, "let me take care of the baby. I'll try to find a job that starts after you get home from work."

That evening, Julianna did not eat supper with the servants. She told them she was bone-tired and just needed to soothe her nerves by taking a hot bath.

Ever since Jean-Claude had become bedridden, Julianna had slept in one of the spare bedrooms. Alone in her room, she sat in the hot tub with eyes closed, soaking in fragrant bubbles.

She stayed in the tub for a long time, lost in thought as she tried to make some sense of all that had happened. Suddenly she noticed that she was shivering, and she realized the water had grown cold.

Julianna was still shivering as she dried off, and it wasn't all because of the cold air on her body. She clad herself in a nightgown and warm robe and walked down the hall to the nursery.

Sapphire had put the baby in her crib and was sitting in a chair beside it, reading her Bible, when Julianna came in.

The nanny looked up and whispered, "She's asleep, Miz Julianna."

The young mother moved close and laid a hand on Sapphire's round shoulder as she looked down at Larissa.

"Ain't that the mos' precious baby in all the world?" Sapphire said.

Julianna smiled. "Yes, she is, Sapphire. I don't know what lies ahead for us, but I'm going to do everything I can to care for her and make her happy." She bent down and lightly kissed a fat little cheek, then said, "I'm going to spend some time with Jean-Claude, then go to bed."

"You sleep tight, Miz Julianna. See you in the mo'nin.."

Julianna opened the door of the master bedroom where her husband lay. A single candle cast a soft glow over the room. The overpowering odor of Jean-Claude's illness made her feel a bit nauseous. She hesitated, then moved quietly into the room.

Jean-Claude did not stir. She could see the even rise and

fall of his chest and knew he was asleep. She wandered about the room, touching the many beautiful pieces of furniture, thinking of happier times. The urge to hate the men who had stolen everything from her welled up, but she fought it.

She was running her hands along the smooth cherry dresser when she heard Jean-Claude's bedcovers rustle, followed by a small moan. Julianna walked toward the bed and sat down in the overstuffed chair beside it. The soft candlelight showed her Jean-Claude's dull eyes.

"Can I get you something?" she asked.

"Water," the sick man said, licking his dry lips.

Julianna poured a cup of water from a pitcher on the bedstand and held it to his mouth. When he had drained it, she sat back down beside the bed. Jean-Claude reached out a shaky hand and took hers in his weak grasp. He looked into her eyes for a moment, smiled faintly, and closed his eyes.

Julianna observed her husband with compassion. Though he had brought this deadly illness on himself, it hurt to see him suffer. He had been her husband for three years, and he was Larissa's father. He'd made life miserable for her at times when the liquor was in control of him, but now, as he lay dying, her heart went out to him.

Jean-Claude squeezed her hand with what little strength he had and opened his eyes. He stared at her for a long moment, then said in a feeble whisper, "Julianna...I..."

Leaning close to hear him better, she said, "Yes, Jean-Claude?"

"I...I'm sorry for all the misery I've caused you. You've had a hard life living with me. I really do love you, and I wish I had treated you better. Can...can you find it in your heart to forgive me?"

Julianna felt tears collect in her eyes. She gently squeezed his hand and said, "I forgive you."

Jean-Claude swallowed hard and said, "And when Larissa

grows up…would you ask her to forgive me for not being a good father to her?"

"I will."

He managed a smile. "Thank you."

She squeezed his hand again. "You rest now."

Jean Claude closed his eyes and drifted into a troubled sleep, rolling his head back and forth on the pillow.

Julianna was still holding his hand, pondering his words, when she heard a light tap on the door.

Hattie Vaughn came in, carrying a tray. "I know you've got to be hungry, Miz Julianna," she whispered. "I brought you some sandwiches an' hot tea. You've got to keep yo' stren'th up fo' the tasks ahead."

Julianna gave her a lopsided smile, flashing one deep dimple, and whispered back, "Hattie, dear, you are a gem. I think I could eat a little something. Thank you."

Jean-Claude stirred and came awake suddenly. He gritted his teeth, and seeing Julianna beside the bed, he said, "I'm in a lot of pain. Laudanum. Would you give me some laudanum, please?"

"Of course." Julianna went to a small table and mixed the proper amount with water, then raised Jean-Claude's head with one hand and gave him the bitter brew.

"Thank you," he said weakly after he had drained the cup.

"You relax as much as possible and let the laudanum do its job," Julianna said, adjusting the covers at his neck.

It wasn't long before a deep, drug-induced sleep overtook him.

Julianna studied Jean-Claude's face in the candlelight. It was pallid and drawn. She wondered if he would live another day. Though she was weary, she couldn't leave him. She would sleep in the chair.

But first she went to the dresser, took paper and pencil out of a drawer, and began writing down things she needed to do.

Gradually the strain of the day overcame her, and she curled up in the overstuffed chair. As she laid her head back and closed her tired eyes, she could hear Jean-Claude's heavy, even breathing in the stillness of the room.

Julianna came awake, feeling a bit stiff from her position in the chair. She opened her eyes and looked around the room. The candle still burned faithfully.

She sat very still for a moment and listened for the repeat of some sound that might have disturbed her sleep.

Nothing. Absolute silence. She straightened her legs and stood up, her heart thumping hard. Leaning over Jean-Claude, she put her ear close to his mouth, then laid her head against his chest to listen for a heartbeat.

Jean-Claude was dead.

A lump rose in Julianna's throat, and tears surfaced in her eyes. She sat on the bed and took his lifeless hand in both of hers, bringing it up to rest on her cheek. Her tears sought release, and with a great gasping sob, she let them flow.

After weeping for several minutes, her tears subsided. Gently she lifted the covers and placed Jean-Claude's hand beneath them, then drew the covers over his face and left the room.

The next morning, the young widow sent Grover Reed downtown to wire a message to Jean-Claude's parents in Idaho, informing them of his death. The wire also told them of what had happened to the estate, and that Julianna and Larissa would be forced out of the mansion by October 18.

On Wednesday, a wire came back. The LeCroixs were

saddened by their son's death and expressed their regret that they would not be there for the funeral. The body would have to be buried long before they could travel from Boise to New Orleans.

The wire also contained an invitation for Julianna and Larissa to come to Boise and live with them. Arrangements had been made for money for travel expenses to be delivered to Julianna from a New Orleans bank. The LeCroixs would eagerly await her reply, telling them when to expect her and the baby's arrival.

The heavyhearted young widow gathered her servants together and read them the telegram.

"You're going to do it, aren't you, Miss Julianna?" Grover asked. "You and the baby will have a home that way."

Julianna looked at him sadly, then ran her gaze over the faces of the female servants. "All of you know that I've never been close to Jean-Claude's parents. I would rather not live with them, but this is far better than for me to try to earn enough money to support Larissa and myself, and to provide a decent place to live. I must do it for Larissa's sake."

"That is so right," Pearl said. "Bes' thing is fo' you and that sweet baby to go to Idaho. But we's all stayin' on right here till the day you and Larissa leave."

On Thursday, Jean-Claude LeCroix was given a pauper's burial. Overhead, the sky was iron gray and heavy with threatening rain. Only the servants and Julianna attended the funeral.

A minister hired by the undertaker stood at the head of the coffin and read a passage of Scripture, then offered a short prayer. He moved to Julianna, shook her hand and those of the servants, and was gone.

Julianna handed the baby to Sapphire and stepped to the

coffin. Two men with shovels stood nearby. The young widow tenderly caressed the coffin, spoke a few words as if she were talking to Jean-Claude, then nodded to the gravediggers.

Grover helped Julianna into the nearby carriage and handed her the baby as the other women climbed into the backseat. Then he settled onto the driver's seat and gave the reins a slight snap.

As the carriage rolled out of the cemetery, Julianna held Larissa close to her heart and heaved a big sigh. She lifted her chin, fixed her eyes straight ahead, and thought of the new life she and the baby would have in Idaho.

A few days later, the New Orleans bank delivered money to Julianna, and Grover was sent to the railroad station to purchase her tickets for the trip west. To get to Boise from New Orleans, they would go by rail to Chicago, change trains, and go to Denver. They would take a train north from Denver to Cheyenne City, Wyoming, then travel by stagecoach across Wyoming into Idaho.

Julianna and Larissa were scheduled to leave New Orleans on Saturday, October 11. Grover sent a wire to the LeCroixs that she and baby Larissa would arrive in Boise—if on schedule—on October 22.

In the days that followed, Julianna grew heavy of heart as the time drew near to leave. Giving up the mansion, the company, the investments, and everything her father had worked so hard to provide seemed unbearable. The thought of no longer having Grover, Hattie, Pearl, and Sapphire a part of her life was also grievous.

One evening, when Julianna was in the nursery with Larissa, Sapphire entered the room. She watched as Julianna held the giggling baby above her head and jiggled her. A long string of baby drool landed on her mother's forehead.

Julianna laughed and said, "Oh, Larissa! You got Mommy's face all wet!"

The baby was still giggling as Sapphire said, "You two ladies are gonna have to call it quits fo' the night. It's Larissa's bedtime."

"Did you hear that, Larissa?" Julianna said. "That bossy nanny of yours is here to ruin our fun!"

Later, when the baby was asleep, and Julianna was about to go to her bedroom for the night, Sapphire said, "Miz Julianna, could I ask you a question?"

"Why, of course, Sapphire. What is it?"

"Honey, pardon me, but you look awfully tired."

"Well, to tell you the truth, I'm not sleeping so well. There's so much on my mind. You know…having to go off and leave you and the other servants, maybe to never see you again. I feel terrible that the three of you have lost your jobs. I'm dreading the long trip with the baby, and I'm afraid I won't be happy in Boise. It's…well, it's as if my pillow is made of stone. I can't get comfortable enough to sleep."

The nanny grinned and said, "Honey, there was a man in the Bible who slep' with his head on a pillow of stone. His name was Jacob, an' he later was named Israel by the Lord. Did you ever read 'bout him?"

"I haven't read much of the Bible. It's something our family never did."

Sapphire went to the small table by her chair and picked up her Bible. "It's really a very interestin' story, honey," she said, flipping pages. "Let me show it to you. Here…read it to me out loud." As she spoke, she placed the Bible in Julianna's hand. "Right there, honey. Genesis chapter 28."

Julianna let her eyes fall on the page and read it to Sapphire: "'And Jacob went out from Beersheba, and went toward Haran. And he lighted upon a certain place, and tarried there all night, because the sun was set; and he took of the stones of that place, and put them for his pillows, and lay down in that place to sleep. And he dreamed, and behold a ladder set up on the earth, and the top of it reached to heaven: and behold the angels of God ascending and descending on it.'"

"All right, honey," Sapphire said, "now go over to verse 18 an' read that one to me."

Julianna smiled faintly and proceeded: "'And Jacob rose up early in the morning, and took the stone that he had put for his pillows, and set it up for a pillar, and poured oil upon the top of it.'"

"See, honey? You mentioned that yo' pillow seemed like it was made of stone. That's what made me think of Jacob. See that? When Jacob's head was on that pillow of stone, he saw God's angels goin' up and down on that ladder from heav'n. Since yo' pillow seems to be a stone, you should look fo' them angels and let 'em he'p you relax an' get some sleep. We're all gonna fin' jobs, an' you an' that baby will have a good and happy home in Idaho. We mus' trust the Lord an' His angels to take care of all of us."

Julianna closed the Bible and handed it to Sapphire. She thanked Sapphire for her concern and told her good night.

As Julianna headed down the hall to her room, she decided that maybe tonight she would sleep better, and maybe it would work out that she and Larissa would have a future in Idaho.

It was almost noon on Saturday, October 4, as the crowd emerged from Temple Emmanuel, New York's Jewish synagogue in Manhattan.

It was a warm day, but a nice breeze was blowing off the Hudson River, making it more comfortable.

Rabbi Joseph Feldman stood at the door, shaking hands

with his people as they were leaving after Sabbath Day services. When the Kates brothers, Henry and Jacob, filed by, Feldman shook Henry's hand, then looked around and said, "Where's Naomi?"

Henry smiled. "Where is my wife usually, Rabbi? Talking to someone!"

Feldman laughed, then spotted Naomi Kates in conversation with a small group of women a few feet away. "Well, you tell her, Henry, that I feel slighted that she did not come through the line to shake my hand."

Henry laughed. "I'll tell her, Rabbi."

Feldman then turned to Jacob Kates, who, like Henry, was a slender man who stood exactly five and a half feet tall. He was bald, with a fringe of wavy salt-and-pepper hair, and he had snappy brown eyes and a ready smile.

The rabbi took hold of Jacob's right hand and gripped his upper arm as he said, "Jacob, my dear friend. I am going to miss you very much. You will be in my prayers, and I sincerely hope you will find happiness in the Wild West."

Jacob blinked at the tears that welled up in his eyes and said, "I will miss you, too, Rabbi. Perhaps one day I can return to New York for a visit. If that happens, rest assured, I will come and see you."

"Please do," Feldman said as he let go of Jacob's hand. "I will look forward to it."

CHAPTER FOUR

The land lay golden under the brilliance of the October sun as a large crowd gathered on Main Street in the town of Fort Bridger, Wyoming. Fort Bridger was in the southwestern part of Wyoming Territory, where the wind blew free across the surrounding hills and plains, and broad-winged hawks ruled the sky.

A few miles farther to the southwest stood the jagged Uintah Mountains. Puffy white clouds, rambunctious in a northern wind, billowed over the towering peaks, patching them with drifting shadows.

Between Fort Bridger and the Uintahs, the valley floor was a forested tapestry of tall green pines and Douglas firs, with the waters of the Little Muddy River glistening through wind-stirred branches.

The excited citizens of Fort Bridger, along with most of the army personnel and the officers' families from the military installation, were gathered on Main Street in front of Cooper's General Store. Also in the crowd were a few Crow Indians led by Chief Two Moons, his squaw Sweet Blossom, and teenage son, Broken Wing.

A huge canvas sign fashioned by the men of the town stretched across the slender balcony of the store, announcing:

GRAND REOPENING! COOPER'S GENERAL STORE!
CONGRATULATIONS, HANNAH COOPER!

Hannah Marie Cooper stood on the porch of the general store building with her four children gathered around her. Brown-eyed Hannah wore a pretty gingham-checked dress of blue and white, covered with a crisp white apron. Her long, dark brown hair lay softly on her shoulders with waves adorning her temples and complementing her prominent cheekbones. She noticed some stragglers still making their way to the store. She would wait for all to arrive before delivering her short speech.

Wagons and buggies were parked along the boardwalks for over a block in both directions, and saddle horses were tied to the hitching rails. The crowd had formed a large half circle in the street, and traffic could no longer pass through.

While a din of voices rode the air, Pastor Andy Kelly and his wife, Rebecca, stood close by the porch. Hannah had asked him to close the event with prayer, dedicating the new store to the glory of God. With the Kellys stood Captain John Fordham, his wife, Betsy, and their children, Ryan, Will, and Belinda.

Betsy Fordham smiled and said, "The people of this town dearly love Hannah. Just look at the turnout for this dedication."

"She's given them plenty of reason to love her," Rebecca said.

"Amen," said John Fordham. "She's quite a lady."

At that moment, Hannah stepped to the edge of the boardwalk, and the crowd grew quiet.

"Friends," Hannah said in a voice loud enough to carry to the fringes of the crowd, "my children and I deeply appreciate your coming for the opening of our new store. I see some of you ranchers and farmers who come into town only once every few months, and you might not have met my children."

Turning to the two boys and two girls on the porch with

her, Hannah had them lined up according to age. "My oldest is Christopher, who will soon turn fifteen. He plans to be a soldier like his father was in the Civil War."

There were some cheers from the army personnel.

Tall and slender, with dark brown hair like his mother's, hazel-eyed Chris gave them a snappy salute. His best friend, Broken Wing, waved at him. Chris gave Broken Wing a tiny wave back, and the people applauded.

"Next in line is my daughter Mary Elizabeth," said Hannah, "better known as Mary Beth. Her greatest desire is to be a schoolteacher."

Sundi Lindgren, the town's only schoolmarm, waved a hand and said, "Yay, Mary Beth!"

Everyone applauded. Mary Beth did a perfect curtsy, and the applause gained volume.

Smiling, Hannah said, "Mary Beth is twelve, going on twenty-one."

The crowd laughed appreciatively.

"My third child," said Hannah, "is this husky boy with the freckles on his face. His name is Brett Jonathan, but everybody calls him B. J."

B. J. Cooper grinned at the crowd. He had blue eyes and medium brown hair with a blond streak in it.

"B. J. is eight years old," Hannah said. "He hasn't declared yet what he wants to be when he grows up. Right now, he's quite accident prone. He's an accident looking for a place to happen!"

Some of the people in the crowed laughed especially loud because they knew B. J. usually had a bandage somewhere on his body or a scab that was trying to heal.

Hannah glanced down at her youngest. "Ladies and gentlemen, last but not least is my five-year-old daughter Patty Ruth."

There were cheers for the little redhead with bright blue

eyes, who wore her hair in long pigtails and had a sprinkling of freckles across her nose and cheeks. In her arms was her stuffed bear, Tony. And pressed close to her legs was the family dog—a small black-and-white rat terrier.

Patty Ruth had watched her big sister do a curtsy. Since the cheering continued, she decided to do the same. As she positioned herself to curtsy, she lost her balance, stumbled sideways, and lost her hold on Tony. She tried to grab the falling bear and completely lost her balance, landing hard in a sitting position.

Some of the children in the crowd snickered, and some of the adults were trying to hide their smiles.

Chris quickly went to her, picked her up, and placed Tony back in her arms. She turned to her mother and buried her face in Hannah's skirt.

Hannah laid a hand on Patty Ruth's head and said, "It's all right, honey. Everybody loses their balance once in a while."

"That's right, Patty Ruth!" called out Curly Wesson, who managed the Wells Fargo office in town along with his wife, Judy. "Thet was a right purty curtsy!"

The little dog went to Patty Ruth, realizing that something was wrong, and yapped twice.

"Oh yes, folks!" Hannah said. "And this is the family dog, Biggie, short for Big Enough!"

The crowd clapped for Biggie.

While the applause continued, the town mayor and barber, Cade Samuels, stepped out of the crowd and onto the porch. The noise died down, then all was quiet.

"Hannah," Samuels said, "as mayor of this fair town, I want to say something before you officially open the store."

Hannah kept a hand on Patty Ruth's head and nodded.

Samuels ran his gaze over the crowd, then looked at Hannah and said, "I believe I can speak for everybody in the town and the fort, Hannah. We all love you and your little family, and we'll love that new one when he or she is born. The Coopers are a vital part of Fort Bridger, and we've all come here today to show you what you mean to us. Right, folks?"

There was a rousing cheer, punctuated by whistles.

With that, Cade Samuels stepped off the porch and joined his wife, Regina.

Mary Beth bent down to Patty Ruth, who was still clinging to Hannah's skirt, and spoke so only Patty Ruth could hear. "Come over here and stand with me. Mother wants to talk to the people for a few minutes."

At first, the little redhead stiffened and shook her head, but when Hannah said in a low voice, "Patty Ruth, you stand with Mary Beth," Patty Ruth obeyed, but hid her face in Mary Beth's skirt.

As Hannah took a deep breath to speak, Glenda Williams called out, "We love you, Hannah! Just like Mayor Samuels said!"

This brought on louder cheers, more applause, and higher pitched whistles. Happy tears misted Hannah's eyes as she ran her gaze over the faces of her friends and neighbors. Even Chief Two Moons and his handful of people were cheering.

The care and kindness of the crowd brought a warmth to her heart, and she silently thanked the Lord for all His provisions and blessings. A radiant smile lit her face as she brushed tears from her face and said, "Thank you, each and every one! Now, before I say what's on my heart, then open the store for business, my good friend Alex Patterson has asked if he could address all of you. Alex…"

Tall, lanky Alex Patterson stepped up on the porch and faced the crowd. "Folks, I won't take but a minute here, but my family and I owe this dear lady so much, I just gotta say a few words."

Many tears were shed as Alex told them Hannah Cooper's love and kindness had shown him what a real Christian was.

And now, as a child of God, he had more joy than he'd ever dreamed possible. His home was filled with joy because Jesus lived there.

There were "Amens!" from the Christians in the crowd, and the loudest came from Pastor Kelly.

Alex wiped tears from his face as he turned to Hannah and said, "God bless you, dear lady. And thank you for caring for my soul." With that, he stepped off the porch and joined his family.

Hannah had to clear the lump out of her throat before she could speak.

The people listened intently as she thanked the Powells for providing the money so she could have the store rebuilt, and the Williamses for providing a place to stay while it was being built. She thanked her helpers in the store—Glenda Williams, Betsy Fordham, Julie Powell, Judy Charley Wesson, Mandy Carver, and Sylvia Bateman for helping her behind the counter whenever she needed them.

Hannah closed by expressing her appreciation to all the people for their patience in waiting for the new store to be built.

"As you all know," she said, running her gaze over their faces, "the sutler's store is quite small. This has forced me to carry fewer goods. But now, in this new building, the shelves are once again loaded with goods of every description. I know you're all eager to enter and make your purchases, so if my helpers will go inside first, we'll open the store!"

Patty Ruth, having finally overcome her embarrassment, was ready to go into the store with her mother to help her wait on customers.

Hannah glanced at B. J. and said, "Take Biggie back up to the apartment, son."

B. J. picked up the dog and cradled him in his arms. He caught Patty Ruth's eye and grinned at her mockingly.

The five-year-old made sure her mother wasn't looking, then made a bug-eyed face and stuck out her tongue.

Soon the store was crowded, and a long line formed along the boardwalk.

Chris Cooper had his mother's permission to ride back to the Crow village with Broken Wing. Mary Beth and Sundi Lindgren were going to the Crow village too. On Saturdays, Sundi held classes for the Crow children. Mary Beth was happy as a lark to be counted worthy to be Miss Lindgren's associate teacher of the Indian children.

As they were climbing into the wagon, Sundi's older sister, Heidi, smiled up at Mary Beth and said, "You really look happy every time you climb into this wagon to go teach at the village. I'm glad you can do it."

"Not as glad as I am, Miss Heidi. This is what the Lord made me for...to be a teacher."

"Well, you two have a good time today. I've got to get my shop opened. If anybody in that long line over there has any money left after they've done business with Hannah, maybe I'll sell a dress or two today!"

When Patty Ruth Cooper entered the store, she started to go behind the counter where she had often stationed herself to help her mother. But with Glenda, Mandy, and Sylvia back there, too, she found little space.

She drifted to the rear of the store and smiled at the Wessons standing near the storeroom door. Even though Patty Ruth sometimes had trouble understanding Curly and Judy Wesson, she loved to hear them talk. It was when she tried to imitate their lingo at home that she got into trouble with her mother.

The Wessons had come to town recently to open the Wells Fargo stage office. Twice, instead of sitting in church with "Grandpa" Dr. Frank O'Brien and "Grandma" Edie, Patty Ruth had sat between the Wessons. She liked to hear them "sang them thar hymns," as they put it. Neither one of them could sing on pitch, but they both talked about how they loved "sangin'" and what good "sangers" they were.

A steady stream of customers came into the store, and soon the Wessons were rushing back and forth from the store-room to restock shelves. Patty Ruth stood near the storeroom door, watching them.

Busy as he was, Curly stopped and bent down to her level. "Whut's your name, li'l girl?"

"Patty Ruth."

Curly drew in a sharp breath. His eyebrows lifted, and his eyes widened. "Really? Your name's Patty Ruth?"

She giggled. "Mm-hmm."

"How old are you?"

"Five."

"Five years old?"

"Mm-hmm." She giggled again.

By this time they had an audience. A few customers and Judy Wesson were looking on, smiling, as were the ladies behind the counter.

Curly said, "Wal, whattya know? Do ya know whut I do when I meet a li'l girl whose name is Patty Ruth, an' she's five years old? Do ya know whut I do?"

"Hmp-mm."

Curly encircled her with his arms and said, "I hug 'er!"

Patty Ruth giggled and hugged him back, and everyone watching laughed.

Curly carried a box of goods from the storeroom, emptied its contents onto the shelves, and headed back again. It was Patty Ruth's turn to match his routine.

"Hey, mister," she said as he drew near.

Curly stopped and said, "Whut, li'l girl?"

"Whut's your name?"

"Why, my name's Uncle Curly."

Patty Ruth widened her eyes in surprise. "Really? Your name's Uncle Curly?"

"Yes, ma'am."

"How old are you?"

Curly giggled like Patty Ruth and said, "Wal, li'l punkin, how old do ya think I am?"

Patty Ruth rolled her eyes as if she were concentrating. "Um...'bout thirty-six."

Curly smacked his forehead with a palm and said, "Wal, whuttya know! You guessed it 'zactly!"

The little redhead giggled. "Do ya know whut I do when I meet a nice man whose name is Uncle Curly an' he's thirty-six years old? Do ya know whut I do?"

The old man shook his head. "Hmp-mm."

Patty Ruth giggled. "I hug 'im!"

The people looked on with pleasure as Curly let the little girl put her arms around his neck and hugged her in return. Some applauded while others, touched by the scene, said, "Aw-w-w-w."

Business was finally starting to slow down when Judy walked past Patty Ruth and gave her a big smile and a wink.

Patty Ruth noted the single snaggletooth. She had wondered about it since the first time she'd seen the sweet woman. When Judy returned, Patty Ruth said, "Aunt Judy Charley..."

"Yes, honey?"

"Where did you put your other teeth?"

"Patty Ruth, you don't ask people questions like that!" Hannah called sharply.

Judy cackled while customers looked on, and said, "Aw, Hannah, dear, it's all right fer as I'm concerned. The li'l thang is jus' curious."

Curly cackled and said, "Wal, honey pot, tell Patty Ruth and all these nice people. 'Zactly where did you put your teeth?"

Judy grinned impishly and replied, "Wal, dear husbin' o' mine, I put 'em the same place whar you put your hair!"

Patty Ruth giggled and said, "Uncle Curly, did you put your hair in a drawer?"

Hannah frowned again. "Patty Ruth, I think it would be best if you come over here behind the counter. I can make room for you."

That night at bedtime, Hannah gathered her children in her bedroom to pray together.

"Mama, are you feeling all right?" Mary Beth asked.

"I'm fine, honey, why?"

"You look tired, and maybe a little pale. Don't you think it's time to let the ladies work the counter every day?"

"I am tired, honey, but it's only because this was an especially hard day. I think I can work the counter for another couple of months…maybe even longer."

Concern showed in Mary Beth's sky blue eyes. "I just don't want anything bad to happen to you or my new little sister because you overdo."

"I don't either, Mom," spoke up Chris. "You shouldn't be on your feet so much anymore." Then to Mary Beth: "And, sister dear, I'll have you know, what we're getting is another brother."

"Yeah!" put in B. J. "Another brother! Mom's gonna have another boy!"

"She ain't neither!" spoke up the little redhead. "Mama's gonna have another girl!"

"Patty Ruth…" said Hannah.

Big blue eyes settled on Hannah's face. "Yes, ma'am?"

"We don't say 'ain't.' You should say, 'She isn't either.' Not, 'She ain't neither.'"

"Yes, ma'am," said the little one, dipping her chin.

"Now, it's prayer time," said Hannah. "We'll pray in the usual order."

As the Cooper family bowed their heads, Patty Ruth held her stuffed bear close and closed her eyes. She was the only one in the family who didn't lead out in prayer. Her mother would help her pray later, just before she kissed her good night.

While the others prayed in order of age, Patty Ruth peeked periodically, making sure everyone kept their eyes closed.

Mary Beth's prayer asked the Lord for a little sister, and when the boys prayed, they pleaded for a little brother. Hannah closed in prayer, then said, "Okay, everybody. Night-night time."

Patty Ruth looked at one brother, then the other. "I know why you boys don't want another girl in the family."

"And why is that?" asked Chris.

"'Cause then you'd really be in the mirorinty. Counting Mama, there are already more girls than boys."

"Honey," said Hannah, "the word is minority."

Patty Ruth tilted her head to one side and tried to shape her mouth to get it out right. "Mirorinty."

"Minority," corrected Hannah.

Patty Ruth grinned. "Yeah, that."

CHAPTER FIVE

T he bell in the church tower pealed in the bright, crystal clear morning, calling the people of Fort Bridger to worship. Carriages, buggies, wagons, riders on horseback, and people on foot began gathering at the church.

The air was cool but comfortable, and several church members were standing in front of the glistening white frame building in conversation when a wagon pulled up with a man, woman, and three children aboard.

"New folks," Dr. Frank O'Brien said to Gary Williams. "Look like ranchers."

"Let's go meet them," Gary said. He was an amiable sort and always wore a ready smile.

As the man pulled the wagon to a halt next to a carriage, he spotted the two men coming toward them and said in a slow, Southern accent, "Looks like we got us a welcomin' committee, Nelda."

"Howdy, folks," Gary said. "I'm Gary Williams. My wife and I own the Uintah Hotel down the street. This is our town's beloved physician, Dr. Frank O'Brien."

"Mighty happy to see you folks here," added the rosy-cheeked Irishman. "What are your names, and where are you from?"

While the big man stepped down, he said, "My name's Buford Wynn...W-Y-N-N." He shook their hands, then reached up to help his wife down. She smiled at them as Buford said,

"This is my wife, Nelda." He motioned for his three children to climb down. It was obvious they were strictly disciplined by the way they sat so still, then reacted immediately when they were given the signal to alight.

"These are our younguns, gentlemen. Norman is fifteen, Betty Sue is thirteen, and Donna Rae is eleven."

Norman shook hands with both men, and the girls curtsied politely.

"We came to Wyomin' from Georgia," Buford said. "Arrived here 'bout two weeks ago. Moved onto a ranch some seven-eight miles to the south. Neighbors ain't churchgoin' folks, but they told us 'bout the church here in town, so we decided to attend the services today."

"Well, we're plenty happy to have you," Dr. O'Brien said. "Adult Sunday school class is held in the auditorium, folks. I'll lead you in."

"And I'll show these fine-looking young people to their classes," Gary said.

He delivered the girls to their classes, then said to Norman, "Teenage boys' classroom is the last one on the right side of the hall."

Three boys were standing outside the classroom door as Gary and Norman drew up.

"Morning, boys," Gary said. "We have a family visiting today who just moved into the area. This is Norman Wynn."

Chris Cooper and his friends welcomed Norman, and Gary went on his way.

"Where are you from?" Chris asked.

"Georgia," came the reply in a noticeable Southern drawl. "We bought a ranch south of here a few miles."

"Well, we're glad to have you with us today. Our teacher is Mr. Abe Carver. He's the blacksmith here in Fort Bridger. I'll sit with you in class and take you to the auditorium for the preaching service."

Other boys were coming down the hall toward them.

"Let's go on in the room," Chris said, laying a friendly hand on Norman's shoulder.

Abe Carver was a big muscular black man with a warm personality and a winning smile. He was writing some Scripture verses on the blackboard when the boys came in.

Chris felt Norman stiffen and saw his smile disappear when Abe turned from the blackboard and said, "Good morning, boys. Ah! We have a visitor today! Is this a friend of yours, Chris?"

"I just met him, Mr. Carver," Chris said. "This is Norman Wynn. Norman, this is our teacher, Mr. Abe Carver."

Abe extended his hand, "Welcome, Norman. I hope you'll enjoy our class and our church today."

Norman was slow to take hold of Carver's hand. He finally did so reluctantly.

After class, when Chris led Norman into the auditorium for the preaching service, Norman thanked him and went to sit with his parents and sisters. Chris saw that as Norman sat down beside his father, he whispered something into his ear. Buford Wynn's eyes widened and his face reddened.

Both Abe and Mandy Carver sang in the choir. Just before the offering was taken, they left the choir loft, went to the pulpit, and sang a duet. Abe had a deep bass voice, and Mandy's clear soprano was beautiful, as was the expression on her shining face as the two of them glorified the Lord Jesus Christ in song.

While the Carvers sang, Chris stole a glance at the Wynns, who were seated across the aisle from him.

At the close of the service, Pastor Kelly and Rebecca were standing at the door to greet the people. When the Wynn family approached, the Kellys smiled at them and were about to say how happy they were to have them in the services when they noticed Buford Wynn's angry eyes.

"I'm gonna tell you somethin', preacher," said the rancher, "you got no business havin' a black man teachin' that Sunday school class! And what's worse is lettin' him and his wife sing in the choir and then get up there behind the pulpit! You shouldn't even allow 'em inside the buildin'!"

Wynn's outburst plainly embarrassed his wife and got the attention of everyone on the church grounds who had not yet departed. Among them were Abe and Mandy Carver, and their young children—Tyrone, Leroy, and Annie Frances. The boys stood wide-eyed, glancing at their father to see what he was going to do. Annie Frances clung to her mother's skirt. Abe started to move back toward the door, but Mandy, with tears filling her eyes, laid a hand on his arm.

"Please, Abe," she said, "let Pastor Kelly handle it."

Hannah Cooper moved up beside Mandy and slipped an arm around her waist.

Every eye was on Pastor Kelly, who was struggling to hold his temper as he looked Wynn square in the eye and spoke softly. "Mr. Wynn, the Carvers are fine Christian people and faithful members of this church. They have as much right to enter the building as anyone else. They have as much right to sing in the choir and from behind the pulpit as anyone else in this church. Abe Carver knows his Bible well, and he's absolutely qualified to teach. And what's more, those boys love him."

"That's right!" Chris Cooper said loudly. He was standing a few feet away with his siblings. "Mr. Carver is the best Sunday school teacher I've ever had!"

Hannah turned to Chris and silently mouthed, "Let Pastor Kelly handle it by himself."

Chris started to defend his action, but the look in his

mother's eyes changed his mind. His close friend, Lieutenant Dobie Carlin, who had recently been saved because of Chris's testimony, stepped up and laid a hand on his shoulder.

"Well, I'm from the South," Wynn said. "And where I come from, they don't let black folks in white churches!"

Kelly forced himself to stay calm and held his voice level. "Mr. Wynn, you're not in the South now. People here feel differently about it. A man's soul has no color, and in the eyes of God, the color of a man's skin makes no difference. God created all men, and Jesus died on the cross of Calvary that all sinners might have the opportunity to be saved. Every person who is born again is a child of God, Mr. Wynn. If you're a born-again man, Abe Carver is your brother."

Buford Wynn started to say something, but Alex Patterson stepped up and said, "Mr. Wynn, my name's Alex Patterson. I'm from Alabama. I was taught when I was a boy that black people don't even have souls. But when I got saved, I had to unlearn a lot of things I'd been taught. Jesus changed my thinking completely when He saved me. It sounds to me like you need—"

"Bah-h-h!" Wynn said, pivoting around. He stomped toward his wagon, saying, "C'mon, Nelda! Let's go!"

Nelda Wynn gave the Carvers an "I'm sorry" look and hastened away with her three children beside her. The crowd watched as the Wynns piled into their wagon and Buford snapped the reins violently, putting the team to a gallop. Dust clouds billowed up behind the wagon.

Hannah wrapped her arms around Mandy as she broke into sobs. Tyrone and Leroy began to cry, and Abe put a comforting arm around each of them. When little Annie Frances began to cry, Patty Ruth ran to her and hugged her, saying, "Don't cry, Annie Frances."

A moment later, Mary Beth knelt down beside the two little girls and said, "Here, Patty Ruth, let me have her." Mary Beth picked Annie Frances up, kissed her cheek, and held her close.

"It's all right, sweetie," she said. "Everything's going to be fine."

The church crowd waited quietly as Pastor Kelly and Rebecca comforted the Carvers.

Soon Mandy was in her husband's arms, and the Carvers were thanking the pastor and the others for their kindness.

The first person to approach from the crowd was Judy Charley Wesson, who left her husband's side and said, "Abe, Mandy…if ever I see thet thar loudmouth Wynn feller again, he'll git a piece of my mind fer shore!"

The rest of the people crowded close, each one assuring the Carvers they were loved, respected, and wanted in the town and in the church.

Glenda and Gary Williams, with their "adopted" daughter Abby Turner, had invited Hannah and the children home for Sunday dinner.

Abby's parents had been killed a few weeks earlier by hostile Blackfoot Indians at a small town called Buffalo Lodge, some twenty miles west of Fort Bridger. Since coming to Fort Bridger, Abby had opened her heart to the Lord Jesus for salvation because of Mary Beth's witness to her, and the two girls had become best friends.

As the group walked toward the Williams home, they talked about what had just happened.

"I feel so bad for the Carvers," Abby said. "They're such precious people."

"We all feel that way, honey," said Hannah. "It's sad that some people in this world look down on others."

"I was that way about Indians," Abby said, "because they killed my parents. I looked on all Indians as bad people. But when I got saved, my feelings toward them changed. I came to realize that some bad Indians do not make them all bad."

"'Specially Mr. Two Moons an' his fam'ly," put in Patty Ruth.

Patty Ruth noted that Chris was walking beside Abby. She

hurriedly stepped between them and said, "'Scuse me, big brother. I wanna walk next to Abby."

Chris picked up Patty Ruth and set her down on his other side. "You walk on this side of me, little sister," he said.

Patty Ruth giggled. "I know why you wanna walk so close to Abby. 'Cause you really like her. Mary Beth said you have a smash on her."

Chris sent a glance to his other sister, whose features tinted.

"Well, everyone can see that you like her," Mary Beth said.

Now Abby was blushing.

Mary Beth directed her gaze at the little redhead. "And, Patty Ruth, as usual, you got it wrong."

"What?"

"It's not a smash, it's a crush."

"Oh. Okay. Chris has a crush on Abby."

"Patty Ruth," said Hannah, "that's enough."

"Yes, Mama."

Mary Beth, who was walking on Abby's other side, said, "I don't understand people who are prejudiced against minorities. In the Southwest, it's prejudice against the Mexicans. On the West Coast, it's prejudice against Orientals. In the Northeast, it's prejudice against the Jewish people, and in the deep South, it's prejudice against the black people. I have a hard time with this.

"Our memory verse in Sunday school last week was Luke 6:31: 'And as ye would that men should do to you, do ye also to them likewise.' If the whole world would live by Jesus' words, there wouldn't be any prejudice. No one likes to be treated mean and looked down on. People want to be treated with kindness and respect. So they should treat others the same way."

"That's right, Mary Beth," said Patty Ruth. "People shouldn' be predijuced against mirorinties."

"You're right, honey, they shouldn't. But it's not predijuced. It's prejudiced. And it's not mirorinties. It's minorities."

The little redhead frowned as she concentrated on the two words for a moment, then said, "Yeah, that. That's what people shouldn' be."

On Monday morning, Marshal Lance Mangum trotted his horse down the alley and drew up behind his office. It was a nippy October morning, and the breaths of horse and rider plumed out on the cold air.

Mangum dismounted and led the horse into the small corral with shed that served as a barn. He noticed ice crystals around the edge of the stock tank and pumped fresh water into the tank. "There you go, boy."

Mangum crossed the alley and unlocked the back door to the office. He removed his hat and hung it on a peg behind his desk, but left his jacket on. As he unlocked the front door, he noted there was quite a bit of activity on Main Street.

He dropped a fresh supply of kindling in the potbellied stove, stuffed some old newspapers around it, and struck a match. When the paper was burning, he dropped the heavy lid, opened the flue, and moved toward the cell block.

His only prisoner was sitting up on the bunk in cell one, huddling under a pair of blankets. "Well, Jed, did you sleep it off?" Mangum asked.

Jed Smith was somewhere in his late fifties, but looked older. He had a scraggly gray beard, and what little hair he had was almost totally gray. Smith put his fingertips to his temples and said, "Yeah. I guess so. What time did you throw me in here?"

"About eleven-thirty. You don't remember?"

"No. But I sure do have a headache."

"You'd think after thirty-two hours, the headache would be gone."

Smith's head bobbed as Mangum inserted the key in the cell door. "Thirty-two hours?"

"Yeah, Jed. It was Saturday night when you got drunk and started shooting up the sign at the saloon. This is Monday morning."

"Oh."

"You won't find any money in your pockets. I gave it to Lester Coggins to get his sign repaired." Mangum swung the door open. "Okay, Jed. You can go now."

"You ain't gonna fine me?"

"What good would it do? Main thing is that Lester gets his sign repaired. You might steer clear of him. I think it's going to cost more than you had in your pockets. In fact, the smart thing is to steer clear of the Rusty Lantern altogether. Liquor will kill you, Jed."

"Aw, now you sound like that there preacher Kelly. He's always tellin' me I should get saved and get offa the drink."

"Maybe you'd better listen to him."

"Well, how 'bout yourself? You don't drink, but you ain't a Christian, are you?"

"No, but I've been doing a lot of thinking about it. Come on now, I've got work to do."

When Jed Smith passed through the front door and shuffled down the boardwalk, Mangum dropped a couple of logs in the stove and hung his jacket on a peg next to his hat. He was about to sit down at his desk when the front door swung open and Mandy Carver stepped inside the office.

Mandy was usually a happy, cheerful person, but when she rushed up to Marshal Mangum, her eyes were filled with sadness and fear. She blurted out, "Marshal, did you hear about the incident at the church yesterday mornin'?"

"Yes, I did. Some of the church folks told me about it yesterday afternoon. I was proud to hear of Abe's restraint when he probably would have liked to punch that loudmouth a good one. You look worried, Mandy. Is something wrong?"

"Abe couldn't sleep all night, Marshal. He's gone to find that Mr. Wynn."

Mangum's eyes widened. "You mean to get back at him?"

"No, no," she said, shaking her head. "Abe feels he should talk to Mr. Wynn and see if he can make friends with him. But I'm afraid of what might happen. Especially when Abe shows up on Mr. Wynn's property. That man hates black folks, Marshal. Would…would you ride out there and see if you can keep anything bad from happenin'?"

"I sure will," Mangum said, reaching for his jacket and hat. "Do you know where Wynn lives?"

"On a ranch about seven or eight miles south o' town."

"How long ago did Abe ride out?"

"'Bout ten minutes."

"I'm on my way."

"Thank you, Marshal," she said, brushing tears from her cheeks.

"You go on home, Mandy. Abe and I will be back soon."

Mandy stepped out onto the boardwalk and watched the marshal put a sign in the window, indicating that he would be back later. It wasn't long until she caught a glimpse of the marshal on his horse as he swung onto Main Street at the intersection ahead of her and rode south out of town.

Abe swung onto the Cameron Mayfell ranch and trotted down the lane to the house, where he found Mayfell working at the back porch, putting new hinges on the door.

It took Mayfell only a minute to give Abe directions to the Wynn ranch, and soon he was galloping farther south over the hills. The sun's warm rays were beginning to warm up the air, and while riding, Abe slipped off his jacket.

Buford Wynn had just forked hay to his cows and horses in the barn and was passing through the corral gate, when he saw the lone rider turn off the road and trot toward him. He recognized Carver instantly and made a dash for the house.

Nelda and the children were in the kitchen when Buford rushed in with fire in his eyes. He was taking his shotgun off its rack when Nelda said, "What's wrong? What are you going to do with the shotgun?"

"We've got company, Nelda," Buford said, breaking the double-barreled shotgun open to check the loads. "The big black Sunday school teacher is ridin' toward the house right now."

"By himself, Pa?" Norman asked.

"All I saw was him," Buford replied, snapping the barrel closed.

"Then he isn't here to start trouble," Nelda said. "Don't go out there with that shotgun!"

"You just stay in here and keep the kids with you!" Buford said, and headed out the door.

Abe was drawing near the house when he saw Buford come around the back corner with the shotgun in his hands. He drew rein at the edge of the front yard, threw up his palms, and called, "Mr. Wynn, I've come here peaceable to talk to you, sir. I would like to be your friend, and I'd like to see you come back to church."

Abe could see the troubled faces of Nelda and the Wynn children at a side window of the house.

Buford's face darkened into a scowl as he said, "I don't want to be your friend! And as long as they allow you and your family in the church, we won't be back! Now get off my property!"

Abe's horse moved forward slightly without being prompted.

Keeping his voice steady and low, Abe said, "Please, Mr. Wynn. Couldn't we jis' sit down like decent human beings and talk about this? Fort Bridger is the only town within forty miles. You'll need to buy your groceries and other needful things in Fort Bridger. I don't want there to be trouble if my family or I should meet up with you in town. If our families could—"

"Turn that horse around and ride, or I'll blow you outta the saddle!"

Just as Buford finished his threat, both men heard pounding hooves. Buford's line of sight flicked to the oncoming rider, who was galloping down the lane as fast as his horse could carry him. Sunlight glinted off a badge on the rider's chest.

Mangum drew up beside Abe and said, "Mr. Wynn, I'm Marshal Lance Mangum from Fort Bridger. Why are you holding that shotgun on Abe?"

Wynn didn't answer.

"Did Abe threaten you?" Mangum said. "Or has he done something else to cause you to hold the gun on him?"

"He's black, Marshal! And he had the gall to ride onto my property without an invite! That's enough to bring out this shotgun! I told him to ride, or I'd blow him outta the saddle."

Mangum dismounted and walked toward Wynn. "That kind of attitude is bound to get you into trouble, Mr. Wynn," he said. When he was three feet from the dual black muzzles of the shotgun, he looked back over his shoulder and said, "Abe, why did you ride onto this man's property?"

"I jis' wanted to make friends with Mr. Wynn, Marshal."

"Did you tell him that?"

"Yessir."

Mangum turned back to Wynn. "Is he telling the truth?"

The look on Buford's face was a mixture of anger and discomfort. He lowered the shotgun and pointed the barrels toward the ground. "Yeah."

"Then why don't you lighten up? Life will go better for

you and your family in these parts if you're friendly with folks."

Wynn looked at him coldly. "Tell me, Marshal, is it against the law to pick and choose your friends?"

"What are you getting at?"

"I'll be friends with whom I choose, and I'll not be friends with whom I choose. That's not against the law, is it?"

"You know it's not."

"Good. End of discussion. You can leave now, Marshal, and take Carver with you."

Mangum held the man's gaze for a long moment, then said, "We'll go, but remember what I told you. Your attitude is liable to get you into trouble."

"Let me worry about that, Marshal," Buford said.

Mangum swung into his saddle. "All right, Abe. Let's go."

As Mangum and Carver trotted up the lane toward the road, they saw a rider coming toward them.

"It's Pastor Kelly," Abe said.

When the riders drew abreast, Kelly said, "Marshal...Abe...what's going on? Is there a problem?"

"Abe came out here alone to try to make friends with Wynn, Preacher," Mangum said. "Mandy came to my office right after he rode out, and asked me to follow him. She was afraid there'd be trouble. And there almost was. When I got here, Wynn was holding a shotgun on Abe and making threats. He lowered the gun when I talked to him, but he still wouldn't budge on his attitude toward Abe."

Kelly glanced toward the house and saw that Buford and his family were standing outside, looking their direction. "I'm pleased at what you did, Abe," he said. "You certainly showed the spirit of love to ride out here and try to make a friend out of the man who so vehemently spoke out against you at church."

The wide-shouldered blacksmith shrugged. "All I could do was try, Pastor."

Kelly nodded. "Well, I was just coming out here to make a

friendly visit and talk to them about salvation. I'll go ahead and make the call. If Mr. Wynn would come to know the Lord, he'd get over his prejudice."

CHAPTER SIX

It had been a long night, with several stops, as the train pulled out of Memphis, Tennessee, on its northbound journey to Chicago. The sun was climbing into the morning sky, casting a glare on the broad Mississippi River just west of the high ridge where the tracks ran.

A weary Julianna LeCroix glanced at the river's surface below. It was glittering so brightly that she could only look at it for a few seconds at a time. Movement overhead caught her eye, and she saw the dark V-shaped silhouette of ducks winging their way south.

She covered a yawn and looked down at little Larissa Catherine as she stirred on the seat beside her. The long-lashed eyelids fluttered momentarily but didn't open. Larissa raised a small plump hand and thrust her thumb into her mouth. Her tangled ringlets were a dark contrast across the white pillow.

When Larissa finally slept, Julianna laid her head back and closed her eyes. Once more she felt the pain of leaving her faithful servants and the house where she had grown up. Her mind went back to the previous afternoon, when Grover was at the barn out back, hitching the horses to the carriage...

Pearl Littlefield, Hattie Vaughn, and Sapphire Johnson gathered at the front door, waiting for Julianna to come down the stairs.

When Julianna appeared at the top of the winding stair-case, she lovingly caressed the banister railing as she slowly descended. She had already been through the rooms on the ground floor, touching tapestries, paintings, and pieces of furni-ture, and spilling tears as she went along.

Grover pulled the carriage up in front of the house and loaded her two small pieces of luggage and the overnight bag, which doubled as a diaper bag. Julianna had to leave most of her clothes behind.

Grover came back into the house and said, "All loaded, Miss Julianna."

Julianna's eyes were swimming in tears. She took a deep breath and said, "I'm going to miss all of you so terribly."

Sapphire's cheeks were wet as she kissed the baby and said, "I'm gonna miss this sweet li'l darlin'. I wish I could've had the joy of watchin' her grow up."

Julianna sniffed. "Maybe someday, when she's older, we can come back to New Orleans for a visit."

"We'd love that, Miz Julianna," Pearl said.

"We sho' would," said Hattie.

Grover cleared his throat gently. "We'd best be on our way, Miss Julianna. They won't hold that train for you."

Julianna nodded, then wrapped her arms around Pearl. They held each other tightly for a long moment, weeping and speaking words of love. She repeated the embrace with the other two women, then said, "All right, Grover. You and I will say our good-bye at the depot. Let's go before I change my mind."

Julianna could hear the three women crying as Grover helped her into the carriage with Larissa in her arms. She gazed at their faces as the carriage started to roll, and kept them in view as long as she could.

At the depot, Grover checked Julianna's luggage with the baggage handlers, who put it into the baggage car, then carried her overnight bag on board and helped her find a seat. He placed the bag at her feet for easy access, then said, "Good-bye, Miss Julianna. I will never forget you."

Julianna put Larissa on the seat and stood up to wrap her arms around Grover's neck and kiss his cheek. "Nor will I ever forget you, dear Grover. I hope you enjoy your new job."

"It will be all right, ma'am," he said, his lips quivering. "Thank you for always being so good to me." He turned and hurried out of the coach.

As the conductor gave his last call to board, Julianna looked out the window. Grover was standing on the platform, weeping. When he saw her looking at him, he forced a smile and wiped tears from his face.

The whistle blew, the big engine hissed, and the train lunged forward.

"Good-bye, Miss Julianna," Grover called above the noise of the engine. "I love you!"

Julianna felt weary to the bone. It had been a trying trip so far, and it was only the beginning. Idaho was a long way off, and though she was hoping things would work out for some happiness there, she still wasn't looking forward to living with her in-laws. But she would give it everything she had for Larissa's sake.

She leaned over and took out the map the ticket agent had given Grover when he bought the tickets. She was booked on two Wells Fargo stagecoaches, and the company had provided the map so she would know the route all the way to Boise. She had only glanced at the map when Grover gave her the railroad tickets. Now she unfolded it and spread it on her lap. The route was marked with red ink. She would board the first stage at Cheyenne City, Wyoming. The trip westward would take her through Laramie and across the Rocky Mountains to Rawlins, with a few stops in small towns and settlements in between.

The next large town would be Rock Springs. From there, she and Larissa would go to Green River, then to Fort Bridger. She had read of Fort Bridger, named after the famous mountain man and explorer Jim Bridger.

From Fort Bridger, they would go on to Evanston, where they would take another stagecoach north to Montpelier, Idaho, and head west for Boise. There would be stops in Pocatello and Twin Falls, with stops in smaller towns and settlements in between.

Just the thought of the long trip by stagecoach made Julianna feel tired. And none of this would be happening, she thought, if those vile men hadn't stolen every dollar and piece of property that was rightfully hers.

Hot tears pushed against Julianna's eyelids as she thought back on all that had been taken from her. Bitterness welled up inside as she dwelled on the wickedness of the men who stole her fortune. She wanted to just let go and hate them with all her being.

Mandy Carver had sent Tyrone off to school over two hours ago. Leroy and Annie Frances were playing together in the boys' bedroom while she paced the floor in the parlor. It was time for Abe and the marshal to be back, she told herself.

Had Marshal Mangum arrived too late? Maybe the man from Georgia had shot Abe…Mandy breathed a word of thanks to the Lord when she saw her husband and the marshal ride up. She opened the front door and stepped onto the porch.

"Hello, sweet wife of mine," Abe said, smiling as he dismounted.

"Is everything all right, Marshal?" Mandy asked.

Mangum swung down and stepped toward the porch

beside Abe. "Well, as you can see, ma'am, your husband is in one piece. When I arrived, Wynn was holding a shotgun on him, but he calmed down in my presence."

"Well, I'm glad you're all right, honey," Mandy said. "I hope you aren't upset at me for askin' Marshal Mangum to follow you."

"Of course not. I'm plenty happy to have a wife who cares."

"I sure wish I had a wife to look after me," Mangum said.

Mandy grinned. "One of these days, Marshal, there'll be a lovely young lady come walkin' into your life."

"You really think so?"

"Of course. It'll happen sooner or later, Marshal. Don't you despair. As handsome and rugged as you are, there's bound to be a female come along and fall head-over-heels in love with you."

"Well, far be it from me to argue with you about the handsome and rugged part, ma'am," he said with a grin, "but maybe she'll come riding into my life. You know, in one of those wagon trains that stops here."

"Or even riding in a stagecoach," suggested Abe.

"Oh, yeah!" Mangum said. "I'm not used to having the stage office here, yet. Maybe Miss Right will come riding in here on a stage and fall head-over-heels in love with me!"

When Julianna LeCroix and her baby daughter arrived in Chicago, they had four hours to wait till the Denver-bound train was scheduled to leave.

It was eight-thirty in the morning, and Julianna had rested little during the night. She carried Larissa and the overnight bag into the terminal and found a bench to sit on. She noticed a vendor pushing a cart through the terminal and said to the baby, "Mommy will get something to eat and drink, sweetheart, then she'll check your diaper and feed you. Mommy doesn't have much appetite, but I have to eat and drink so I can take care of you."

Julianna signaled as the vendor drew near. When she had devoured food and drink, she picked the baby up and said, "All right, sweet Larissa, let's take care of you. Mommy saw a sign back that way that says 'Ladies Washroom.' That's us."

Julianna threaded her way through the crowd. When she entered the washroom, she found that a table had been provided for exactly what she needed. She changed Larissa's diaper, then took a handkerchief from her purse inside the overnight bag and moistened it with water from a flowered pitcher sitting on a small stand.

She wiped Larissa's face, then her own. There were also a couple of wooden chairs provided. Julianna sat on one while she fed Larissa.

When the feeding was done, Julianna returned to the hard bench in the terminal to await the departure of their train. The big clock on the wall over the main door told her it was almost nine-thirty. There were hundreds of people moving about the terminal.

Julianna made Larissa comfortable on the bench beside her, and soon—with a full tummy—the baby fell asleep.

The young widow sat quietly and watched the people hurrying by. An overwhelming sense of homesickness and loneliness came over her. She missed her home—the mansion, the servants, the familiar surroundings. A lump came to her throat, and she began to cry.

Larissa was asleep, but she began to stir when her mother's weeping met her ears. Julianna pulled a hankie from under her sleeve, pressed it to her eyes, and wept as quietly as she could.

Suddenly she became aware of a hand touching her shoulder. She gasped and looked up through her tears to see a kindly woman with silver hair and eyes of compassion.

"You poor dear," said the woman, "is there something my husband and I can do for you?"

Julianna drew in a shaky breath, dabbed at her tears, and noted the tall, thin man who stood beside the woman. He also had compassionate eyes. "We'd like to help if we could," he said in a tender tone.

Julianna swallowed with difficulty and replied, "I appreciate your kindness. Both of you. I'm going through a very trying time in my life, and I'm just having a hard time handling it."

"What's your name, dear?" asked the woman.

"Julianna LeCroix. And my baby is Larissa."

"Larissa," echoed the woman. "That's a beautiful name for a beautiful baby. She really is darling."

The man moved a little closer. "Mrs. LeCroix, where in the South are you from? No, wait a minute. Let me guess. New Orleans?"

A smile touched Julianna's lips. "How did you know?"

"Oh, it wasn't too hard. LeCroix is a French name, and even though it is your married name, I can tell that you are French yourself."

"Well, you are right."

"Mrs. LeCroix, I am Dr. Charles G. Finney, and this is my wife, Matilda. I'm an evangelist. We're from Oberlin, Ohio, a few miles southwest of Cleveland. Matilda and I have been in a meeting here in Chicago, and we're about to catch a train to Cleveland."

"I'm very pleased to meet both of you," Julianna said. "And I appreciate your kindness, but there's really nothing you can do."

"We'd like to hear about it, dear," Matilda said. "Our train doesn't leave for another hour and a half. Sometimes it helps just to talk to someone."

"Well, all right," Julianna said, glad to have some company. "Please sit down." She felt quite comfortable with the Finneys, who were so tenderhearted and compassionate.

When the couple sat beside her, Julianna said, "Let me explain first of all that I am a widow."

"Oh, we're so sorry," Finney said. "Did this happen recently?"

"Yes, sir. Less than a month ago. But since there's ample time, let me go back a ways."

"We're listening, dear," Matilda said.

Julianna began her story at the time she was fourteen, when her parents arranged her marriage to Jean-Claude. She went on to tell about her parents being killed during the Battle of New Orleans, and of her disappointing marriage. She explained how her father's attorneys had conspired with the executives of the Daguerre Shipyards to steal her wealth from her. And then how Jean-Claude had died.

"So now," she concluded, "I am unhappily going to Idaho to live with my dead husband's parents, because I have nowhere else to go. This has been very difficult for me. Most of all I lament the loss of my wealth."

Larissa began to fuss, and woke up. As Julianna started to pick her up, Mrs. Finney jumped to her feet and said, "Oh, may I hold her?"

"Why, of course," said Julianna.

Matilda picked the baby up, cooing to her, and Larissa's fussing soon stopped.

While Matilda entertained Larissa, Finney said, "Mrs. LeCroix, I—"

"Oh, please, Dr. Finney, call me Julianna."

"All right," he said with a smile. "I was about to ask you a very important question that relates to all of this sorrow and loss of material things you've been talking about."

"Certainly. Go ahead."

"Life here on earth is really quite short, wouldn't you say?"

"Well, yes."

"More important than what has happened to you these past

few weeks, Julianna, is where you are going to go when you die. Let's say that you were to die today...where would you go?"

Julianna looked at him blankly for a moment, then replied, "Well, I suppose I would go to heaven."

"You suppose?"

"Yes."

"But you don't know?"

"Nobody can know, can they? I mean, it all depends on what kind of life you live. If you're bad, you go to hell, and if you're good, you go to heaven."

Charles Finney smiled. "That's the general consensus, Julianna, but it's based on man's philosophies and religious tradition, and not on the Word of God. The Lord Jesus Christ said, 'Except a man be born again, he cannot see the kingdom of God.' And that's heaven, of course. If a person doesn't go to heaven when they die, God's Word says they go to hell."

"Born again," Julianna said. "I've heard of it, but I never really knew what it was."

As Finney read Scriptures to Julianna, he explained that when a person was born again—born of the Spirit—there was once again spiritual life because they became children of God. The new birth placed them in the family of God.

With his Bible open to John 1, Finney placed his finger on verse 10 and said, "Read me verses 10 through 13, Julianna. It's speaking here of the Lord Jesus Christ."

She looked down at the page and read aloud: "'He was in the world, and the world was made by him, and the world knew him not. He came unto his own, and his own received him not. But as many as received him, to them gave he power to become the sons of God, even to them that believe on his name: which were born, not of blood, nor of the will of the flesh, nor of the will of man, but of God.'"

Julianna looked up at the balding, thin man, and waited for his comments.

Finney said that to be born again, Julianna would have to believe on the name of the Lord Jesus Christ and accept the fact that He died on Calvary's cross, shed His blood, was buried, and rose again from the dead. There was no other way of salvation.

He showed her that Jesus said, "Except ye repent, ye shall all likewise perish." That repentance was a change of mind about sin, a complete turning away from her unbelief and turning to the Lord Jesus by faith, acknowledging her sins, asking for forgiveness, and believing that Jesus does all the saving, from start to finish.

Finney looked at Julianna expectantly. She was listening, yet she seemed a bit preoccupied.

"Do you understand what I've shown you so far, Julianna?" Finney asked.

"Why…yes, sir."

"Do you see now why I said the general consensus that bad people go to hell and good people go to heaven is wrong?"

"I…well, yes."

"Julianna, you seem quite preoccupied. Let me ask you something."

"Yes, sir?"

"You made the statement that most of all you lament the loss of your wealth."

"Yes."

"But your eternal soul is much more important than material goods and money. Your wealth could never buy you a place in heaven. Let me show you something." Finney flipped pages and stopped at Matthew 6.

"Jesus says here: 'Lay not up for yourselves treasures upon earth, where moth and rust doth corrupt, and where thieves break through and steal: But lay up for yourselves treasures in heaven, where neither moth nor rust doth corrupt, and where thieves do not break through nor steal: For where your treasure is, there will your heart be also.' You know about thieves, don't you? From what happened to your estate in New Orleans."

"I sure do."

"What we hold onto in this world can be taken away from us in the blink of an eye, Julianna. You need to lay claim to a place in heaven, which no one can steal from you. You need to set your heart on things in heaven, and not on earth. Unless you're born again, you'll not only lose whatever you've clung to in this world when you die, but you'll lose your own soul. And Jesus said, 'For what shall it profit a man, if he shall gain the whole world, and lose his own soul?'"

Julianna blinked, but didn't speak.

Finney flipped pages again, and said, "Julianna, let me show you the story of a rich man who died lost. It's in Luke chapter 16."

Julianna listened closely as Finney read her the story of the two men who died and went into eternity—Lazarus and the rich man. He pointed out how the rich man died and instantly lifted up his eyes in hell, crying for water, saying that he was tormented in the flame. After he died, the lost man was never called "the rich man" again. He had lost his earthly riches the moment he died, and he would be in hell forever.

As the evangelist spoke, Julianna felt an inexplicable discomfort.

Finney read the conviction on her face and said, "Julianna, you can be born again right here in this train station if you will open your heart to the Lord Jesus. You need to settle this before it's eternally too late. Jesus will wash your sins away in His precious blood the instant you call on Him for salvation."

Julianna kept seeing the rich man in the flames of hell begging for water. She shook her head to clear the picture from her mind and said, "Dr. Finney, I appreciate your talking to me, but please understand, it's all so new to me. I have never heard these things before. Not as clearly as you have stated them. I...I just need time to think on all of this."

"I understand," he said. "Just don't put it off. God warns in His Word not to boast about tomorrow, for we don't know what a day may bring forth."

"I understand, sir. Please know that I appreciate your concern."

"Would you mind if I pray for you?" he asked.

"Why, of course not."

"All right. Would you bow your head with me while I pray?"

"You...you mean, right now?"

"Yes, of course."

"In front of all these people?"

"Oh, I'm sorry. Would it embarrass you?"

"Well, I'm just not used to—"

"I promise to pray quietly."

"All right."

Matilda Finney was walking the baby close by and was praying in her heart that what seed her husband had sown would soon take root and bring home the harvest of Julianna's salvation.

The evangelist asked God to help Julianna open her heart to Jesus soon, and to give her and the baby a safe journey to their destination. When he finished praying, he looked up at the big clock and said, "We need to head for our train now. Thank you for allowing me to talk to you, Julianna. Matilda and I will be praying for you."

He reached into a vest pocket and handed her a card, saying, "Our address in Oberlin is on this card, Julianna. Please write and let us know when you get to Boise, and even more important, please write to us when you open your heart to the Lord."

Julianna smiled and reached for the baby. Matilda kissed

Larissa's fat cheek and handed her to her mother. She then embraced Julianna, saying she would be praying for her, and the Finneys hurried away to catch their train.

Julianna watched the couple until they melted into the crowd, then sat down and pondered the words of the last hour or so. No one had ever talked to her like Dr. Finney had. Sapphire Johnson had dropped little things now and then, quoting Scripture, but she refrained from going any further probably because she was a servant.

But the Finneys...there was something special about them. They seemed to have an inward peace and a glow on their faces like she had never seen before. Maybe there really was something to this born-again, washed-in-the-blood-of-the-Lamb business. She would give it more thought later.

CHAPTER SEVEN

The conductor paused as he walked through the rocking, swaying coach and looked at the elderly woman sitting behind the sleeping young mother with the baby girl. "Should I awaken her, ma'am?"

The silver-haired woman looked at Julianna, who was moaning and twitching. "It looks like she's having a nightmare of some kind, sir, and if I were her, I'd want to be awakened."

"All right."

The conductor leaned past the sleeping baby and touched Julianna's shoulder. "Ma'am?"

Julianna gave a cry and came awake, and the conductor found himself staring into fear-filled eyes.

"Ma'am, are you all right?" he asked.

Julianna shook her head and blinked, looking around. Cold sweat beaded her brow. "Y-yes, sir. I'm...I'm fine. Thank you." She looked at the darkness outside, and said, "Where are we now?"

"Eastern Iowa, ma'am."

"Can I do anything for you, dearie?" came a feeble voice from behind.

Julianna turned and looked over her shoulder. "No, thank you, ma'am. I'm all right now. It was just a dream."

Larissa was awake and fussing. Julianna picked her up and held her close, speaking softly to her while the nightmare clung like cobwebs to the walls of her mind. It was the rich man in the flames of hell, crying for water and begging for Lazarus to be allowed to go back to earth and warn his five brothers.

In the nightmare, Julianna was there on the edge of hell, looking down at the poor man. The heat of the flames were scorching her face. And it felt as if something was pushing her toward the flames.

Larissa began to cry. "Okay, honey," Julianna said, "let's go to the washroom and take care of things."

When mother and baby returned to their seats some twenty minutes later, Julianna held Larissa until she was asleep, then laid her on the pillow beside her.

Julianna sighed as she stared out the window at the sparks from the engine riding the night air. Her thoughts went back to her conversation with Dr. Finney. After pondering it for a while, she convinced herself that she needn't let it upset her. She was young and healthy and had plenty of time to prepare for eternity.

At seven-thirty the next morning, the train rolled into Des Moines. Some passengers got off, but more boarded. When Julianna saw that the coach was filling up, she lifted Larissa from her pillow and said, "Looks like Mommy's going to have to hold you now, honey. Somebody will need this seat."

No sooner had she spoken than a young woman paused at the seat and said, "Is someone sitting here?"

"No, but there will be when you occupy it," Julianna replied, smiling warmly. She pulled her overnight bag closer to her feet to make room.

The young woman laughed. "Well, I guess you're right about that!" When she had placed her own overnight bag in the rack overhead, she sat down and laid her purse between them. "My, what a beautiful little girl!" she exclaimed.

"Thank you."

"How old is she?"

"Almost ten months."

"And the two of you are traveling alone? Her daddy's not with you?"

"No," Julianna said softly. "My husband died a couple of weeks ago."

"Oh, I'm so sorry. How inconsiderate of me!"

"Please don't apologize. I'm Julianna LeCroix, and this is Larissa. We're from New Orleans on our way west to Boise, Idaho."

"And I'm Kathleen Lindley from right here in Des Moines, and I'm on my way to Omaha. Just a short trip."

The conductor's voice outside the train was calling for all passengers to board. Moments later, the whistle blew and the train was in motion.

Kathleen's attention was drawn back to Larissa. She asked if she could hold her, and the two of them got along fine until Larissa needed changing. Julianna excused herself and took the baby to the washroom. When they returned, Larissa was happy and cooed herself to sleep in her mother's arms.

Kathleen scooted as close to the edge of the seat as possible and said, "I think there's room for her to lie here on the seat."

Juilanna smiled. "Thank you." She laid the baby between them, then eased back in the seat. "I didn't get much sleep last night, Kathleen. If you'll excuse me, I'm going to try to get some right now."

"Sure. Go right ahead."

Julianna had no idea how long she'd been asleep, but when she opened her eyes, she saw that Larissa was still asleep on the pillow, and Kathleen was reading a small Bible, which she had apparently taken from her purse.

Kathleen looked up and said, "I can never get enough of this Book. Do you read the Bible?"

Julianna licked her lips and said, "Oh, sometimes."

"Do you know its Author?" Kathleen asked.

"Do I what? Do I know its author, did you say?"

"Yes. Are you a Christian, Julianna? The genuine kind, I mean. The born-again kind?"

"Well, I...I had a long talk with a preacher about it at the Chicago railroad station yesterday morning."

"Oh, really?"

"Mm-hmm. I think he may be quite well known. He's an evangelist. Finney was his name. Dr. Charles Finney."

Kathleen's eyes bulged. "You talked with *the* Dr. Charles Finney? The Charles Finney who used to be president of Oberlin College in Ohio?"

"Yes. That's him."

"My, oh my! What a great preacher! I've heard him twice, when he came to Des Moines to hold revival services. And you got to talk to him!"

"And his wife."

"Well, isn't that something! Did he lead you to the Lord?"

"Well...no. Actually, I had never heard the things he showed me from the Bible. I told him I needed time to think on them."

"Just don't wait too long, Julianna. God's Word warns us not to put it off."

"I understand that. Dr. Finney told me the same thing."

The conductor came through the car, calling out that the train would be in Omaha in ten minutes.

Julianna looked out the window at the broad, open land of low rolling hills and shallow washes. She could tell winter was coming. The grass was tawny, and what few trees she could see were losing their leaves.

She was relieved when she saw Kathleen put the Bible back in her purse.

She was even more relieved when, fifteen minutes later, Kathleen got off the train in the Omaha station.

Julianna waved to Kathleen as she drifted away in the crowd, then picked up Larissa, who was awake and wanting to be held.

With the baby in her arms, Julianna watched the people milling about the depot like busy ants and pondered her encounters with Kathleen Lindley and Charles Finney. She wondered if God was picking on her for some reason. Why did He keep sending people to talk to her about being saved? She would attend to spiritual matters when she was older.

Hannah Cooper made sure her three oldest children were bundled up warmly as they prepared to leave the upstairs apartment above the store. The door of the apartment was on the back side of the building, overlooking the alley.

"I want all three of you to study hard in school today," she said. "Especially you, B. J."

"I always study hard, Mama."

"Then why don't your grades show it? Seems to me you're daydreaming in class or something. Your arithmetic grades last time were especially low. Am I going to have to talk with Miss Lindgren and set up extra sessions just for you?"

B. J.'s face was red. "I'm sorry, Mama. I'll do better from here on out."

Mary Beth giggled. "Too bad Miss Lindgren doesn't give grades for how quick you can get out of the schoolhouse when she dismisses us, B. J. You'd be a straight-A student!"

"Okay, so I don't hang around in the classroom any longer than necessary," said the eight-year-old. "Other than arithmetic, my grades aren't so bad."

"And you just promised me you'd do better in that, didn't you, B. J.?"

"Yes, Mama. And I will."

Patty Ruth was cradling Biggie in her arms as she looked on.

"Well, we'd better be going," Chris said. "Don't want to be late for school!"

The little redhead laughed. "Don't wanna be late for makin' eyes at Abby, neither!"

Chris stabbed her with a look of mock anger and opened the door. B. J. kissed his mother and hurried out ahead of the others.

"B. J.!" Patty Ruth called. "You're s'posed to be a gennul-man an' let Mary Beth go out first!"

Mary Beth kissed her mother and followed, saying, "B. J., don't you do it!"

Chris kissed his mother and headed out the door.

Patty Ruth called out, "Hey, Chris! Aren't you gonna kiss Biggie?"

There was no answer.

Patty Ruth ran to the open door and said loudly, "You ain't gonna kiss Abby, are ya?"

The older children paused at the top of the stairs as Patty Ruth took hold of Biggie's paw and moved it up and down so Biggie was waving to them.

The early morning air had a bite to it, and there was a stiff breeze.

"Bye, kids," said Hannah. "See you this afternoon."

As she pulled the door closed, Mary Beth could be heard saying, "B. J., don't you do it!"

Just as the door clicked shut, there was a thundering noise on the stairs. Hannah shook her head, knowing that B. J. had once again teased his big sister by stomping his feet on each stair to give it the sound of thunder. She rolled her eyes toward the ceiling and said, "Just like Grandma Cooper said your papa used to do, Patty Ruth."

Patty Ruth giggled. "B. J.'s a whole lot like Papa, isn't he, Mama?"

The mention of Solomon brought a lump to Hannah's throat. "Yes, honey. He sure is."

They could hear Mary Beth bawling out her younger brother and B. J. making a retort that was indistinguishable. Chris also said something Hannah and Patty Ruth couldn't make out, then Mary Beth said loud and clear, "Boys! They're the stupidest creatures God ever made!"

Patty Ruth giggled. "Mary Beth's pretty smart!"

Hannah smiled. "Well, Patty Ruth Cooper, we need to get down there to the store and stock a few shelves before opening time."

"All right, Mama Hannah Marie Cooper." Then she looked into the little dog's dark brown eyes and said, "You have to stay up here, Biggie Marie Cooper."

Hannah moved down the hall toward her bedroom, shaking her head and smiling to herself. "Lord," she said in a whisper, "what would I ever do without my little Patty Ruth? Is this baby in my womb going to be another corker like her?" She called aloud over her shoulder, "Patty Ruth, put your jacket on. It's cold outside."

Hannah went to the closet and took out her coat. As she was slipping it on, her attention went to the gold-framed photographs on the dresser—precious treasures that by the hand of God were not in the previous apartment the night Alex Patterson set the building on fire. One photograph was the handsome Captain Solomon Cooper in his Union Army uniform. The other was their wedding picture.

She picked up the picture and felt warm tears fill her eyes as she let sweet memories flood her mind. She set the wedding picture down and picked up the other frame. "Darling, I miss you," she said. "God's grace is proving sufficient for us, but we still miss you and love you so very much."

"Mama, who are you talkin' to?" Patty Ruth stood at the open bedroom door with her jacket on. Tony the Bear was under one arm.

Hannah placed the picture back on the dresser and wiped tears. "I was talking to Papa's picture, honey."

"We miss him a awful lot, don't we?"

"Yes, sweetheart."

As mother and daughter walked toward the door, Patty Ruth said, "Mama, every day in heaven do Jesus and Papa talk to each other?"

"I'm sure they do, honey."

"Good. 'Cause when I pray quiet in my bed at night, I ask Jesus to tell my papa I love him. So He does, doesn't He, Mama?"

Fresh tears threatened to spill over as they pressed against Hannah's eyelids. She tried to blink them back, but down they came.

Hannah knelt down and folded her little daughter in her arms. "Patty Ruth, that is absolutely the sweetest thing I have ever heard. Of course Jesus tells Papa you love him, when you ask Him to."

Mother and daughter descended the stairs together, and Patty Ruth helped stock the shelves that needed it—those she could reach, of course.

It was soon eight o'clock, and when Hannah went to the front door to unlock it, she found several customers waiting on the porch.

Among the women from the fort were Betsy Fordham and her five-year-old daughter, Belinda, Patty Ruth's best friend. It was Betsy's custom to take Patty Ruth to the Fordham house inside the fort on Tuesdays and Thursdays. This was a help to Hannah, and it gave Patty Ruth some variety and plenty of playtime with Belinda.

It was also Sylvia Bateman's day to help behind the counter. Sylvia came in behind the others, out of breath. She hurriedly picked up a white apron, saying, "Sorry I'm late, Hannah. Army officers are rough and rugged and all that, but when they get to Ross's age, sometimes they need a little attention from a female before they go out to face the world for a new day."

Hannah smiled. "It's all right, Sylvia. It's a little hard for me to dock your pay, since you refuse to take any."

The other women laughed, and the day's business was under way.

Before Betsy and Belinda left with their purchases, Betsy reminded Patty Ruth that tomorrow was Thursday. She and Belinda would come by to get her as usual at eight.

Hannah and Sylvia stayed busy as customers came and left in a steady stream. It was about nine-thirty when two squaws from the Crow village entered. They were dressed in the customary Indian tradition—soft doeskin dresses trimmed with fringe and colorful beadwork. They wore soft-soled leather boots that laced almost to their knees. Both of them fashioned their shiny black hair in a long braid that reached to their waists.

Hannah smiled at Sylvia as they watched the Indian women chatting with the women of the fort and town. "I wish we had that kind of friendliness with some of the other Indian tribes," she said quietly.

Sylvia nodded. "Me too."

It was almost one o'clock when Patty Ruth—feeling a bit bored—was standing at the big window, watching people pass by on the boardwalk. She was also watching for the stagecoach from Evanston. She was fascinated by the stages with their six-up teams, bright colors, and big wheels.

Patty Ruth's heartbeat quickened when she heard the rumble of the six-up team's hooves, the rattle of the stagecoach, and the driver's shrill whistle. She pressed her nose to the glass and shouted, "Mama! I hear the stagecoach!"

"That's good, honey."

Suddenly the coach passed by, and within a few seconds was out of sight. Patty Ruth carried Tony back to the open area in the store around the potbellied stove. The warmth it gave off felt good. She climbed onto one of the chairs where men sometimes sat to play checkers and shuffled the black and red pieces around on the checkerboard. "Okay, Tony," she said, "me an' you are gonna play us a game of checkers."

A few minutes later, Patty Ruth's attention was drawn to the front of the store when the bell jangled above the door. She heard Leroy Carver say, "Look, Annie Frances! Patty Ruth's back by the stove!" Both children ran to greet the little redhead.

Mandy Carver called for her children to be good and not to touch anything on the shelves, then began picking out items for purchase. Patty Ruth was glad to have playmates for a few minutes and set about to teach her little friends how to play checkers—her way, at least.

Moments later, Mayor Cade Samuels came in and chatted with Mandy and others as he picked up a few items. Shortly after Samuels entered, two husky sergeants from the fort came in—Boris Griffin and Ben Shanahan. They greeted everyone they could see, even the children by the stove, then got into a conversation with the mayor near the counter.

When Mandy approached the counter with her goods and saw that Sylvia was busy and Hannah was resting on a stool, she said, "You just stay seated, Hannah. I'll wait for Sylvia."

Hannah slid off the stool. "I will not stay seated. I'm fine. I can wait on you."

Mandy sighed and laid her goods on the counter. "You

know, Mrs. Cooper, one of these days you're going to have to let somebody else do all the work around here."

"Not till delivery time gets a lot closer, Mrs. Carver," Hannah replied with an impish smile.

While Hannah totaled the bill, Mandy leaned close and said, "Have you heard what happened when Pastor Kelly visited the Wynn ranch yesterday? Abe and I haven't had a chance to talk to him."

"Yes," Hannah said. "Pastor stopped by the store when he came back from his visit. He told me about it."

"How did it go?"

"Pastor said Wynn told him in no uncertain terms that all black people ought to be slaves in this country in spite of Abraham Lincoln's Emancipation Proclamation. He said until 'those black people' were thrown out of the church, he and his family wouldn't be coming there. Pastor Kelly said he started to give Wynn the gospel, and Wynn told him he was already a Christian."

"Oh, really?" said Mandy, with raised eyebrows.

"Mm-hmm. Pastor asked him, if he was a Christian, why didn't he have the same attitude toward all people that Jesus did. Wynn cursed Pastor and ordered him off his property."

Mandy's eyes misted. "I've been praying for the Wynns, Hannah, and so has Abe. We don't want them to be our enemies."

"I've been praying for them, too, Mandy. Well, let's see…your bill comes to $11.31."

Mandy ran her gaze over the purchases. "I figured it to be more than that, Hannah. You'd better check it again."

"Well, it was more before I figured in the discount."

Mandy put her hands on her hips. "Now, Hannah Marie Cooper, I told you not to give me any discounts just because I come in here one day a week to help you."

Hannah smiled and was about to counter with loving

words when the bell over the front door jangled, and Buford Wynn and his wife entered the store. Hannah saw them and said in a low tone, "Mr. and Mrs. Wynn just came in."

Mandy's heart pounded. She stole a furtive glance over her shoulder. "Hannah, what should I do?"

Hannah placed Mandy's change in her hand and said, "Just be your sweet self. If that man starts trouble in here, Sergeants Griffin and Shanahan will handle him, I guarantee you."

Hannah watched Buford Wynn as his eyes fell on Mandy. A deep scowl passed like a shadow down his face, but with his hand on Nelda's back, he never broke stride. Nelda turned a bit pale when she noticed Mandy at the counter.

They passed the sergeants and the mayor and drew up at the counter. Wynn looked past Mandy and spoke to Hannah in his usual loud voice: "We need to load up on groceries and supplies. Do you have any boxes we might use, or should I get some elsewhere?"

"I probably have enough empty boxes in the storeroom," Hannah replied.

Buford nodded. "Okay, then we'll start pickin' out the stuff we want."

Nelda avoided eye contact with Mandy, but Buford met her gaze then looked away.

By this time, Buford's voice had the attention of everyone in the store, including the sergeants.

Mandy smiled nervously and said, "Hello, Mr. and Mrs. Wynn."

Nelda followed her husband and moved toward a long row of shelves.

Both sergeants bristled at what they saw. Excusing themselves to the mayor, they strode toward the unsuspecting couple. "Hey, mister!" Sergeant Shanahan said.

Wynn looked over his shoulder, and the scowl returned

to his face. "You addressin' me?"

Nelda's eyes widened in fear. "Buford," she whispered, "let's leave."

Buford glared at Shanahan. "You got a problem?"

"Yeah. The lady spoke to you folks, but you ignored her. She called you by name, so I know you're acquainted with her. Fort Bridger is known for being a friendly town, and we like it that way. Now, can't you folks be courteous and return the lady's greeting?"

Buford set his jaw in a stern line. "No black woman is a lady, and we ain't returnin' no greeting."

CHAPTER EIGHT

Hannah could see down the row of shelves. She was praying silently that if Buford Wynn resisted Ben Shanahan, the store wouldn't get torn up.

As Shanahan drew close, Nelda touched her husband's arm and said in a shaky voice, "Buford, hold your temper."

Shanahan set kind eyes on Nelda and said, "Ma'am, you're free to walk around behind me, out of the way. It's your husband I'm dealing with."

"I...I don't think my husband is going to give you any trouble, Sergeant."

Shanahan looked at Buford, his eyes narrowed to wicked glints, and said, "Is she right?"

"Why...uh...I don't want no trouble, Sergeant."

"Good. Then let's go out here where the lady is standing. I want an apology from you. Number one, for ignoring her when she spoke to you so nicely. Number two, for making the asinine statement that no black woman is a lady. Understand?"

Wynn cleared his throat. "Yeah."

"All right. Come on."

Nelda looked up at her husband as they followed the sergeant out of the long aisle of shelves to where Mandy stood beside Hannah.

"Mrs. Carver," Shanahan said, "this Southern gentleman would like to say something to you."

"I...uh...I'm sorry, ma'am, for ignorin' you when you spoke to the missus and me. And...I'm sorry for sayin' that no black woman is a lady."

"Wait a minute, mister," Ben said. "When Mrs. Carver greeted you, she smiled. I want to see a smile. Start over. Smile this time."

Buford forced a smile on his lips and said, "I'm sorry, ma'am, for ignorin' you when you spoke to the missus and me. And I'm sorry for sayin' that no black woman is a lady."

Mandy stood like a statue.

"Mrs. Carver, please forgive my husband and me," Nelda said. "We are truly sorry for the way we treated you."

Mandy nodded. "I forgive you. Both of you." With that, she picked up her groceries and said, "Leroy. Annie Frances. Let's go home." She took a few steps, then stopped and looked at Ben Shanahan and said, "Thank you."

Ben grinned. "You're welcome. Tell Abe hello for me."

"I'll do that." She looked at Hannah. "See you tomorrow, honey."

"I'll look forward to it," Hannah said.

When Mandy and her children were gone, Buford said, "Well, Nelda, let's get our shopping done."

Ten minutes later, the Wynns returned to the counter and Hannah totaled up the bill. Smiling at them, she said, "So you folks are from Georgia."

"Yes, we had a farm outside of Augusta," Nelda said. "You are Hannah Cooper?"

"I am."

Patty Ruth looked on quietly as she sat at the checkers table. Her legs, far too short to reach the floor, swung rhythmically to a tune she was humming to herself.

"Must be quite a load for you to handle," Nelda said. "I mean, carrying the baby and all."

"I have lots of help," Hannah said, her gaze flicking to

Sylvia, who stood beside her. "A few of the ladies from the fort and from the town come in to help me periodically."

"That's nice. What does your husband do?"

When Sylvia noticed the look on Hannah's face, she said, "Mr. Cooper died three months ago."

"Oh, I'm so sorry."

Hannah smiled faintly. "Thank you."

When the bill was totaled and the money collected, Buford said, "Let's go, Nelda," and picked up one of the big boxes.

The two sergeants stepped forward. Boris Griffin said, "Here, Mr. Wynn. Let us help you."

Wynn blinked in surprise. "Oh. All right."

Between them, the three men had all the boxes in their arms. As they started toward the door with Nelda following, Hannah said, "Mr. and Mrs. Wynn, please come back to church and visit us again." Buford ignored her. Nelda gave her a weak smile.

Patty Ruth left her chair and moved to the counter, watching the Wynns and the sergeants leave. Tony the Bear was in her arms.

Before they reached the door, a gray-haired man opened it from the outside and held it for them. The sergeants thanked the man, as did Nelda. The gray-haired man came inside and drew up to the counter.

Hannah excused herself to the woman standing before her and said, "Hello, sir. Something I can help you find?"

Running his gaze between Hannah and Sylvia, he asked, "Is one of you the proprietor?"

"That's me," Hannah said.

"I just need to talk to you, ma'am. I'll wait till you're through taking care of the lady."

Hannah nodded, taking in the fact that his clothing was clean but worn, including his tattered overcoat. His hat had seen better days, too.

Patty Ruth looked up at him and studied his leathered, time-worn face. He smiled at her and winked. She tried to wink back, but found that both eyes closed at once.

"My name's Patty Ruth Cooper," she said. "What's your name, mister?"

The man pressed a hand to his back as he bent down to her level. "My name is Clem Cooper."

Patty Ruth's eyes widened. "Your last name is Cooper, too?"

Clem Cooper's pale blue eyes twinkled as he showed Patty Ruth another smile. This time she noticed his two shiny gold teeth. "Yes, little lady, my last name's Cooper, too."

"Are you alated to my Papa?"

Clem chuckled and stood up, straightening his back. Looking down into her eyes, he said, "I don't know, honey. Could be. But don't you mean related, not alated?"

Hannah had heard the conversation. Looking past her customer, she said, "My daughter sometimes gets her words wrong, sir."

"That's 'cause I'm jis' a little girl," Patty Ruth said. "When I get bigger and go to school, I'll learn my words better."

Clem laid a hand on her head and said, "Sure you will, honey."

While Hannah counted change back to her customer, Clem noted the stuffed bear in Patty Ruth's arms. "What's your bear's name?"

"Tony Cooper."

"Ah…that's a nice name. Tony Cooper. I never heard of a bear with a name like that."

"We have a dog upstairs in the apartment, an' his name's Biggie Cooper."

Clem laughed. The lady in front of him smiled and walked away, carrying her package. Moving up to the counter, he said, "Mrs. Cooper, that's quite a little gal you have here."

"Oh, don't I know it!" Hannah said, chuckling.

"I guess you heard me tell Patty Ruth my name's Clem Cooper."

Hannah extended her right hand over the counter. "I'm glad to meet you, Clem Cooper."

He shook her hand gently.

"Now, what can I do for you, Mr. Cooper?"

"Well, ma'am, I live alone in a shack about thirty miles north of here. I'm a widower. I only get to town once every few months. I come into town a little while ago and went inside the fort to do business at the sutler's store. Them soldiers told me that Judge Carter went out of the sutler business since the last time I was in town, and there was a new general store on Main Street. So here I am."

"I'm glad you're here," Hannah said.

As the Wynns rode out of town in the family wagon, Buford's features were set in hard lines. He stared straight ahead, gripping the reins as if he were trying to squeeze something out of them.

"Buford," Nelda said, "I'm glad you restrained yourself back there. I didn't want to see you get into it with those two sergeants."

"I could've whupped up on both of 'em," he growled. "I would've if I'd been alone. Didn't want to embarrass you, so I backed off. So let 'em think they scared me. No skin off my nose. I still hate those blacks. And now I hate white sergeants, too."

Nelda looked skyward and bit her lip.

Clem Cooper looked around the store. "Nice place. Whole lot more stuff than Judge Carter had in the sutler's store."

"We have quite a bit more room for shelves and storage," Hannah said. "Allows us to carry a larger range of items."

"That's good. Patty Ruth asked if I was related to her papa. Where is Mr. Cooper from?"

"Illinois. My husband died three months ago when we were traveling here on a wagon train."

"Oh. I'm very sorry, ma'am."

"Thank you."

"Well, I guess since he was from Illinois and I'm from Maryland, if we're related we'd have to be distantly related."

"I would suppose so. You said you wanted to talk to me. What can I do for you?"

"Mrs. Cooper, I did a dumb thing and came off from the shack without my pocketbook. I don't have any money on me. I'm almost out of everything at home. I was going to ask Judge Carter to extend me some credit so I could go ahead and load up on the supplies I need. He knows me. I realize you don't, but would you allow me to take enough on credit to last a few days? I'll come back with the money to pay you and to buy the big load I need so's I can stock up for winter."

Hannah's heart went out to the ragged old man. "Tell you what, Mr. Cooper, I—"

"Oh, you can call me Clem, ma'am."

"All right. Tell you what, Clem, I'm going to let you take what you need for the winter. I don't want you to make a sixty-mile trip back for your big load just so you can pay me. You can cover the bill when you return next spring."

"Oh, I couldn't do that, ma'am. I'll take what I need to get me by for a few days, then I'll come back for the big load. And I'll have money in my pocket to pay you."

Hannah smiled. "All right, if you insist. Just pick up what you want, and I'll total the bill so you'll know how much it is."

As Clem started down the rows of shelves, Patty Ruth laid Tony on a box behind the counter and ran after him. When she caught up, she said, "Mr. Cooper, I'll help you carry stuff to the counter."

The old man looked down at her and smiled. "Okay, but only if you'll call me Clem."

Her countenance sagged. "I can't do that, sir. My Papa and Mama told me I can't call big people by their first name unless I put mister or missus with it. Could I call you Mr. Clem?"

"Why, sure."

"Okay, Mr. Clem. I'll help you."

While Clem and his helper were carrying items from the shelves to the counter, Dr. O'Brien came in. He greeted Hannah and Sylvia, then went to a shelf and picked up a bag of coffee. When he started for the counter, Clem and Patty Ruth appeared from between two rows of shelves.

"Hello, Doc," Clem said.

"Grandpa!" Patty Ruth exclaimed. She had adopted the O'Briens as her Fort Bridger grandparents.

While the doctor was getting a hug from the little redhead, he said, "How are you, Clem?"

"Other than this arthritis in my back, I'm doin' pretty good."

"You need some powders for the pain?"

"I think I'm pretty well supplied, Doc. You gave me quite a bit when I was in town the last week of July."

Doc nodded. "All right. Good to see you again."

"You too, Doc."

Clem and his helper placed their items on the counter and went back for more.

Dr. O'Brien set the bag of coffee in front of Hannah and handed her the proper amount of money. While she opened the cash drawer, he said, "I suppose you haven't met Clem until today, have you?"

"No."

"He's a widower."

"Yes, he told me."

"Veteran of the Mexican War. Lives a lonely life in his shack about thirty miles north of town. Makes his living by doing odd jobs on ranches. Quite the handyman."

"Seems real nice. He sure hit it off with Patty Ruth."

"If a person couldn't hit it off with that precious bundle of love, something's wrong with them!"

O'Brien left, and two women came in a minute or so later. Hannah totaled Clem's bill, and he picked up about half of his packages, saying he would take them out to his wagon and come back for the rest. When he returned, he loaded his arms again, but there was one small package he couldn't pick up.

"I'll carry it out for you, Mr. Clem," Patty Ruth volunteered. "Can I carry it out for him, Mama…please?"

"Excuse me, Louise," Hannah said to her customer. "Clem, is your wagon parked on this side of the street?"

"Yes'm. 'Bout fifty feet down to the south."

"All right, Patty Ruth, you can carry the package out for Mr. Clem. But you know the rule. You are to stay on the boardwalk. Don't go into the street. You almost got yourself trampled by a horse back in Independence when you forgot that rule."

"I 'member, Mama. I won't go in the street. Promise."

"All right. Put your coat and cap on."

Patty Ruth dashed behind the counter, quickly donned coat and cap, and picked up the package.

"Thanks for extendin' me credit, Mrs. Cooper," Clem said. "I'll be back in town in a few days."

"Now, don't you make a special trip just to pay me," she told him.

"I won't, but I'll be back soon, anyhow."

Hannah smiled at him and turned back to her customer.

Patty Ruth followed on Clem's heels as he led the way down the boardwalk. People greeted him and Patty Ruth along the way.

A team of husky chestnut horses was hitched to Clem's wagon. They bobbed their heads and snorted when he drew up.

The child's attention was quickly drawn to a yellow-haired dog on the wagon seat. Looking at Clem, he made a low, whining sound and attempted to wag his tail.

"Miss me, boy?" Clem asked, grinning at the dog. "We'll be on our way home pretty soon."

Patty Ruth cocked her head and scrutinized the dog, who didn't take his eyes off his master. His right ear had been all but chewed off. His right foreleg was nothing but a stump. He had only one eye, and his tail was broken where it joined his body, making it wag in a lopsided manner.

As Clem took the package from Patty Ruth, he noticed that she was studying his dog. He grinned, placed the package in the wagon bed, and said, "You like my mutt, Patty Ruth?"

"Uh-huh," she said with a nod, unable to take her eyes off him. She had never seen a dog with so many things wrong with him.

"I found him wanderin' on the prairie one day 'bout six months ago," Clem said. "He needed a home, and I needed some company, so I took him in. Didn't know his name, so I gave him one."

"What did you name him, Mr. Clem?"

"I call him Lucky."

Suddenly there was a burst of laughter from behind him. Clem turned around to see who it was. Lieutenant Dobie Carlin and his wife, Donna, had stopped to look at the unusual dog. Clem didn't know the Carlins, but he grinned as they kept laughing and repeating the dog's name.

"You folks got it, didn't you?" he said, breaking into laughter himself.

"You've got quite a sense of humor, mister!" Carlin said. "Don't you think so, Patty Ruth?"

The little redhead gave the lieutenant a blank look. "I...guess so."

The Carlins went on down the street, laughing.

"Mr. Clem..." Patty Ruth said, tugging on his coat.

"Yes, honey?"

"What was so funny?"

The old man laid a hand on her head and said, "Tell you what, sweetie face, you'd have to be a little older to understand."

Patty Ruth shrugged. "Could I pet Lucky? Please?"

"Of course. Lucky likes kids."

Clem picked her up and set her on the wagon seat, saying, "Get ready for a face wash."

Lucky wagged his broken tail, climbed into Patty Ruth's lap, and started licking her face. She giggled and petted him. She was used to face washes from Biggie and didn't try to avoid Lucky's kisses. There was an instant bond between the two.

While Patty Ruth and Lucky were getting acquainted, a man drew up on horseback and greeted Clem, calling him by name. They knew each other well, and got into a conversation.

After a few minutes, Hannah stepped out of the store, wondering what was keeping her daughter. She quickly spotted Patty Ruth and the strange-looking dog on the wagon seat. She noted that Clem and Farley Wilson—a local rancher—were talking.

Patty Ruth was giggling as her mother approached.

"Hi, Mama!" said the happy little girl. "I've got a new friend!"

Hannah smiled as she drew up. "I guess so. He really seems to like you!"

"He's so cute, isn't he?"

"I won't tell Biggie you said that."

Rubbing the dog's head, Patty Ruth said, "Mr. Clem found him out on the prairie a long time ago. Mr. Clem was lonely, so he took him home to live with him and gave him a name."

"So what did Mr. Clem name him, honey?"

"He named him Lucky, Mama."

Hannah put her hand to her mouth and nose as she

snorted and broke into a laugh. "Lucky? Really? Clem, you named this poor beat-up animal Lucky?"

Laughing with her, Clem nodded. "Yep, I sure did!"

When Hannah's laughter subsided, she rubbed her arms and said, "Come on, Patty Ruth. Mr. Clem has to head for home, and I'm getting cold out here."

Patty Ruth kissed the top of Lucky's head and told him good-bye. She got another kiss or two from the dog, and Clem lifted her down from the seat. He thanked Hannah once again for extending him credit, and as he climbed into the wagon, mother and daughter headed back toward the store.

Lucky started barking and wagging his tail as he looked directly at Patty Ruth. She glanced back and waved, saying, "Bye, Lucky! Come back an' see me!"

Clem pulled away, and Patty Ruth hurried to the edge of the boardwalk and cried, "Bye, Lucky-y-y!"

The little yellow dog was still yapping when the wagon passed from view.

Sylvia was waiting on a customer as mother and daughter moved behind the counter. While removing her cap and coat, Patty Ruth said, "Mama, what's funny about Lucky's name? You laughed when I told you what it was, and so did Mr. Lieutenant Dobie and his wife."

"Well, honey, it's just that the little dog has had so many bad things happen to him, that he really isn't what people would call lucky."

She screwed her face up. "Huh? I don't understand."

"It's all right, sweetie. When you get older, you'll understand."

That night at the supper table, Hannah told her other children about the little beat-up dog and what Clem Cooper had named him. Chris and Mary Beth started laughing right away, and soon B. J. caught on too.

Biggie was next to Patty Ruth's chair because she often slipped him little morsels of food.

"I still don't see what's so funny about Lucky's name," said Patty Ruth.

"You will someday, honey," Mary Beth said.

Patty Ruth looked down at Biggie, who was expecting more for his stomach. "Biggie," she said, leaning over to meet his gaze, "I met a dog today who only had three legs. One of his eyes was gone, his tail was broken, an' one of his ears was almos' gone. His name is Lucky."

When there was no reaction to her words, Patty Ruth looked around at her family and said, "See there? Biggie didn't get it either."

Chapter Nine

Jacob Kates had been staring out the window on the left side of the swaying coach since boarding the train in Denver late in the afternoon. While the train rolled due north toward Cheyenne City, he gazed at the majestic Rocky Mountains and marveled at their jagged, saw-toothed peaks. He had never seen sky so blue, and the wide-open country around him took his breath away.

The Rockies looked as if they were taking a bite out of the lowering sun as it sent its golden light eastward, creating a red-orange glare on the passenger coach windows. The plains rapidly changed color as the sun dropped.

Jacob faced this new chapter in his life with excitement and trepidation. He had wanted to travel to the Wild West almost since arriving in this country at six years of age. He had learned of it in school and had told himself that one day, when he was grown up, he was going west. The dream had taken some fifty years.

He had never been farther west than Hoboken, New Jersey, until climbing aboard the train in Grand Central Station and riding it into the sunset. Large, busy, congested cities were all Jacob had ever experienced. But in spite of his lifelong dream, he felt some fear of the unknown as the towering Rocky Mountains loomed up on his left and the vast prairies spread out before him. There seemed to be so much emptiness—great expanses of windblown sagebrush, few trees, and nothing to hinder the endless wind until it encountered the mountains.

Since crossing from Illinois into Iowa, it seemed there was a tremendous distance between towns and villages. And now, much farther west, the distance between ranches appeared almost endless.

And so here he was drawing closer to Cheyenne City, where his longtime friend, Eli Goldman, waited at the depot with the man who was going to give him a job that was mostly out of doors—something Jacob had yearned for since growing into manhood.

"Dear God of Israel," he said in a whisper, "I am a bit frightened. I implore You, help me as I begin this new life."

By the time the conductor passed through the coach to announce that Cheyenne City was less than fifteen minutes away, the prairie twilight was rapidly succeeding the sunset. It accentuated the forlorn loneliness of the wide-open spaces.

The Cheyenne City depot's lamplighter had been moving from lantern to lantern along the platform for several minutes when Eli Goldman and his goods supplier, Manfred Collier, slipped into the crowd waiting for the Denver train.

"As I told you," said Goldman, a small, wiry man like Jacob Kates, "Jacob knows how to market goods and how to sell. He's going to do well as a peddler."

"Well, if he's anything like you, my friend, he will."

The whistle could be heard in the gathering darkness, and soon the blinding headlight of the engine illuminated the station. As the train came to a hissing stop, people inside the coaches waved to friends and loved ones, while others took luggage down from the overhead racks.

Eli let his gaze roam from car to car, looking for the familiar face of his friend. Suddenly there he was, stepping down from the front of car number three. Eli pointed, and Collier followed him as he threaded his way through the crowd, smiling and waving.

Jacob saw Eli, and his face lit up. Eli was the first familiar thing Jacob had seen since pulling out of Grand Central Station almost five days ago.

"Jacob!" Eli cried.

"Eli, you old scoundrel!" Jacob set his small bag down so they could embrace.

They pounded each other on the back for what seemed an age to Manfred Collier, then Eli turned and introduced the two men.

When they shook hands, Collier said, "Welcome to the wild and woolly West, Jacob!"

"Thank you."

"And how was your trip...other than tiring?" Collier asked.

"It was fine. I got to see a lot of country my eyes had never beheld before. I especially love your Rocky Mountains, though I've only seen them from a distance."

"You'll get closer looks, I promise," Collier said, chuckling.

"You have more luggage, I assume?" Eli asked.

"Yes. A trunk and a couple of suitcases."

"We'll find us a porter and have them wheeled to the carriage out in the parking lot," Collier said.

Some twenty minutes later, the three men were riding in a carriage with Eli at the reins.

"We'll take you to your hotel, Jacob," Eli said. "Get you settled in your room. Then we'll eat in the dining room."

"First thing in the morning," Collier said, "we'll pick you up and take you to the warehouse where the goods are stored. As I told you by mail, I have a boxed-in wagon ready for you, along with a team of mules. And as we agreed, you can pay me back a little at a time for the wagon and team. We'll sign our contract at the warehouse in the morning."

"Sounds good to me," Jacob said, a lilt in his voice.

"I want to be there when you sign the contract, Jacob," said Eli. "Then I've got to pull out on my run and head for Nebraska Territory."

Jacob Kates was excited the next morning when the carriage pulled onto the grounds at the warehouse with a huge sign declaring the building to be the business place of Collier Distributors, Incorporated. Near the office door stood a bright-colored boxed-in wagon with yellow wheels. Painted on both sides in large letters was:

JACOB KATES
Peddler with the Goods
You Name It, I've Got It

"Looks great to me," Jacob said. "Let's get that contract signed!"

They sat down in Manfred Collier's office, and Collier went over the contract carefully, making sure Jacob understood it.

When the papers were signed, Eli stood and said, "Well, old friend, I've got to be moving out. Glad to have you aboard."

"Thank you, Eli. I'm truly grateful to be here."

When Eli was gone, Jacob and Collier sat down again, and Collier said, "You recall, I'm sure, that there will be a three-day training period, Jacob, then you'll be on your way, too."

"Yes, sir. I can hardly wait."

Collier opened a desk drawer and pulled out a map. "This is a map of Wyoming Territory, Jacob. It will be yours to keep.

Take a look as I point out your route."

Jacob noted a red line drawn across southern Wyoming. Collier took him through the route slowly, pointing out every stop he was to make from Cheyenne City to the Utah border. He would stop in every town, village, and settlement along the route. The main towns were Fort Sanders, Laramie, Walcott, Rawlins, Wamsutter, Rock Springs, Green River, Fort Bridger, and Evanston.

When Collier was satisfied Jacob understood the route, he said, "We're not far from winter, Jacob. Coming from New York, you know what snow is. But out here, it's different. It snows more, and the high winds make for blinding blizzards. You don't want to get caught out on the plains between towns. As you saw on the map, there's never more than thirty miles from one stop to the other.

"Rely on advice from the locals when it looks like bad weather is in the offing. If they tell you not to chance the next leg of the route, you stay put till the weather clears. There are always barns where you can keep the mules, and there'll be places where you can park the wagon and stay in a warm house. If there's a Wells Fargo office where you're forced to lay over, those folks'll be glad to give you a warm place to stay. They'll let you keep your mules in their barn, too."

"All right, Mr. Collier."

"Now, as you'll see when I take you outside to your wagon, it's equipped with a small potbellied stove for heating and cooking, and the box is well insulated to keep out the cold. There's plenty of room for food and firewood, as well as your wares. Do you know how to use a gun?"

"I've never fired one."

"Well, I've supplied you with a .44-caliber nine-shot Winchester rifle and plenty of ammunition. There are hostile Indians about and robbers on the plains. I'll show you how to work the rifle. Of course, I hope you'll never need it."

"Me too."

"With Indians, don't try to outrun them with your mules. Those pinto ponies are too fast. Best thing to do if you see them riding toward you is to wave, smile, and act friendly. Chances are, since you offer no threat to them, they'll pass on by. If you're forced to defend yourself, get inside the wagon and fire through the small window in the door."

Jacob nodded again. "Same with robbers?"

"Ordinarily, all a robber will want is what cash you're carrying. Carry enough in your pockets to make it look good, but hide the bulk of your money in the small compartment in the false floor of the wagon. I'll show it to you."

"Okay."

"Any questions?"

"Yes. When are we gonna go look at my wagon?"

Four days later, Jacob Kates rolled out of Cheyenne City in his bright red wagon with yellow wheels and headed west for Fort Sanders.

The eighteen miles seemed to pass swiftly as he enjoyed the scenery, and soon he pulled into the small town that lay just south of the army's fort.

The novelty of having a peddler in town caught on quickly. Jacob parked his wagon on the main thoroughfare in the middle of town, set up his table, which was hinged to one side of the wagon, and had a large crowd around him as he lifted his voice and began advertising his wares.

Sales were excellent for the size of the town, and Jacob was encouraged. He slept in his wagon that night and headed out for his next stop the next morning.

Julianna and Larissa LeCroix arrived in Denver late in the afternoon. The railroad people had made her a reservation at the Rocky Mountain Hotel. The Cheyenne City train was scheduled to leave the next morning at six o'clock.

A carriage from the hotel provided transportation for Julianna and Larissa, along with several other Cheyenne City-bound passengers, from the depot to the hotel.

Mother and baby settled into their room, and by the time Larissa had been changed and fed, it was time for Julianna's supper. She didn't look forward to eating alone in the hotel dining room, but she entered the dining room anyway with Larissa in her arms and was seated by the host at a table where she could lay the baby on a chair next to her.

Even while Julianna was reading the menu, several people stopped to admire the chubby baby girl.

Julianna's appetite was dull, but she ordered a nutritious meal. Once she began to eat, she realized she was actually quite hungry and finished every bite of the hearty meal, including a sizable piece of dried-apple pie.

Before going upstairs, Julianna stopped at the desk and ordered hot water and a tub sent up to her room. When the tub and water arrived, she mixed hot and cool water in a small washbowl and bathed Larissa, dried her off, and put her in warm nightclothes. Larissa's eyes were already droopy, and by the time Julianna laid her in the crib and pulled the covers snugly up around her, she was asleep.

The buckets of hot water were still steaming as Julianna poured the water into the tub, saving enough to rinse with. It felt good to slip down into the soothing hot water all the way up to her neck. On the train it had been quick spit baths only.

She bathed thoroughly, then sat for a long time in the

soapy water, almost dozing. When the water became too cool to enjoy, she roused herself, used the last of the water in the buckets to rinse, and stepped out of the tub.

After drying off, she put on a warm nightgown, then went to her sleeping baby and adjusted the blanket. She lightly caressed Larissa's ringlet-covered head and tenderly kissed her soft, rosy cheek.

A weary and lonely Julianna padded to the nightstand, doused the lantern's flame, slipped between the cool sheets, and pulled the covers up to her chin. Sleep, however, eluded her.

How could this horrible tragedy have happened? How could they steal everything she had and get away with it? Was there no justice? Didn't God care?

Julianna continued to toss and turn, periodically fluffing her pillow. It felt to her as if it were made of stone. She thought of her talk with Sapphire and of the Scripture Sapphire had shown her about Jacob, his pillow of stone, and the angels.

The angels...should she do as Sapphire had said and ask help from God's angels? She thought on it a moment, then decided that Julianna René Daguerre LeCroix had always handled her own problems in life. Somehow she would get herself through this horrid time.

The next morning, weary from lack of sleep, Julianna boarded the train with Larissa in her arms. The conductor came through the coach as the train chugged out of Denver's Union Station, announcing that there would be three stops—Longmont, Loveland, and Fort Collins—before they reached Cheyenne City.

On a large cattle ranch in the mountains west of Fort Collins, rancher Wes Goodloe left the big ranchhouse with his son,

Buck, at his side. Buck had married and bought himself a ranch in Montana. He and his wife were back for the first time since leaving Colorado two years ago.

Father and son strode the fifty yards between house and bunkhouse, meeting up with cowhands, some of whom knew Buck and welcomed him back.

The ranch was in a valley, with towering mountain peaks on all four sides. The highest peaks were already glistening white with snow.

"So this fella doesn't want to stay on as one of the regulars?" Buck asked.

"No. Jack's a drifter, son. Mighty good with horses and with a gun. He'd sure make a good regular here, but he doesn't seem to want to put his roots down. So, whenever he comes by lookin' for work, I put him on."

Buck looked at a long-legged gray roan that stood near the bunkhouse door, reins looped on the pommel of the saddle. "That his horse?"

"Yep. Good for herdin' cattle, as you can see."

The door opened, and a tall, slender, sandy-haired man emerged. He was handsome in a rugged sort of way and had a Colt .45 slung low and tied down on his right hip. He wore a plaid mackinaw and a gray, wide-brimmed Stetson.

"Good morning, Mr. Goodloe," he said. "This your son?"

"Sure is," said the rancher. "Buck, shake hands with Jack Bower."

The two men exchanged friendly greetings, then Wes took a small envelope from his jacket pocket and handed it to Bower. "Here's your pay, Jack. The offer still stands, you know. Anytime you're ready to settle down, you've got a regular job waitin' for you right here."

Jack stuffed the envelope in one of the mackinaw's side pockets. "I really appreciate that, sir. Maybe someday I'll get the urge to roam out of my system."

"That usually happens when a man finds the right woman, Jack. Seems like that's what it's gonna take to get you to sink your roots."

Jack chuckled. "No woman would be interested in the likes of me."

"Never know," Wes said with a laugh. "I didn't think Buck here would ever lasso him a woman, but he did. A mighty fine one, too. Your day'll come."

Jack grinned as he swung into the saddle to the squeak of stiff leather, touched his hat, and said, "See you next time, Mr. Goodloe. Pleasure to meet you, Buck."

Father and son watched Jack Bower ride away.

"Dad, you said the man's good with a gun. From the way he wears that sidearm low and tied down, I'd say he's more than good. Has the air of a gunfighter, seems to me."

"Not in the sense you're thinkin'. Jack has no desire to be a gunfighter. But driftin' around this country like he does, he's got to use his natural ability with a gun. And believe me, he can draw and shoot plenty fast and accurate. I've watched him put on a show for the cowhands. He's good. Plenty good."

It was midafternoon when Jack Bower rode down the dusty main thoroughfare that bisected the town of Fort Collins. Outside the town to the north was the fort. The town's business section was bustling as Bower angled toward the hitch rail in front of the general store. A new canteen, some beef jerky, and he would ride on.

As he was dismounting, Bower's line of sight fell on a ranch wagon across the street with the well-known T-Slash-L brand on its sides, matching the brands on the hips of the two horses hitched to it. The wagon was parked in front of the Colorado Outfitters Clothing Store.

Bower had been in Fort Collins and the surrounding area before, but never for very long. He had been there enough, however, to know about the T-Slash-L Ranch and its owner, Tack Lombard. The T-Slash-L was a large spread west and a bit north of Fort Collins, near the foothills of the Rockies. It boasted the most cattle of any ranch for fifty miles in any direction.

Tack Lombard was known to be a ruthless, hard-nosed "range bull," and when men had crossed him, more than a few had strangely disappeared. Sometimes their bodies turned up, and other times no trace of them was ever found. Though local authorities had suspicions that Lombard was behind the disappearances, he had never been charged by the law.

Larimer County Sheriff Walt Craw believed that Lombard had secretly hired men to eliminate his enemies, but there simply was no convicting proof.

Eyeing the Lombard wagon closely, Bower crossed the boardwalk and entered the general store.

Inside Colorado Outfitters, Derek Lombard—Tack's son—was buying new boots, Levi's, and hat. His six-year-old son, Danny, was with him. Derek was Tack's foreman, and in spite of his father's unpopularity in the area, most everyone liked Derek.

"You gonna be a cowboy on your grandfather's ranch someday, Danny?" Stan Meade, one of the clerks, asked.

The little boy's eyes glistened brightly. "I sure am, Mr. Meade. I'm gonna ride a big horse like Grandpa's, too!"

"You're the apple of your grandpa's eye, aren't you, boy?"

"Yes, sir. Me and Grandpa are bestest pals!"

"That's for sure, son," Derek said. "Your grandpa thinks the sun rises and sets in you."

Vern Newman, owner of the store, came from the back room and spotted Derek and Danny. "Howdy, Derek," he said.

"Hey, that's a nice-looking pair of boots."

"I kind of like them myself," said Derek, rising up and down on his toes.

Turning to the boy, Newman said, "Danny, do you suppose your dad would let me give you a piece of horehound candy? I've got some back in my office."

"Oh, boy! Could I have some, Daddy?"

"Sure, son. One piece."

Jack Bower strolled out of the general store, stepped around the end of the hitch rail, and stuffed the beef jerky into his saddlebags. He took the canteen to the water tank that stood nearby and worked the pump handle to begin filling the canteen. He decided he'd drift eastward for a while. There were a couple of ranchers out toward Fort Morgan that he'd worked for in time past.

He capped the canteen, returned to his horse, and hung the canteen on the pommel. He was about to mount up when his gaze swung down the street to a rider just pulling up to a hitch rail.

Howie Spence!

The infamous gunfighter owed Bower a gambling debt from a poker game down in Las Cruces, New Mexico, two years ago. It was time to collect.

Spence was wrapping the reins around the hitch rail when Bower stepped up behind him and said, "Well, look who's here! If it isn't my old poker-playing pal, Howie Spence!"

The cold-eyed man turned and set his gaze on Bower. His face remained impassive as he said, "Hello, Jack."

"Long time no see, Howie."

"Been a year or two, I suppose."

"Two, to be exact. Las Cruces."

"Oh, yeah. 'Bout this time of year, wasn't it?"

"Little later. November 14."

"My, how time flies, huh? So what're you doin' now?"

"Thinking about the money you owe me."

"Money? I owe you money?"

"Yeah. I beat you in a poker game at the Wagon Wheel Saloon. You remember."

Spence tugged at his gun belt, adjusting it. "You must be thinkin' of somebody else."

"You're lying, Howie, and you know it. It was almost midnight. You wrote me an IOU. Said you'd go to the bank the next morning, cash a check, and pay me. You took off in the middle of the night. I want my eleven hundred dollars, Howie."

"You got the IOU?"

"Wasn't worth the paper it was written on."

Spence shrugged his shoulders. "Without proof, whattaya got?"

People on the street were stopping to watch and listen, and customers began coming out of stores after hearing that Howie Spence was on the street, being pressed by some unidentified man to pay him a gambling debt.

The residents of Fort Collins had seen Spence around on several occasions of late and knew his reputation. The crowd was growing fast.

"What have I got?" said Bower with a sneer. "I've got a lying dude who welshed on his debt."

Spence's nostrils flared. He backed up a few steps into the street and took his stance. "If you want your money, you'll have to outdraw me and take it off my dead body."

CHAPTER TEN

T he door of Colorado Outfitters burst open and a teenage boy dashed in, wide-eyed. "Mr. Newman! Looks like there's gonna be a gunfight out here! It's Howie Spence!"

Every eye in the store turned to the boy.

Vern Newman was helping a woman pick out a gift for her husband. Turning from her, he said, "Who's Spence gonna draw against?"

"I don't know who he is. I think I might've seen him around town before, but I'm not sure. He says Howie owes him money, and Howie just said to collect it he'd have to outdraw him and take the money off his dead body!"

Derek Lombard was at the counter, paying Stan Meade for the items he had purchased. One thing he couldn't resist was watching a gunfight. "I'll came back in and pick up this stuff and my change, Stan," he said. "Come on, Danny."

Newman said to the teenage boy, "Has somebody gone for Sheriff Craw?"

"I heard a man say he was going after the sheriff, but someone told him the sheriff and his deputy were seen riding out of town about half an hour ago."

Newman's features tightened. "Why now?" he muttered more to himself than the others. "Just when we need them!"

The teenaged boy whirled about and returned to the

street, and some of the customers were already filing out the door ahead of Derek and Danny.

Excitement showed on the faces of the gathering crowd, and whispers ran among them as Jack Bower said, "Howie, I don't want to draw on you. But if you had an ounce of decency in you, you'd pay your debt like a gentleman."

Spence reached into his pants pocket with his left hand and flashed a wad of green bills. "There's more than eleven hundred here! Beat me to the draw and it's yours!"

"Why force bloodshed, Howie?" Jack said. "All I'm asking is that you pay me what you owe me."

"Well, ol' pal, you're gonna draw on me! I'm callin' you!" His words carried a flat finality.

Slowly, Bower moved away from the hitch rail and stepped into the street. Spence watched him closely, turning to square off with about thirty feet between them.

Just as Bower stopped and took his stance, Vern Newman's voice split the air.

"Wait a minute!"

Both men eyed Newman as he pushed his way through the excited crowd.

"Hold it, you two!" he blared, stepping into the dust of the street and halting after taking a couple of steps. "There's a big crowd here! Don't you care that you endanger the lives of these people? If you have to shoot it out, take your fight else-where and settle your differences where you won't put others in peril!"

Bower kept his eyes on Spence and said, "There won't be any shoot-out, mister, if Spence will simply pay me the money he owes me. His debt is eleven hundred dollars. All of these people heard him say there's that much and more in that wad he just flashed. I have no desire to draw on him. Man has a debt, he should pay it."

Newman looked at Spence. "That so, Howie?"

Spence went for his gun. Bower's weapon was out of its holster a split second sooner. The bullet struck Spence in the left shoulder, causing him to jerk sideways as his own gun fired.

Women screamed and a man shouted as Spence's bullet plowed into the crowd.

Bower stepped to the fallen Spence, kicked his gun out of reach, and bent over, saying, "You said I could have the money if I outdrew you. This time, I'll take you at your word."

Spence was gripping his bleeding wound. He looked up with dazed eyes as Bower reached into his pocket and relieved him of the wad of money. "You said there's more than eleven hundred here. The difference will be the interest you owe me."

A woman's voice was heard over the din of the crowd: "He's dead! Little Danny's dead!"

Everyone began gathering around the place on the boardwalk where Danny Lombard had fallen. His father was wailing.

No one noticed Bower as he dashed to his horse, vaulted into the saddle, and put the animal to a gallop. When he was finally in open country, he realized he was riding due south. He decided the best thing to do was to head into the mountains and find a secure place, then figure out what to do next. Tack Lombard would want his hide.

Marshal Lance Mangum stood before the students of Fort Bridger School and smiled as they applauded him.

Miss Sundi Lindgren was still applauding as she said, "What do we say to Marshal Mangum for taking his time to come and talk to us about law and order, boys and girls?"

"Thank you!" came the response, almost in unison.

"It's been my pleasure."

"And will you come back again sometime soon, Marshal?" Sundi asked.

"I sure will. Bye, boys and girls!"

There was more applause as Mangum passed through the door and closed it. He smiled to himself as he mounted his horse and put it to a mild trot. Lance Mangum loved children. One day he would have some of his own. Of course, first he would have to find a woman who would marry a lawman.

The schoolhouse was at the south edge of town. Mangum was near the business section when he saw a stagecoach racing into Fort Bridger from the east. It turned the corner onto Main Street, charged toward the Wells Fargo office, then slowed to a stop.

Mangum saw the driver and shotgunner hop down from the box, and he could hear a woman's wails. He touched heels to his horse's sides and rode up as the driver was helping the weeping woman from the coach. Judy Wesson was there to help the woman inside the Fargo office. Above the young woman's cries, Curly Wesson said something about the stage being almost an hour late, and the driver told him they had been held up by robbers about thirty miles back.

"Did I hear you say you've been robbed, Alfie?" Mangum asked.

"Oh, hello, Marshal. Yes, sir. Four of 'em. S'prised us by chargin' out from a grove of trees some twenty miles this side of Green River."

"Anybody hurt?"

"No, thank the Lord. They just took our guns and the money and jewelry from the passengers and rode off."

"Were they masked?"

"Yes," said shotgunner Bob Stout, "but Alfie and I both agree that those four are part of the Wade Kilbane gang."

"Kilbane? This is a bit far west for his gang to work. How could you tell?"

"Just the way they acted. Kilbane's bunch all have a way about 'em. We came up against 'em four-five times when we were runnin' the route from Cheyenne City to Sheridan over them years."

They could still hear weeping coming from the office. Looking that way, Mangum said, "What about her?"

"Oh, she just fell apart while they were robbin' us," Alfie said. "Scared her pretty bad, and upset her somethin' terrible when they took a ring offin' her finger. Might help if you talked to her a bit."

"I'll do it. Alfie, write down what description you can of the robbers, and I'll send a wire to the U.S. Marshal's office in Cheyenne City."

"Will do, Marshal."

Curly was talking to the other passengers on the board-walk while Lance Mangum entered the office. Judy and the weeping young woman were sitting side by side on a wooden bench, and Judy had her arm around her.

"Oh, lookee, honey," Judy said, "it's Marshal Mangum."

"Y-you're the marshal here in Fort Bridger?" she asked, her voice quaking.

"Yes, ma'am," he said, pulling up a chair and sitting down in front of her. "I'm going to send a wire to the U.S. Marshal's office in Cheyenne City. We'll try to catch the robbers and get back your ring and whatever else they stole. What's your name, ma'am?"

"Virginia Hallbeck," she said, sniffling. "But most folks call me Ginny. Do you think there's really a chance of getting my ring back? It was a very special gift."

"I can't promise anything, Miss Ginny," he replied, "but we'll sure try. If we should catch the robbers before they sell your ring, where could I get in touch with you?"

"Evanston," she said. "That's where I'll be living now. I'm from St. Louis."

"Do you know where you'll be living, Miss Ginny?"

"Well, I'll be staying at a boardinghouse run by a Mrs. Beatrice Waddell until I get married."

"Oh. You're getting married."

"Yes. The ring was a very special sort-of-engagement ring from my fiancé. Oh, dear. Paul's going to be upset when I tell him it's been stolen."

"Well, if you haven't heard from me by the time you get married, please leave your new address with Beatrice Waddell, and I'll contact you through her. But I caution you, don't get your hopes up. The chance of recovering the ring is pretty slim."

"I understand, Marshal," Ginny said softly. "Thank you."

Jack Bower hid in an old abandoned cabin in the Rockies for two days. On the morning of the third day he rode out, deciding to head north into Wyoming. He would stop in Cheyenne City for supplies, then head for parts yet undecided on. One thing was for sure: he had to make himself scarce in Tack Lombard's territory.

It was midafternoon the next day when Bower rode into Cheyenne City. He dismounted in front of the general store and walked inside. There were customers at the counter and several others moving about the store, picking up items from the shelves. As he began the search for the items he needed, he heard a male voice use the word *sheriff*. It was then that he saw a group of men standing around in the open area by the potbellied stove.

"You say this gunfight involving Howie Spence was three days ago, Sheriff?" one of the men said.

"That's right," said the beefy man with the badge on his chest. "And since it was Tack Lombard's grandson who took Spence's bullet, you can't tell me it wasn't somebody hired by Lombard who snuck into the clinic that very night and smothered Spence to death."

"Gotta be," said another man.

"Problem as always when Lombard has somebody killed is proving he's behind it. They don't have proof. Just talk. Can't arrest a man on talk. And you can bank on it, the big bull has hired a gang of killers to track down the other guy."

"Sheriff Craw have any idea who this other guy was?" one man asked.

"Nope. All Craw or Lombard has is a vague description of him—mainly how he was dressed and that he took off south out of town riding a gray roan."

Another said, "Ol' Tack's got the money to hire the best when it comes to tracking down a man and killing him. No matter where this guy goes, they'll find him."

Jack Bower quietly made his purchases and went back to the street. As he was putting the items in the saddlebags, his line of sight drifted up the street to the railroad station, which was a block away. He also noticed that the Wells Fargo Stagelines office was directly across the street from the station.

Bower took the beef jerky out of the saddlebags, along with a .42-caliber derringer. He put the derringer in his coat pocket and stuffed the beef jerky into one of the packages in his hands.

He walked down the street the opposite direction from the depot to the first hotel he came to. He took a room, left his purchases on the dresser, and returned to the roan. He rode the horse out of town to a place beside a creek. There he removed the saddle and bridle and gave the horse a slap on the rump to send it galloping away. He watched it head west toward the distant mountains, then threw the saddle and bridle into the creek at the deepest spot he could find.

The sun was sinking toward the western horizon when Bower entered the depot and paused to read the chalkboard schedules of daily departures and arrivals. The choice was quite limited, but he decided not to take the train that came in at 9:40 in the morning from Denver. There was a train coming in from Billings, Montana, at 9:20 in the morning. It would head back north to Billings at 10:55.

When he approached the ticket window, a thin, silver-haired man wearing a visor and sleeve garters smiled and said, "May I help you, sir?"

"Yes. I'd like to be on the 10:55 train to Billings in the morning."

"We can fix you up on that, sir."

Moments later, Bower left the depot with the ticket in his pocket and headed down the street. Before reaching the hotel, he stopped at a small café and ate his supper.

With a full stomach, he returned to his room to wait for the hour to grow late. When it was past midnight, he left the hotel by the rear exit and skulked down the alley toward a clothing store he had spotted earlier only a few doors down. He drew up behind the store and leaned for a moment against its back wall. Then he used his revolver butt to break a window.

When he had picked out new boots, Levi's, shirt, hat, and coat by the dim glow from the street lamps, he made his exit the same way he came in, carrying his old clothes, boots, and hat. He left money on the counter that more than covered the price of the clothes and broken window pane.

He went to an ash pit he had seen in the alley and found red embers inside. He dropped his shirt in first, and when it flamed up, he threw in boots, Levi's, shirt, and hat. They were catching fire when he hurried back to the hotel.

Upon rising the next morning, Jack Bower shaved and donned his new clothes. He decided he wouldn't bother carrying the beef jerky and other items he had bought. Making a quick trip out the back door of the hotel, he deposited the packages in the trash barrel and headed for the street.

He ate breakfast at a different café than the one the previous night, then walked to the depot. He went to the area where the trains came in and took a seat. There was a sizable crowd waiting on the side of the platform where the train from Denver would arrive in a few minutes.

Soon he heard a whistle. Shortly after that, the big engine chugged in, bell clanging, and ground to a halt with steam hissing from its bowels.

Bower observed the passengers who alighted, some into the arms of loved ones and friends; others looking about for familiar faces, and still others moving swiftly toward the street.

His eyes searched the crowd, looking for men who might be in quest of him. He could pick out none at the moment.

His attention was drawn to an attractive young woman who stepped off the train carrying a baby wrapped in a blanket. The mother's jet black hair was done in an upsweep, and she was wearing a tiny hat that matched her dress. She seemed to be in a hurry.

A porter hastened up behind her and caught up just as she was passing Jack Bower's bench. Bower heard the porter say, "What time does yo' stage leave, ma'am?"

"In twenty minutes. The train had to stop for a herd of antelope a few miles back. I'm glad we're not any later. The baby and I need to be on that stage."

"All right," said the porter, "I'll hurry, ma'am. I'll get yo' bags from de baggage coach an' be right over to de stage office. You tell 'em I'm comin'."

"Thank you. I will," she said without breaking stride.

Jack Bower's mind turned over a new thought. Tack Lombard's hired killers wouldn't be looking for a man traveling with his wife and baby....

Julianna LeCroix's legs were feeling the strain of her pace as she hurried through the railroad station and finally came out on the boardwalk. She spotted the stage office across the broad street, where the conductor told her it would be; then she took note of the heavy traffic. Buggies, carriages, wagons, and riders on horseback rushed by from both directions. The stage crew was loading luggage in preparation for the trip.

Larissa started to fuss.

"No, honey," Julianna said with a sigh, "not now. Mommy's very tired and in a hurry. Be a good girl, please."

It was as if Larissa understood, for the fussing trailed off into silence.

"Good girl," said Julianna, her eyes darting back and forth with the busy traffic.

Twice she started to cross, then had to step back. Frustration washed over her. She had to make that stage.

She was startled when a deep male voice from behind said, "Need some help getting across, ma'am?" As he spoke, the tall sandy-haired man stepped up beside her.

"Why, yes, I do. My baby and I are supposed to be on that stage over there. My train from Denver was delayed in getting here, and we're running late."

"Let me see what I can do."

Julianna watched as the man removed his hat and moved out into the street, waving it at oncoming traffic. Vehicles and riders began slowing and then came to a stop.

"Mother and baby coming through!" he shouted. He waved at Julianna to follow him.

When they reached the middle of the street, he did the same thing again, bringing traffic from the other direction to a halt. As they drew up on the other side, Julianna smiled and said, "I'm very grateful, sir. Thank you."

"My pleasure, ma'am."

Julianna hurried on toward the stage office. Suddenly she felt someone edge up close and rub shoulders with her. She was surprised to see the same man again and wondered at his boldness to come so close. Before she could speak, she felt a slight jab in her ribs and gasped. Still, she kept walking.

Jack Bower said, "That hard object pressing your ribs, lady, is a double-barreled derringer. Stop right now. I mean it!"

Julianna halted as ordered and looked at him with fear in her eyes, her breath coming in short gasps.

"Now, listen, lady," he said, "you show the least resistance, or try to call for help, and I'll shoot you, then the baby! I'm desperate! Don't test me, or you'll be sorry!"

CHAPTER ELEVEN

Julianna LeCroix's pulse pounded in her temples. Her skin tingled with fear, and her forehead was suddenly damp with perspiration.

Her voice shook as she said in a low tone, "Please don't shoot my baby! I'll do whatever you say."

"I assume you have a reservation on the stage."

She nodded.

"Where's it going?"

"Evanston."

"That's your destination?"

"N-no. I...the baby and I are going on to Boise, Idaho. We change to another stage at Evanston."

"I want you to go inside the stage office right now and tell them your husband met you here by surprise and he needs a ticket too."

"What? You want to ride the stage, posing as my husband?"

"You got it."

"Are you running from the law?"

"Don't ask questions, lady. Now, give me the baby and get in there!"

"I'm not giving you my baby!"

He pressed the derringer against her ribs again, causing her to wince. "Do what I tell you, or I'll shoot you both right now!"

With great reluctance, Julianna loosened her grip on Larissa and handed her to Bower, who slipped the derringer into his coat pocket and took the baby gently. Julianna patted Larissa and said, "You be a good girl, sweetheart, while the nice man holds you. Mommy will be right back."

"You're doing fine, lady," he said.

"What should I do if the seats are all filled?"

"You better pray they're not. If I'm not going, neither are you."

"I'm quite low on money. I probably don't have enough to pay for your ticket."

Jack thrust his hand into a pocket and came up with a small roll of bills. "Here. Take this. But I want back what's left."

Julianna took the money, paused, and looked into his eyes hesitantly.

"Go on, lady. It'll be all right. I'll stay right here. I can see inside the stage office. You'll be able to see me."

Larissa looked up at the man and frowned, but didn't make a sound.

Julianna rushed into the stage office, wondering why her life was filled with so much that was frightening and unpleasant.

After a few minutes, Julianna came out of the office and headed toward Jack, her features grim and pale.

"I got you a seat," she said, handing him a roll of bills. Jack was so relieved he almost smiled. He took the money and stuffed it back in his pocket.

At that instant, the porter drew up, having pushed his cart hurriedly across the street. He glanced at Jack, who was still holding the baby, then said, "Here are yo' bags, ma'am. I'll see that they get put on the stage."

"Thank you," said Julianna, trying to smile.

While her baggage was being loaded, Jack spoke in a low voice: "You're doing fine, ma'am. Just keep it up."

"If you think it's easy, you've got another think coming," she replied.

"Like I said, you're doing fine."

When the porter was gone and the bags were loaded, Julianna reached out her hands and said, "I'll take my baby now."

"Not yet," he said. "I want to know your name and the baby's name."

"I'm Julianna LeCroix. Her name is Larissa."

"What part of the South are you from?" he asked.

"New Orleans."

"Oh, of course. That explains the French name."

"I want Larissa back, now."

"In a minute."

"Now!"

Larissa sensed the tension in her mother and screwed up her little face to cry.

Jack handed her back. "Just don't try to call for help, Julianna."

Julianna held Larissa against her shoulder, patting her back to soothe her. "It's all right, sweetheart. Mommy's fine." Then to her abductor: "I'm not going to invite your wrath, Mr.— I think I have a right to know your name as well."

"Jack Bower."

"And that's the truth?" she asked, doubt showing on her face.

"Yes, ma'am. It's the truth."

"Are you running from the law?"

"No, I'm not. There's a gang of hired killers after me, but they're looking for a man traveling alone on horseback. All I want to do is elude them. You'll be saving my life if you cooperate."

"I don't believe you, Mr. Bower…if that's your name. You act like an outlaw—a desperado."

"Like I said, Julianna, you've been doing fine. Keep it up and all will be well."

Larissa studied Jack from her mother's arms and smiled at him. Jack smiled back and chucked her under the chin. She giggled and snuggled shyly into her mother's arms.

The driver and shotgunner were ready to go. The other passengers were coming out of the office. The agent emerged and said, "Mr. and Mrs. LeCroix, we're boarding now."

"Thank you," Jack said. He turned to Julianna. "Let's get on board, darling."

Julianna gave him a bland look and moved toward the coach.

There were three other passengers—two women and a man. The driver, an aging man with weathered skin the color of mahogany, introduced himself as Biff Hoxton. The young shotgunner was Ollie Finch.

When everyone was seated in the coach, Jack and Julianna were riding backwards, facing the other three. The driver cracked his whip over the horses' heads, and the stage rolled westward out of Cheyenne City.

Jack smiled at the people facing him and said, "Well, I guess we need to get acquainted. My name is Jack LeCroix, and this is my wife, Julianna. And of course, our daughter, Larissa."

"Oh, she's so cute!" said the older woman. "How old is she?"

Jack looked at Julianna, who said, "Almost ten months."

"My name is Chester Downes," said the man, who was in his early sixties. "This lady next to me is my lovely wife, Tess. And the lady next to her is her younger sister, Jean Morden. We're on our way home to Evanston."

"How far are you folks going?" Jean asked.

Jack smiled. "Evanst—"

"Boise, Idaho," Julianna said.

"Well, what I meant," said Jack, "was that we'd be changing stages in Evanston."

The stage was rocking and swaying along the road, and the morning air was quite cool. There were leather curtains on the windows, but they were constructed to allow some light in, which also let in the cold air.

Julianna pressed Larissa close to her and said to Jack, "I think we'd better ask the driver to stop. I should get another blanket for Larissa out of one of the suitcases."

"Let's just wrap her in my coat, honey," Jack said, twisting in the seat to shrug it off. "We'll get another blanket out at the next stop."

When Julianna wrapped the coat around the baby, she felt the weight of the derringer in one of the pockets. She wished there were a way to get her hands on it.

Chester set his eyes on Jack and said, "You've got my curiosity up, Mr. LeCroix."

"How's that?"

"I've never seen a blond Frenchman."

"Well, you see, I'm actually not French. I was adopted by the LeCroixs when I was a small child."

"Everybody alert down there!" came Biff Hoxton's voice from up in the box. "We've got Indians comin' our way!"

Julianna hugged Larissa to her breast as both Chester and Jack rolled up the leather window shades. A band of about a dozen Indians was riding toward them from the south. Jack's hand went to his sidearm, but he didn't pull it from the holster.

Chester squinted, trying to focus on their headbands and the feathers on their lances. After a few seconds, he said, "Shoshone...some Shoshone are friendly."

"I hope these are the friendly ones," said Jean, her face pale.

Hoxton kept the six-up team at a steady pace.

Jack saw the fear in Julianna's eyes and took hold of her hand. She started to jerk it away, then caught herself.

"What'll we do if they start shooting?" Tess asked.

"Shoot back, ma'am," said Bower, his hand still on the butt of his Colt .45.

"It's all right, folks!" came Hoxton's voice again. "They're friendly Shoshone!"

The Indians drew up at a gallop, then rode alongside the coach. The passengers watched and listened as driver and shotgunner shouted friendly words, and the Indians smiled and waved. Seconds later, they veered off the road and disappeared over a ridge.

"Whew!" Chester said. "Glad those were the friendly type!"

"We can all thank the Lord for that," said Jean.

Bower relaxed, moved his hand from the gun, and let go of Julianna's hand.

Julianna kissed Larissa and said, "It's all right, sweetheart. Those are good Indians. But if they had been bad ones, Daddy would've protected us."

Julianna swung her gaze to Jack, and he smiled at her.

The stage made a lunch stop at a way station at the edge of Fort Sanders. After lunch, Jack stood guard outside the ladies washroom while Julianna took care of Larissa's needs. Julianna had taken the extra blanket out of her suitcase, and Jack now had his coat on again.

When Julianna came out of the washroom with the happy, satisfied baby in her arms, Jack said, "I'll carry her to the stage."

As Julianna placed Larissa in Jack's hands, she noticed the baby smiled at him and cooed.

The sun was almost down when the stage rolled up in front of the Wells Fargo office in Laramie. A log building stood behind the office, which had eight rooms with beds for passengers and crew.

While crew and agent took the necessary luggage out of the rear boot and down from the rack, Jack took a walk to the building and checked it out, front and back. Julianna sat in the coach and watched him. He returned quickly, reached inside the coach, and said, "I'll take the baby."

As Julianna climbed out of the stage, she said so only Jack could hear, "You want to act out a little spat so these nice people will think you're sleeping in a separate room because we're mad at each other?"

Jack didn't answer until he'd led her out of earshot from the other passengers and the crew. "If I slept in another room, you'd be free to run away or call for help. I can't afford for that to happen, Julianna."

She bristled. "Now, look, mister, you're not—"

"Just hear me out. You don't have anything to fear. I'll sleep on the floor in front of the door. My life depends on you appearing to be my wife."

"Trying to fool some lawman, aren't you?"

"Let's just say that I like living, and I need to keep up the ruse till I know I'm safe. And I'll do anything I have to in order to survive."

After a meal in the stage stop's dining hall that evening, Jack stood outside the door of the room, pretending to get some fresh air. Inside, Julianna was feeding the baby. When that was done, she prepared herself for the night and put on a robe. The agent had provided a crib for Larissa, which was next to the bed.

Julianna carried Larissa toward the door and kissed her cheek. "We have a strange man here, honey. I'm afraid of him, yet I trust him. Does that make any sense to you?" Julianna opened the door and said, "You can come in now."

When Jack stepped inside, Larissa reached for him. He took her and said, "My, my, little girl, don't you smell good. Are you ready for bed?"

Larissa smiled and made a gurgling sound.

Jack sat down on a straight-backed wooden chair and bounced the baby on his knee.

Weary to the bone, Julianna sat on the bed, bracing her back against the headboard. She watched her abductor with Larissa and marveled at how good he was with her.

"Are you a father, Jack?" she asked. "You know how to handle babies."

"No. I've never been married. But I was the oldest in a family of seven children. I have a lot of experience handling babies."

"Did you grow up in a loving, happy home?"

"Sure. I had a good home. Why?"

"It's hard for me to understand how a man can be brought up in a loving family and end up an outlaw…and a gunfighter."

Julianna put Larissa to bed in her crib and sat back down on the bed. The baby was asleep almost immediately.

Still sitting in the chair, Jack said, "Can I ask you a question?"

"I suppose."

"Why are you going to Boise?"

"Larissa and I are going there to live."

"What about your husband?"

"He's dead."

"Oh. How long ago?"

"Not very."

"So who's in Boise?"

"My husband's parents."

"Your husband didn't leave you any money?"

"No."

"What about your own parents? Couldn't you and the baby live with them?"

"They're deceased, too."

There was silence for a few moments, then Jack said, "Sounds like you've had some rough bumps in life."

Julianna tilted her head back and closed her eyes, then looked again at Jack. "Would you like to hear my story?"

"If you want to tell it. I've got nothing else to do."

Julianna took the next half hour to give him every heartwrenching detail of Jean-Claude's slow death and how the attorneys and the company executives had stolen her fortune.

Jack's heart went out to her, but he didn't let on.

She covered a yawn and said, "Well, we'd better get some sleep. Morning will be here before we know it."

With that, she got up, took the top blanket off the bed, and picked up a pillow. Jack accepted them and said, "See you in the morning. I'll blow out the lantern."

"I'll need the lantern burning low in case Larissa wakes up in the night."

"Julianna, I assure you, as long as you cooperate in this pretense, you're in no danger from me. Try to call for help...you're in big trouble."

With that, he stretched out on the floor by the door, laid his head on the pillow, and covered himself with the blanket.

Julianna turned down the wick in the lantern, leaving the room with a soft yellow glow, and slid beneath the covers. Though she was on edge, her weariness took over, and soon she fell asleep.

At first it sounded like thunder, then Julianna realized it was someone pounding on the door.

Jack was stirring on the floor as a heavy masculine voice boomed, "We know you're in there, Bower! You're outnumbered! There's no way to escape! Open the door or we'll break it down! And we're comin' in, guns blazin'!"

Julianna sat up and stared at Jack as he rose to his feet groggily and whipped out his revolver.

Larissa fussed a few seconds, then began to cry loudly. Julianna took her out of the crib and held her close. Wide-eyed, she said, "You can't resist them, Jack! Don't make them come in here shooting! They could hit Larissa!"

A vicious look claimed Jack's face as he glanced at her, then he bellowed through the door, "I've got a woman and a baby in here! If you come in shooting, you'll kill them!"

Suddenly the door began to shake as something heavy struck it from outside. The hinges rattled with each blow, and splinters went flying.

In desperation, Jack rushed to Julianna, snatched Larissa from her, and went back to the door. Julianna wailed when he cocked the hammer of his gun and pressed the muzzle to the baby's head.

"Stop it!" Bower yelled at the top of his lungs. "Stop it! I've got a gun to the baby's head, and I'll—"

The door gave way and swung open. White flashes of blazing guns stood out against the blackness of the night as bullets ripped into Bower and the baby, buzzing like angry bees as they whizzed by Julianna, chewing into the wall behind her. A bloodcurdling scream escaped her lips as her own body felt the punch of bullets....

Julianna's scream awakened her. She sat up, the thunder of her heartbeat slamming against her ribs.

Jack raised up where he lay on the floor, and Larissa stirred.

Sleepy-eyed, Jack gained his feet and said, "What's the matter, Julianna?"

She threw back the covers and tugged her robe close around her, and picked up the baby. "I…I was having a nightmare."

"Must've been a bad one," Jack said, rubbing his eyes.

Julianna's heart was still pounding as she sat down on the edge of the bed and held the baby close. "It's all right, honey," she said. "Mommy's baby needs to go back to sleep."

"So what was the nightmare?" Jack asked in a whisper.

Keeping her voice low, Julianna told him, giving every detail. "It was awful," she said in conclusion. "Just awful. I knew Larissa had been hit. Then the bullets started hitting me."

Jack stared at her in the dim light. "But it was all right that the bullets were ripping into me? It would be good if it was just me who got killed, wouldn't it?"

"I don't wish you dead, Jack," she said. "I just wish this real nightmare was over."

"Well, Julianna, you keep cooperating like you've been doing, and soon it will be over."

Soon after breakfast the next morning, they were in the stagecoach and rolling westward once again. The day passed without incident, and at sundown they pulled into the Elk Mountain stage stop. Jack scanned the grounds as the crew and passengers went into the eating area, which was in the same room as the office.

Agent Bill Latham's wife, Doreen, was the cook, and while the crew and passengers ate their meal, Bill and Doreen played with Larissa, who quickly captured their hearts.

This time, when Jack entered the room where they were to

stay the night, Julianna was not fearful of any wrong intentions on his part. As before, he slept on the floor in front of the door.

The next morning, the delicious aroma of frying bacon and steaming coffee met crew and passengers when they stepped into the office. Doreen greeted them from where she stood by the stove, as did Bill from behind the counter.

"I'll have it all on the table in a minute," Doreen said, "then I'll take the baby while her mother eats."

"Fine," said Julianna. "In the meantime, I'll just lay her here on the chair between Jack and me."

Suddenly two men wearing bandanna masks burst through the door, guns drawn. One of them barked, "Everybody get your hands in the air! Now!"

The loud voice frightened Larissa. She broke into a shrill cry. Julianna picked her up, keeping her eyes on the two men. Everyone else had their hands over their heads.

"I said everybody with their hands in the air, lady!"

Above Larissa's wails, Jack said, "My wife holding the baby isn't going to endanger you!"

The gunman swore and cracked Jack on the jaw with the barrel of his revolver. Jack fell from the chair and tumbled onto the floor.

"Now, lady," said the first gunman, "put that screamin' kid down and get those hands in the air!"

Julianna laid Larissa on the chair.

"Get up!" the gunman rasped at Jack. "The rest of you lay your guns on the floor."

When each man had complied, the second gunman relieved Jack of his sidearm as he was gaining his feet and shaking his head to clear it.

While the second gunman broke open the guns and

spilled cartridges on the floor, the other one set piercing eyes on Biff Hoxton and said, "We want the Dudley Oil Company payroll that was put on your stage at Cheyenne City."

Biff shook his head. "You're wrong about that, fella. That payroll was on the stage that went out of Cheyenne City three days ago. There won't be another payroll for almost four weeks. You're too late."

The gunman made a swift move, grabbed Julianna, and pulled her to her feet. He rammed the muzzle of his gun against her temple and hissed, "I know the payroll was put on that stage outside, old man! You wouldn't leave the money in it overnight, so it's gotta be in here somewhere. Probably in a safe. We get the money right now, or this lady dies!"

CHAPTER TWELVE

Julianna ejected a tiny, high-pitched whine as the gunman held the muzzle of his revolver against her head. Little Larissa lay on the chair, kicking and crying.

The gunman's eyes bulged as he blared, "I want that payroll money right now! Do you hear me, driver? Or I kill this beautiful lady!"

Biff Hoxton and Bill Latham exchanged glances. With their eyes, they agreed to give the money to the gunmen. But before Biff could speak, Jack was off the chair with the derringer pressed to the skull of the gunman holding Julianna.

"Give me the gun, mister," Jack hissed, "or say good-bye to your head!"

When Bill Latham saw the other gunman's attention go to Jack, he reached under the counter, came up with a Colt .45, and snapped back the hammer in one smooth move.

The sound brought the nearest gunman's head around to find the .45 aimed at his heart.

"You, too," Bill growled.

The gunman who held Julianna stiffened when the cool metal touched the back of his head. His eyes flicked to Latham, then to his partner, who was frozen on the spot. From the side of his mouth, the gunman said to Jack, "If you put a bullet in my head, reflex will pull the trigger and kill her. So you drop your gun."

Jack pushed the derringer harder against his head. "You willing to die, just to kill her?"

The gunman licked his lips, released Julianna, and gave Jack his gun. The other robber was quickly disarmed by Ollie Finch.

Tess Downes dropped her arms and began to weep.

While Chester and Jean attended to her, a shaky Julianna breathed a deep sigh and picked up her crying baby. Doreen went to her and helped her sit down on a chair.

Jack jerked the bandannas off the faces of the gunmen, looked around at Biff, Ollie, and Bill, and said, "These faces familiar to any of you?"

All three shook their heads.

"Well, let's get them tied up," Jack said. "Where's the nearest lawman in these parts?"

"Be Sheriff Roberts in Rawlins," Biff said. "We'll bind these snakes up good and let 'em have a nice ride up in the rack with the luggage."

While the outlaws were bound hand and foot with hemp cord from Bill Latham's supply, Julianna held Larissa close, speaking in soothing tones to her. As soon as Julianna stopped shaking, Larissa's crying subsided. She put a fat little thumb in her mouth and looked around with wide eyes, still holding tears on her long lashes.

Doreen checked the food on the table. "Bill, the food's cold. I'll have to cook breakfast again."

"You boys just relax," Bill said to the gunmen. "You rudely interrupted these folks' breakfast. You can have your ride atop the stage when they've eaten."

The men picked up their empty guns and retrieved the cartridges from the floor.

Biff looked at Bill and chuckled. "Well, my friend, I guess we'd just as well go ahead and take the payroll money out of the safe."

The one who had hit Jack with his gun spat out, "If I had these ropes off, I'd wipe that grin off your face, old man!"

"Shut your mouth," Jack said. "I owe you one, so don't tempt me to pay my debt."

The gunman looked at him coldly but remained silent.

"I'll go get the payroll," Bill said.

He went into a back room and returned a couple of minutes later. He handed a full canvas bag to Biff and scratched at an ear. "I've been thinking...There's only one way these two no-goods could've known what stage the payroll would be on. They either work for the Dudley Oil Company, or somebody at the company office in Cheyenne City tipped them off."

"You're right," Biff said. He turned to outlaws. "Which is it? You work for Dudley, or you got a friend that does?"

"We ain't tellin' you nothin', Grandpa."

"You knew I was the driver of the stage, too," Biff said. "How'd you know that?"

"Like I said, old man, we ain't tellin' you nothin'."

Bower put his nose within an inch of the man's nose and said, "We'll turn you over to the sheriff in Rawlins. He'll get it out of you."

When breakfast was over, the would-be robbers were dragged outside and hoisted by strong hands onto the top of the stage to lie uncomfortably amid the luggage. Their hands were also tied to the metal rack.

"This roof is too hard," complained one of them to the driver. "Every bump you hit is gonna hurt us."

Biff grinned. "I hope you'll be very uncomfortable."

The women had stayed inside the Wells Fargo building while the men were putting the outlaws in the rack.

Jack returned to see Julianna and Larissa to the stage. Tess and Jean went on ahead, and Jack took the baby from Julianna, saying he would carry her. Julianna thanked Doreen for her kindness and stepped out into the brisk air with Jack.

As they moved toward the stage out of earshot from the others, Julianna said, "Thank you for coming to my rescue."

"I was only protecting my own interests. Those two guys were delaying things. I couldn't let the stage sit here much longer. I can't afford to have that gang of hired killers catch up with me."

Julianna looked up at him, squinting against the morning sun. "You mean you can't afford to let whatever lawmen are after you catch up with you."

It was early on a crisp Saturday morning in Fort Bridger. Hannah Cooper and her children were busy with their chores. Chris was on his way to the barn across the alley to tend his horse. Patty Ruth was in the kitchen in the upstairs apartment, wiping the table with a damp cloth. She was also assigned to clean up the cupboard, which Hannah had trained her to do. B. J. was downstairs in the store, sweeping the floor. It was more than an hour before opening time.

In a small room next to the storeroom at the rear of the store, Hannah and Mary Beth were doing the laundry. The storeroom had a potbellied stove, which was there to keep the canned goods from freezing in the winter. They heated their water on the stove.

Mary Beth was rinsing clothes in a cool-water tub while her mother bent over a hot tub and scrubbed clothes on a scrub board.

Even though Hannah was barely halfway through her pregnancy, her back ached from bending over the tub. She paused, slowly straightened up, and kneaded both fists into the small of her back.

Mary Beth happened to look up from her work at that moment. She dropped the wet clothes in her hands and said, "Mother, you go on upstairs and sit down. I'll finish the washing."

Hannah gave her a hug. "Thank you, sweetheart. I'm fine. Just a little backache. If we work together, it'll get done a lot sooner. You've got to be ready when Miss Lindgren comes to take you to the Crow village."

"I can get it done," Mary Beth insisted. "It won't take me much longer to finish washing and rinsing…and I can get the wash on the line before Miss Lindgren gets here."

"We'll work together," Hannah said. "The air is cold out there, and the hours of sunshine are fewer now."

Giving her aching back one final rub, she plunged her hands back into the hot, soapy water.

Mary Beth shook her head. "You know what?"

"What?" Hannah said, without raising her head.

"The other day I looked up the word *stubborn* in Mr. Webster's dictionary."

Hannah paused. "And?"

"It had a picture of you beside the word."

Hannah blinked, then giggled. "Mary Elizabeth Cooper, you're the extreme. The absolute extreme."

Eyebrows arched, Mary Beth said, "The absolute extreme what?"

Hannah left the tub, wrapped her arms around her, and said, "The absolute extremely most wonderful daughter who will turn thirteen on the twenty-fifth day of next month!"

Patty Ruth Cooper moved around the kitchen table, reaching as far as she could to be sure the damp rag picked up all the crumbs left there during breakfast. Biggie was at her feet, looking up with waggly tail, hoping for something to eat.

When Patty Ruth came to B. J.'s place, she made a face and said, "Ugh! Biggie, have you noticed that little boys are really messy?"

Biggie whined and made a snorting sound.

"I thought you had. Now, little boy dogs aren't messy, are they?" She thought on that statement. "Well, most of the time little boy dogs aren't messy. 'Cept when they wait too long to scratch on the door when they need out, like you did last week. 'Member?"

Biggie whined again.

When the table was done, the little redhead scooted a chair up to the cupboard, climbed on it, and went to work. After moving the chair along the cupboard three times, her work was done.

She put the chair back and said to the little dog, "What else could I do to help Mama, Biggie? Oh, I know! I could dust for her. That's us'ally a Saturday job. An' you can help me, Biggie."

Patty Ruth went to the broom closet, which was next to the pantry, and took out a cloth that her mother had treated with beeswax. "C'mon, Biggie," she said, heading down the narrow hallway. "We'll start in Mama's room."

Biggie followed, tail wagging.

The child started at the bed and ran the cloth over the headboard, humming a nameless tune she had made up. Next were the nightstands on each side of the bed. She picked up Hannah's Bible and dusted under it. Showing it to Biggie, she said, "This is Mama's Bible, Biggie. It tells 'bout Jesus an' how much He loves li'l girls like me."

She laid it down and started around the bed to dust the other nightstand. Biggie moved in front of her, cocked his head, and whined.

"Oh," said Patty Ruth. "I think it tells how much Jesus loves little dogs like you, too."

Biggie seemed satisfied and followed her to the other side. She dusted around the lantern on the second nightstand, then picked up the book that lay there. "Mama reads lotsa books, Biggie. She said this one was by Mr. Dickens. It's a story 'bout two towns."

Patty Ruth had to pull a chair up to the chest of drawers, and then could barely reach the top. She dusted the best she could, climbed down, dragged the chair back in place, then ran the cloth over the face of the drawers.

Last was the dresser. Her gaze fell on the two familiar photographs in the gold-colored frames. She paused a moment and studied the wedding picture. A tiny pain lanced through her heart.

She moved to the other picture, the one of her father in his fancy uniform. Her lower lip quivered as she said, "I miss you, Papa. It's been a long time since you went to heaven. Chris 'n' Mary Beth 'n' B. J. miss you too. We talk 'bout you every day. Mama misses you a whole lot. My room's the nex' one, an' sometimes at night when Mama thinks I'm asleep, I hear her cryin' in here. I know it's 'cause she's lonesome for you."

Biggie whined.

Patty Ruth glanced at him, then looked back at the picture and said, "Biggie says he misses you, too, Papa." She took a deep breath, dusted the dresser as best she could, then said to Solomon's photograph, "Bye, Papa. I'll come back an' talk to you some more sometime…like Mama does. I've heard her talk to you lots of times."

While B. J. was sweeping, he noticed some empty space on a top shelf where the boxes of salt and pepper were kept. He finished his sweeping job, then went to the storeroom to get the ladder. When the ladder was in place by the shelf, he returned to the storeroom and loaded his arms with salt and pepper boxes.

He set half the boxes on the floor, tucked the other half under one arm, and started up the ladder. He reached the top shelf and let go of the ladder to slip the boxes from under his arm. As he concentrated on not dropping a single box, he lost his balance.

He let out a wild cry, arms flailing, and boxes going every direction. The knuckles on his left hand struck the sharp edge of one of the shelves on the way down. He hit the floor with a thud and lay there with the wind knocked out of him.

Mary Beth arrived first. "B. J.!" she gasped. "Are you hurt?"

The boy worked his mouth, trying to tell her he couldn't breathe.

"Looks like he just got the breath knocked out of him, Mary Beth," said Hannah. She bent down and gently lifted his midsection off the floor, and it wasn't long before the breath was back in him.

As the eight-year-old continued to gasp, Hannah looked around and saw what he had been doing. "B. J., you didn't have to put those boxes up there. The ladies have been stocking those high shelves for me."

"I just wanted to help, Mama," said the boy, suddenly realizing there was blood dripping from a knuckle.

"Oh, son," Hannah said, "you must've hit your hand on a shelf when you fell. Let's go upstairs so I can bandage it."

"I'll hang the clothes on the line, Mama," Mary Beth said.

"Thank you, honey." Hannah ushered her bleeding son toward the rear door of the store.

As Chris entered the corral, his beautiful strawberry roan nickered and trotted up to him.

"Good morning, Buster," he said, rubbing the horse's muzzle and patting the side of his face. "Want some breakfast?"

Buster gave out a low whinny.

"Okay," said the fourteen-year-old boy, "let's go inside the barn."

Buster knew the routine. He followed his master and went directly to the feed trough. Chris dipped grain from a large wooden barrel that stood in a corner and poured an ample amount into the trough. The horse went to work on it immediately.

"That'll get you started, boy," Chris said, patting a muscular shoulder. "Now we'll take care of your greens."

Chris climbed the ladder to the hayloft and picked up the pitchfork that leaned against the wall, then pitched down a generous supply of alfalfa. Hannah had recently purchased a big load of hay from a local rancher, wanting to have plenty for Buster throughout the cold winter months. The hayloft was packed almost to the roof.

The boy descended the ladder and went outside to work the long pump handle and fill the water trough. There was ice around the edges of the trough from the chilly night. Folks in town and at the fort had talked about Wyoming winters. It got cold in Missouri, and they had snow, but nothing like what the Coopers were told to expect here.

Chris went back inside the barn and took a currycomb from a shelf and brushed his horse while he chomped on grain and hay.

By seven-thirty, all chores were done, the washing was on the line behind the store, and Mary Beth was in her room getting ready for the day at the Crow village with her teacher.

Her face was wreathed in smiles as she sat before the mirror and brushed her long blond hair and tied it back from her face with a shiny blue ribbon. Her weekly visits to the Crow village were the highlight of her life. She loved to teach, and she got such joy when the Indian children learned from her and she saw a sense of pride on their eager faces.

Miss Lindgren was concentrating on teaching the Crow children the alphabet and English words beyond what they already knew. Recently she had begun teaching them how to write their names and how to spell other important words. Miss Lindgren had entrusted the arithmetic lessons to Mary Beth, and when testing the Indian children, found that Mary Beth was doing an excellent job. There was no question in Sundi Lindgren's mind that Hannah Cooper's oldest daughter had been gifted by the Lord to be a teacher.

While she finished getting ready, Mary Beth heard her mother praising Patty Ruth for the good job she'd done in cleaning up the kitchen table and the cupboard, and in dusting the house on her own initiative. Mary Beth smiled to herself. Of course her mother would have to do a measure of work behind the little girl, but Patty Ruth always gave it her best effort.

She could hear Chris and B. J. in their room. Chris was talking about Abby Turner, and B. J. was getting in a few words about his latest injury.

This brought another smile to Mary Beth's lips. Brett Jonathan Cooper. The eight-year-old human accident always finding a place to happen.

Saturday was the busiest day of the week at Cooper's General Store. Hannah was thankful for the different women who worked as volunteers, each on a set day of the week, and two on Saturdays. Others filled in when needed. She had offered to pay them, but not a one would accept money for their services. It was a labor of love.

Hannah knew that when the time drew closer to give birth to her baby, she would need more help. The women would be there, and double up to help, but privately she was asking the Lord to give her someone who could handle the store until she was on her feet again.

Though she planned to keep the baby in a crib in the store when she was able to go back to work, she really wanted to hire someone full-time to help run the store. Business was very good and getting better all the time. She could afford to hire a full-time employee. However, none of her volunteers wanted a full-time job.

Nellie Patterson and Leah Morley both arrived ten minutes before eight, and the three women were ready to open on time. By eight-fifteen, things were bustling. Sundi Lindgren came into the store, waiting for Chief Two Moons and his band of braves to escort her and Mary Beth to the village.

"Good morning, Sundi," Hannah said. "Mary Beth will be down in just a moment."

Sundi flashed her warm smile and said, "I'm a little early. Could you use some help packing those boxes?"

"Well, let's say I wouldn't turn down a nice offer like that," Hannah said.

"I'm helpin' too, Miss Lindgren," came a small voice from behind the counter.

"Oh, hi, Patty Ruth!" Sundi said. "I didn't see you back there."

Sundi removed her coat and laid it over a chair by the checkers table, then moved up to the counter. She spoke to Nellie and Leah, then to the people in the lines. Nearly everyone knew the schoolmarm.

Pert, bright-eyed Sundi Lindgren was clad in a blue-and-red plaid dress with a crisp white collar. Beneath a small hat that matched the dress, her sunshine hair lay in lovely waves on her shoulders.

Mary Beth put in an appearance just as Hannah and Sundi finished loading the boxes and the rancher and his wife who made the purchases began carrying them out.

B. J. came in the front door of the store and announced to Mary Beth and Sundi that Chief Two Moons was out front, along with Broken Wing and four braves.

Hannah had given Chris permission to spend the day with Broken Wing. He now came in the front door and threaded his way through the customers, speaking to them as he moved toward his mother. He kissed Hannah's cheek, saying he would come back when Miss Lindgren and Mary Beth returned in late afternoon.

Mary Beth kissed Hannah and followed her teacher outside to her buggy. They greeted Chief Two Moons, Broken Wing, and the braves. While Mary Beth and Sundi were climbing into the buggy, B. J. rushed out the front door and said, "Miss Lindgren, would you care if I go along with you to the village like I did two weeks ago?"

"Of course not," Sundi said. "You're quite welcome to come along if your mother says it's okay."

"Be right back!"

Mary Beth watched her little brother stumble slightly, catch his balance, then plunge through the door.

"What did B. J. do to his hand?" Sundi asked.

"Banged it on a shelf when he fell off a ladder this morning."

Sundi smiled, knowing B. J.'s tendency toward cuts, scrapes, and bumps.

Chris and Broken Wing were on their horses, talking about the day of riding they had planned.

Sundi looked at Two Moons as he sat astride his pinto and said, "Chief, we'll be ready to go shortly. We may be taking B. J. along."

The chief smiled. "He very welcome at village."

Sundi turned to Mary Beth. "Will it hurt Patty Ruth's feelings if she's the only one who doesn't get to go to the village?"

"Well, I don't think so, but I can go ask her to come along

if you want. Mama might let her."

"Do that."

Mary Beth jumped out of the buggy and ran into the store. She almost bumped into B. J., who was heading for the door.

"Mama says I can go!" he said excitedly.

"Okay. Go on out and get in Miss Lindgren's buggy. I'll be right back."

Mary Beth rushed up to the counter and smiled at the woman Hannah was helping. "Please excuse me, Mrs. Noble. I have to ask my mother something."

"Of course, Mary Beth," said Loretta Noble.

"Mother, Miss Lindgren said that since B. J. is going along today, Patty Ruth could come, too, if she wants to."

Hannah looked down at her youngest. "Would you like to go, Patty Ruth?"

The five-year-old sighed, then laid the back of a hand to her forehead and said, "I'll stay here, Mary Beth. Some of us have to mind the store so we can make a livin' an' pay the bills."

Mary Beth shook her head and raised her eyes toward the ceiling, then said, "Well, all right, Patty Ruth. That is very grandiose of you. Bye, Mama. See you this afternoon."

When Mary Beth was gone, Patty Ruth looked up at her mother. "Mama, what's that word mean?"

Hannah's mind was back on her work. "What word, honey?"

"I ain't gonna try to say it. You know, the word Mary Beth jis' said that what I did was that."

"Oh. Grandiose?"

"Yeah, that."

"It means splendid. Impressive."

A frown penciled itself across the little brow. "What's those words mean?"

Hannah stopped what she was doing, looked at the child, and said, "I'm sorry, honey. Grandiose means good."

"Oh. So Mary Beth was sayin' that 'cause I'm stayin' here to work instead of goin' to the village, I'm doin' good?"

"That's it."

"Okay."

The morning went by with hardly a break. Finally, about noon, business let up. Hannah kept a blue-and-white enameled coffeepot on the potbellied stove. Her regular customers knew they were welcome to a mug and could sit a spell and visit over coffee if they wished.

Since there were no customers at the moment, Hannah sat down with her two helpers and each enjoyed a fragrant cup of hot coffee. Patty Ruth busied herself moving some empty boxes to the storeroom. The three women talked about the Lord and the things that were happening at church.

This led Nellie to say, "Hannah, the change in our home since we all came to know the Lord is nothing short of a miracle. Thank you for caring for me and for leading me to the Lord. You could have been vindictive toward our family, and nobody would have blamed you. But you cared more for Alex's soul than you did for your material loss. If it hadn't been for you, we'd still be headed for hell."

Hannah reached over and patted her hand. "I'm just thankful the Lord could use me, Nellie."

Leah smiled. "It takes a willing person for the Lord to use, Hannah. You've been a tremendous example for the rest of us Christians, I'll say that."

The front door opened to the jingle of the little bell, and from near the storeroom, Patty Ruth exclaimed, "Mr. Clem! Mr. Clem! You came back!" Tiny feet pitter-pattered across the wooden floor as the child ran to Clem Cooper.

Clem swept her up in his arms, hugged her, then planted her back on the floor, and said, "Hello, Mrs. Cooper. I'm back to pay you what I owe you and to take a big load home."

Hannah rose to her feet and smiled. "Hello, Mr. Cooper. Come on over to the counter." She introduced Clem to Leah and Nellie and met him at the cash drawer.

Patty Ruth tugged at Clem's coat. "Is Lucky out there in your wagon, Mr. Clem?"

"He sure is, sweetie."

Patty Ruth headed for her coat and cap behind the counter. "Mama, may I go out and see Lucky?"

Hannah looked at Clem. "Is the buggy on this side of the street?"

"Yes'm. Right outside your door."

Hannah smiled. "All right, honey, you can go and see Lucky, but don't go into the street."

"I won't, Mama. Can I climb up on the wagon seat so I can hug Lucky?"

"Of course."

"Oh, boy!" she shouted as she put on cap and coat and darted out the door.

When Lucky saw her, he wagged his tail as best he could and licked her face when she climbed onto the seat. The reunion was sweet as Patty Ruth and the one-eyed, one-eared, three-legged, broken-tailed dog showed their affection to one another.

CHAPTER THIRTEEN

Jacob Kates pulled his bright red wagon up to the outskirts of Green River, Wyoming, on a Friday evening. His sales had gone well, and he was ready for the Sabbath day. Even though Saturdays were busy days in all the towns, he would not break the Jewish Sabbath for monetary gain.

The night air was frosty. Jacob built a fire in his small pot-bellied stove, ate a quick meal, and began his worship at 6:00 P.M., the beginning of the Jewish Sabbath. The heat from the stove felt good as Jacob read a portion from Genesis, then read from the Talmud. While reading, Jacob heard people pass by a couple of times, commenting on his wagon, and showing excitement that a peddler was parked at the edge of town.

Jacob had been told by both Manfred Collier and his friend Eli Goldman that the people of eastern Wyoming and Nebraska—especially the women—loved to have peddlers come to their towns. They were able not only to purchase new goods that were not available in their local stores or trading posts, but they could also get caught up on any news from the other towns and settlements where the peddlers had been. For residents of settlements where there was no regular postal service, the peddler would carry letters to the next town on his route and post them.

Jacob had reason to believe that once he had established his new route, he would do better financially each time.

He spent the Sabbath Day quietly, venturing outside only when necessary.

Sunday came, and he stood outside the wagon and greeted people as they passed by on their way to church. Smiles lit up faces when they asked if he would be in town on Monday, and he assured them he would. Jacob had learned that Sundays were not good for sales; there were the Gentile church services, and the stores were closed. If anyone was seen on Sundays in the business districts, they were just passing through.

After the church traffic had dwindled, Jacob returned to his potbellied stove and dropped in a couple of logs to keep the fire going.

The after-church traffic went by shortly after noon, and once again Jacob stood outside to greet the people.

It was midafternoon when he sat by the warm stove inside his wagon, reading a recent copy of the *Rock Springs News,* which he had purchased in that town on Friday morning. When he heard voices outside, he looked through one of the small windows and saw four teenage boys standing together, admiring his mules and the wagon.

By their conversation, Jacob realized they had never seen a traveling peddler before and were curious. Putting on his coat and hat, the wiry little man stepped outside, closed the door behind him, and said, "Good afternoon, boys. You live in town?"

"Yes, sir," the one who seemed to be the oldest replied. "We've heard about peddlers like you going through the towns over on the east side of the territory, but we've never had one here."

One boy squinted at the sign on the side of the wagon and said, "Do you really have everything in your wagon? I mean, it says, 'You name it, I've got it.'"

"Well, son," Jacob said in his New York accent, "it has to be within reason. You have something in mind?"

"Not really, but how about licorice candy? We used to live in Pennsylvania, and we could get licorice there, but nobody has it out here."

A smile lit up the peddler's face. "Don't say nobody, son. Ol' Jacob has it!"

"Oh, boy! If I go home and get some money—" The boy stopped. "Oh, I forgot. This is Sunday. Ma won't let me buy anything on Sunday. Are you gonna be here tomorrow?"

"Sure am. I'll be on the street down there in the business district."

"We have to go to school at eight-thirty. Will you be there before then?"

"Sure. I'll have my display all laid out by eight."

The boys grinned at each other.

"Would you boys like to see some of what I've got?"

"Yeah!" they said, almost in unison.

Jacob opened boxes and let them look through various and sundry items. They were excited about things they had never seen before, some of which they had never even heard of. The boys thanked Jacob for allowing them to see his wares and told him they would tell their parents and anyone else they saw.

Monday was a good day for Jacob. His sales were excellent. He ran out of licorice.

As the sun was going down, he took inventory. If the rest of the route did as well, by the time he reached Evanston, his inventory would be depleted. He would return to Cheyenne City, load up on supplies, then start his route over again.

On Tuesday morning, Jacob pulled out of Green River and continued westward. He arrived in a small settlement two hours later and did well there. Moving on, he stopped in two villages, then guided his mules farther west. He reached a small town called Grass Hollow and knew by his map that he was now twenty-eight miles from Fort Bridger. He figured he'd do very well there because of the town and the fort.

Sales were good in Grass Hollow. When the sun went down he put away his display, moved into the wagon, and built a fire in the potbellied stove.

Soon Jacob had a cozy fire burning and his supper cooking. He thought of his family so far away in New York. An emptiness filled his heart as his mind went to his beloved Miriam. He recalled how he'd fallen in love the first time he saw her. The courting months were filled with sweet memories. Then he thought of the wedding.

Suddenly he was brought back to the present when he smelled something burning. The beans had gone dry in the skillet, and smoke was beginning to fill the place.

He jumped up, knocking his small stool over, and lifted the skillet off the stove. After letting the smoke out of the wagon and starting over, Jacob finally sat down to his supper. While eating, a slight smile captured his lips as he thought of the hearty, delicious meals Miriam always had ready for him when he came home at the end of a busy day at the store.

It was late in the afternoon as the women looked out the windows of the listing stagecoach while Ollie Finch, Chester Downes, and Jack "LeCroix" Bower stood beside it, waiting for Biff Hoxton to come out from under the coach. His feet and legs were visible, but the rest of him was lost beneath it.

They heard a sigh, then Biff scooted out on his back and said, "Yep, we've got a broken axle, all right. This stage has gone as far as it will go."

Ollie looked westward toward the uneven rooftops of Rawlins and said, "Well, if we had to hit a deep rut covered with tumbleweeds, I'm glad we did it only a couple miles from town."

One of the gunmen up on top frowned and said, "You

ain't got no mercy at all, do you, Hoxton? We're black and blue from ridin' up here."

Biff grinned and said, "Cheer up. You'll soon be much more comfortable in your nice jail cells."

"Well, who's gonna walk into town and get help?" Chester asked.

"I'd say that's my job," Finch said. "Sit tight. I'll be back with help as soon as possible."

The shotgunner was back in a little more than an hour with the Wells Fargo agent, Conrad Thomas, who drove a carriage for the passengers to ride in, and a wagon driven by a friend to carry the luggage. Right behind Thomas and his vehicles were two deputy sheriffs from the Carbon County Sheriff's office, driving a wagon.

The would-be robbers were taken away, and driver and shotgunner were asked to come to the office the next day to make a formal statement against the gunmen.

Biff walked behind the six-up team and drove them to the Wells Fargo barn.

When the passengers arrived in Rawlins, they were taken immediately to the hotel since the Fargo station there did not have an eating place nor facilities for passengers staying overnight.

Thomas informed them he would wire Cheyenne City and see if they had a spare coach they could send. If they could send one right away, change horses at the relay stations, and drive straight through day and night, they could arrive in Rawlins in a day and a half.

The weary passengers ate a simple but filling supper at the café next to the hotel, then went to their rooms.

When Jack and Julianna entered their room, Julianna laid the baby in the crib that had been provided and said, "Jack, I'm going to ask you to find something else to do for a while. I've just got to have a bath."

Jack nodded. "I'll order the hot water for you and wait out in the hall."

There was a knock at the door. Jack opened it to find Conrad Thomas standing there. "Yes, Mr. Thomas?"

"I've let your stage crew know, and I just told Mr. and Mrs. Downes and Mrs. Morden about the wire I received back from our office in Cheyenne City. They said they'd send a stagecoach through nonstop, except to change teams, once they can free one up. They have very few spare coaches, and they're not sure when they'll be able to send one. Could be a week or more. We'll pay for your hotel room and meals, of course, while you're here."

Julianna's heart felt like it had turned to lead, and Jack's countenance fell.

"All right," Jack said. "If that's the way it is, that's the way it is. Thanks."

When Jack closed the door, Julianna said, "The hot water, please."

"I'm going to lock the door from the outside. Don't start screaming for help while I'm gone. You might get somebody hurt besides yourself. Understand?"

"I understand," she said.

Jack pulled the skeleton key from the door, stepped out into the hall, and locked it. Julianna stared at the door after Jack closed it and heard him turn the key in the lock. She looked at Larissa, who was playing with a rattle Julianna had brought along, and said, "Baby doll, Mommy's got to find a way to get us free of that man." She turned away from the baby, drew her fists up to her temples, and choked out the words, "How much longer will this torture last?"

Julianna finished her bath, slipped into her robe, and took care of Larissa's needs. When the baby was fast asleep, she went to the door. Her nerves felt as though they would snap as she turned the knob. She looked at Jack, who was leaning against the opposite wall in the hallway, and said, "You can come in now."

When he stepped in and locked the door, Jack said, "You look like you're going to bawl."

Julianna threw herself on the bed facedown and began to sob.

"What are you crying about?" Jack said brusquely.

She raised up, gave him a disgusted look, and said, "If you had any heart at all, you'd know what I'm crying about! I've lost everything I had in this world except Larissa. I lost my husband. I lost my house. I lost all my money. And on top of that, I'm having to make this awful trip to Idaho as hostage of an outlaw!" She sniffed and wiped tears from her face. "It's all too much! It's more than I can stand!"

Burying her face in the pillow, Julianna sobbed uncontrollably, her entire body shaking.

Jack was surprised Larissa did not awaken with Julianna weeping so loudly. He stood there watching her cry her heart out and thought, *Julianna, I'd like to take you into my arms. I'd like to hold you and comfort you...even kiss you but—*

Jack was amazed at how this beautiful French woman had affected him. He had never felt like this toward any woman before.

There was a knock at the door.

Julianna lifted her head and looked at Jack. Her sobbing had stopped, and she was drawing one shuddering breath after another, trying now to bring herself under control.

Jack's hand went to the gun in his holster. He caught Julianna's eye and put a finger to his lips.

"Who is it?" he called, easing up to the door.

"Chester Downes, Mr. LeCroix."

"What do you want?" Jack called through the door.

"We're in the room next door. Tess and I heard Mrs. LeCroix crying like her heart was breaking. Is something wrong? Is there something we can do?"

Jack motioned for Julianna to come to him. She sniffed, left the bed, and crossed the room, wiping her tears.

"Mr. LeCroix?" Downes called through the door. "Is there anything we can do?"

"Just a moment, Mr. Downes!" Jack said as Julianna drew up to him. He whispered, "Let me do the talking. Understand?"

Julianna nodded, sniffed again, and brushed away more tears. He slipped his arm around her, pulled her close to him, and opened the door. She leaned against him, giving in to his strong embrace.

Chester studied Julianna's swollen, bloodshot eyes, but smiled when he saw the way she was leaning into Jack.

"My wife is just tired and homesick, Mr. Downes," Jack said softly. "It all surfaced a few minutes ago."

Julianna pressed a weak smile on her lips. "I very much appreciate your concern, Mr. Downes, but I'll be all right. My husband is here to comfort me. Like he said, I'm tired and I miss our folks back home. Sorry to have disturbed you."

Downes smiled. "No need to apologize for that, Mrs. LeCroix. I'm glad to know it's nothing serious. Tess will be glad to know it too. Good night."

Both wished him good night, and Jack closed the door.

The instant it clicked shut, Julianna's knees gave way. Jack wrapped both arms around her to keep her from falling. She began to weep again.

"It's not my intention to keep you frightened, but my life's at stake here," Jack said. "My only hope of survival is you and Larissa."

She straightened herself within his embrace and said, "I…I've got to get some rest."

When Jack released her, she bumped his right side, closed her hand on the butt of the Colt .45 in his holster, and gave it a yank.

Jack Bower's strong fingers clamped on her wrist. She struggled against him in desperation, as if somehow she could overpower him with what little strength she had left.

Jack looked at her angrily and snapped, "Let go, or I'll break your arm!"

Breathing hard from the exertion, Julianna ejected a tiny, hopeless whimper, and released her grip on the gun. Jack, in turn, released his hold on her wrist. She turned and moved shakily to the bed and sat down.

After a moment, Julianna rose and stood over the crib, looking down at her daughter. Julianna was overwhelmed with an intense love for her beautiful, innocent little girl. She wiped a tear from her face and drew a shaky breath, steeling herself against the hopelessness of her plight. With her eyes on Larissa, Julianna promised herself and her baby that against all odds, she would make a good life for the two of them.

She bent over and placed a warm kiss on Larissa's brow and gently ran the back of her hand down the baby's velvety soft cheek. She stood erect again and squared her tired shoulders. She felt more at peace than she had in a long time.

She stood quietly, watching her sleeping baby, and absently rubbed her bruised wrist.

Jack remained by the door, looking at the back of Julianna's head, wishing he had not had to hurt her.

The next morning, Jack and Julianna were sitting at a table by a window, eating breakfast in the café. Jack watched the traffic passing by on the street. He wondered how many killers Tack Lombard had on his trail...four...five...more?

A familiar face caught his attention on the boardwalk. Conrad Thomas.

Seconds later, Thomas came through the café door and

headed for their table. When Jack saw the dismal look on his face, he said to Julianna, "We've got company, and he's got bad news."

Thomas drew up. "Good mornin', Mr. and Mrs. LeCroix."

"Good morning. I have a feeling that what you're about to say isn't going to make us happy, Mr. Thomas," Jack said.

The Fargo agent sighed. "Not exactly. I just received a wire from our Cheyenne City office. They can't get another stagecoach to us inside of a week. I'm sorry."

Jack felt a surge of panic well up inside him, but he subdued it. "You don't have to apologize, Mr. Thomas. It's no fault of yours. We'll just have to wait."

When Thomas was gone, Jack saw the disappointed look on Julianna's face as she stared down at Larissa, who lay on a chair next to her.

When she looked up at him, he said, "You're not going to try to get my gun again, are you?"

Her lips pulled into a thin line. "If I thought I could succeed next time, I would. What do you expect, Jack? Put yourself in my place. Wouldn't you try to escape if you were me?"

Jack was silent a moment, then said, "I'm sure if I were you, I'd try to bring this to an end. But don't try it, Julianna."

CHAPTER FOURTEEN

The Wyoming sun painted the dawn horizon a vermilion hue, then lifted its flaming head over the edge of the world to send bright beams across the rolling hills around Grass Hollow.

Jacob Kates guided his mules out of the small town and pointed their faces due west. He planned to make the two stops after Grass Hollow and pull into Fort Bridger about noon on the next day.

He was about a quarter mile out of Grass Hollow when he noticed the town's cemetery alongside the road. A wagon was parked just off the road, and Jacob saw three young children—two girls and a boy—near the wagon, and a man and woman standing at a small mounded grave.

The children stood in the tall, tawny grass, watching Jacob's approach. They were bundled up in heavy coats and stocking caps.

As Jacob drew nearer the spot, the parents started toward their wagon, and the children called their attention to the bright red wagon coming down the road.

"Oh, it's a peddler, Will!" the young mother cried. "Look!"

Her husband smiled and gave a friendly wave to Jacob.

Now that he was closer to them, Jacob saw that the children's coats were tattered and worn. They were clean but had seen better days. The mother and father were also clad in well-worn clothing and footwear.

Jacob pulled rein and heard the mother explaining to the children what a peddler was. When they heard that peddlers carried candy, they asked if they could have some. The mother said they would have to wait until some other time.

The man eyed the sign on the side of Jacob's wagon and said, "It's been a long time since my wife and I have seen a peddler's wagon, sir. We're from western Kansas. Used to have one that came to our little town quite often."

"Is this your regular route, sir?" asked the woman.

"It is now. This is my first run. I started in Cheyenne City and will go all the way to Evanston."

"I see by the sign that you're Jacob Kates. My name's Will Summers. This is my wife, Wanda, and our children. Melissa is nine; Scott is seven, and Caroline is five."

"Well, I'm very glad to meet you," Jacob said warmly.

"We had another brother, mister," Caroline volunteered, "but he died. His name was Nathan and he was eleven. That's his grave over there." She pointed to the small grave where her parents had been standing.

"I'm sorry," said Jacob. "When did it happen?"

"Almost two months ago," Will replied. "Nathan contracted a lung disease the medical profession knows little about. Doesn't even have a name. A few people back east have come down with it and ended up dying with pneumonia. I took Nathan back to New York on advice of a doctor in Cheyenne City, but they said they couldn't help him. I brought him back home, and he died a month later."

"You must have spent a lot of money, going to New York and all," Jacob said.

"It took quite a bit, yes, sir." Will paused, then said, "You sound like you might be from New York, if I'm not mistaken, Mr. Kates."

Jacob smiled. "I'm from Manhattan. Came out here quite recently to start this route."

"I see. Is it going all right for you?"

"I've done quite well."

"That's good."

"You live over here in Grass Hollow?"

"Just outside of town on the east, sir."

"Farmer? Rancher?"

"Farmer. Wheat, mostly."

"Good honest outside work. The kind I like. Well, I guess I'd better get on down the road. Got a couple of stops today, then I'll be in Fort Bridger about noon tomorrow. Nice to have met you."

"Papa," spoke up Caroline, "could we buy some candy from this nice man? Please? We haven't had any candy in a long time."

"Yeah, Papa," said Scott. "It's been a real long time. Huh, Melissa!"

The oldest girl nodded but didn't reply.

Will's face flushed. "Kids, we can't buy any candy right now. Maybe after next year's harvest we'll be able to get you some."

Jacob felt a tug at his heart and said, "Tell you what, Mr. and Mrs. Summers, if you would allow it, I'd like to give your children some candy."

"Oh, we can't let you do that, Mr. Kates," Wanda said. "You have to make a living like the rest of us."

The little man smiled as he left the wagon seat and climbed down. "I can spare a little," he said. "Come on, children, let's see what we can find inside here."

Will and Wanda exchanged glances and smiled. They followed their excited children to the rear of the wagon.

Three bright faces watched as Jacob opened the door of the cabin and said, "Come on in."

The parents stood at the door as Melissa, Scott, and Caroline scrambled inside. Jacob reached into a cabinet and brought down

AL AND JOANNA LACY

three glass jars. "Let's see, here. Who likes lemon drops?"

All three assured him they did.

Jacob used a small scoop to make three piles of lemon drops on his table. Screwing the lid on the jar, he picked up the next one. "Anybody here like peppermint sticks?"

Big eyes watched as three piles of red and white peppermint sticks were laid beside the lemon drops.

Next were butterscotch drops, and Jacob was assured by all three that they loved them. Jacob filled three small paper bags with the candies and gave each child a bag.

They thanked him and asked their parents if they could eat some now. They were allowed one piece of each flavor and told to go climb in the family wagon.

Will and Wanda Summers were touched by Jacob's kindness to their children and thanked him for it.

The little man smiled and said, "You folks are pressed for money right now, aren't you?"

"Things are a bit tight, Mr. Kates," Will said, "but come harvesttime next year, we should be back on our feet again."

Jacob nodded. Turning toward his wagon, he said, "Just a minute."

Jacob's slight limp was evident as he moved to the cabin. He went inside, knelt on the floor, and opened the secret compartment where he kept his money. He opened the leather pouch and counted out two hundred dollars, the better part of his profits since leaving Cheyenne City. He folded the currency neatly and placed it in the palm of his hand.

Jacob emerged from the cabin, smiled at Will and Wanda, and said, "Folks, I'd like to help what little I can to get you through the winter." Extending the money to Will, he added, "I hope this two hundred dollars will be of benefit."

Wanda gasped.

Will began shaking his head, saying, "Mr. Kates, this is very kind and generous of you, but we can't accept it. You have to get through the winter yourself."

"I'll be fine," Jacob said, pressing the folded bills into Will's hand. "Please. Let me do this for you and your family."

Tears were streaming down Wanda's cheeks, and she pressed a trembling hand against her mouth.

Misty-eyed, Will said, "Mr. Kates, I—"

"You can call me Jacob. You know…like Jacob in the Bible. That's who I was named after."

Through a tight throat, Will said, "Jacob, who became Israel, a prince of God. You are well named, Jacob. How can we ever thank you?"

"Just seeing the happiness on your faces is enough thanks. I must be going now."

Wanda rushed up and embraced the little man, surprising him. "Thank you!" she said. "And God bless you!"

Will shook Jacob's hand, then put an arm around Wanda as they watched the bright red wagon with the yellow wheels roll on down the road.

When he had gone about a hundred yards, Jacob stood up, looked back over the roof of the cabin, and saw the young couple still standing beside their wagon, looking his way. He waved, and they waved back.

Jacob sat down again and smiled to himself.

The road west carried the peddler over hills, down into valleys, and through small streams. He had gone some seven or eight miles since leaving the Summers family when his eye caught a dark object on the ground about two hundred yards ahead.

A few more minutes showed Jacob that it was a man sitting in the grass, watching the wagon's approach. As Jacob drew near, the man rose to his feet, but not without difficulty. He stood, favoring his left leg.

Hauling to a stop, Jacob saw that the man's face was bruised, and his coat was torn and dirty. "Looks to me like you're in some kind of trouble, mister," Jacob said.

"You might say that. My name's Clyde Little. And I see by the sign that you are Jacob Kates."

"Yes, sir. What happened to you?"

"Well, you see, I'm a rancher from just over the Utah border. I'd been visiting some rancher friends a few miles north of here and was riding my horse at a gallop over those hills, heading down here to the road. My horse lost his footing and tumbled down the slope all the way to the bottom of that ravine. Fortunately, I flew out of the saddle before he went down. I think I sprained my ankle. It hurts pretty bad. It was all I could do to get to the road so I could maybe catch a ride toward home."

"What about your horse?"

Little patted his sidearm. "Had to shoot him. His right foreleg was broken."

"Well, Mr. Little, I'm heading west. I've got some stops to make in the next few days, but you're welcome to ride along if you wish. I'll be turning around at Evanston."

A smile spread over Clyde Little's lips. "Sounds good to me, Mr. Kates. I know some folks in Evanston. I'll impose on them to take me home. My ranch is only about ten miles the other side of the border."

"Well, hop aboard! It'll be nice to have some company."

"Thank you," said Little, then turned and limped to a thick clump of grass a few feet away and picked up a brown leather satchel.

Jacob wondered why the man had the satchel hidden in the grass, and when he saw him pick it up, he could tell it was quite heavy.

"Where could I put this?" Clyde asked.

"Just open the door back there and put it inside."

Jacob heard the door open, felt the weight of the satchel

as it thumped on the cabin floor, and heard the door close. He smiled at the man as he struggled up to the wagon seat. As he settled in the seat with a grunt, Little looked northward, scanning the hills and the horizon.

Soon they reached the first settlement for the day's business. Noting that Jacob had a limp of his own, Little helped him set up his display while people gathered around the wagon.

Clyde watched with interest as Jacob went into his spiel before the growing crowd.

Sales were good, and after about an hour, they took down the display and moved on to the next settlement some five or six miles farther along the road. Sales were good again. While Clyde was taking things off the hinged table outside the wagon's cabin, Jacob placed all his money in the secret compartment for safekeeping. Then he joined Clyde on the wagon seat, picked up the reins, and said, "Okay, ol' mules, let's head for Fort Bridger!"

As the wagon rocked and swayed along the rough road, Jacob said, "I understand the winters are pretty rough in these parts."

"You could say that. Lots of snow, and often with powerful winds behind it. Makes for some real blizzards at times. And then, of course, in December, January, and February, it gets really cold. I'm talking about thirty below zero, and sometimes even colder. You'll want to find a nice warm place to hole up when that cold stuff hits Wyoming."

"I'll work on that," Jacob said, grinning.

Wade Kilbane was a mountain of a man. He tipped the scales at better than three hundred pounds and was six and a half feet tall. He laid a hand on the dead horse's neck and said, "He ain't been dead more'n a few hours, boys. That thievin' skunk can't be too far ahead of us."

The other three men were still in their saddles.

"Not carryin' all that gold," said Mack Jarvis.

"He could be hurt, too," put in Eldon Ray. "By the looks of that slope, his horse really took a tumble all the way to the bottom. Figures that his rider had to have taken a pretty good tumble, too."

"For sure," Kilbane said, raising his line of sight to the south. "Now, if I was that dirty thief, I'd head for the road over there and see if I could pick me up a ride."

Wade Kilbane swaggered to his big bay gelding, stepped into the stirrup, and settled in the saddle. The horse blew, as if to say the load was more than he really wanted to carry.

"One thing we have to have an understandin' about, boys. When it's time to send Clyde Little out of this world, it's me that's gonna do it. I know the gold he run off with belonged to all of us, but I get first priority on him. Any discussion?"

"He's all yours, boss," said Fielder. "Personally, I don't care who takes him out, just so it happens and I get my portion of the gold back."

"So how did you get lined up in this peddler business from way back in New York?" Clyde Little asked Jacob.

"Friend of mine from back there came west, wanting to get a taste of the frontier. Got into it and wrote to tell me how good he was doing. He knew I'd long had a desire to see the West. I wrote back and told him I wanted to come. He said he'd line me up with his distributor, who was wanting to get a route started across southern Wyoming. Since my wife was gone, I figured I might as well do what I'd dreamed about, and come west. So, here I am."

"Well, I sure hope it works out good for—"

Little saw four riders come up out of a draw on the north side of the road at a full gallop. Though they were a good distance away, he knew who they were. He gripped the seat, white with terror.

Jacob saw the riders coming and Clyde's sudden pallor. "What's wrong?" he asked.

"How fast can your mules run?"

"I don't know. I haven't needed them to run."

"Well, crack that whip, and put 'em to it!"

"What's going on?"

"Those riders are outlaws. They're after me."

"Why?"

"They think I stole somethin' from 'em. Hurry! You've got to outrun 'em, or they'll kill me!"

Jacob pulled out the horsewhip from the tube at his left and cracked it over the mules' heads, shouting, "Hee-ya-a-a-h-h-h!"

The well-trained mules instantly broke into a gallop, laying their ears back. Dust clouds lifted from pounding hooves and spinning wagon wheels.

But it was too late. Wade Kilbane and his men sped up, angling toward the road in front of the bounding wagon to cut them off.

"No chance, Clyde!" Jacob shouted. "We can't outrun them!"

"We've got to!" Little cried, his voice strained with fear. "They'll kill me! And they might kill you, too!"

The riders were closing in, guns drawn. The big one out front was shouting at them. Though Jacob couldn't make out what he was saying, he knew he was being commanded to stop.

"I've got no choice, Clyde!" he shouted above the rumble of pounding hooves and bounding wagon. "They'll shoot us for sure if I don't stop!"

Clyde stared at the oncoming outlaws with cold dread.

Jacob pulled back on the reins, shouting, "Whoa, boys! Whoa!"

Kilbane and his men drew up, guns in hand, as the wagon rolled to a halt. It was Kilbane who rode up beside the wagon and leered at Little with steely eyes. He lined his gun on him and said through his teeth, "Okay, Clyde, climb down."

"Look, Wade, you're makin' a mistake. I didn't—"

"Shut up and climb down!"

Trembling all over, Little started to climb down.

"Your gun, Clyde," said Kilbane, extending his free hand.

Little's hand shook as he lifted his revolver from its holster and reluctantly gave it to Kilbane. He left the seat and climbed down.

Wade Kilbane hefted himself from the saddle and met Clyde as he touched ground. He towered over the cowering man.

"When one of my own gang members turns on me and steals from us, he's in real trouble, Clyde."

"Wade, I didn't—"

"Shut up!" Kilbane looked at the others and said, "Check inside the wagon, boys."

Mack Jarvis gave Little a hard look as he dismounted. "Will do, boss."

The other two left their saddles and followed Jarvis to the rear of the wagon.

Kilbane eyed Kates and said, "You sit tight, pal."

The door of the cabin creaked open. Seconds later, Jarvis's voice boomed, "It's here, boss! All of it!"

Kilbane scowled at Little as Jarvis and the other two came around the rear of the wagon. Jarvis was carrying the heavy satchel.

Suddenly Kilbane swore at Little, and his big meaty fist lashed out. It connected solidly, and Little went down hard. The other three swore at him, kicking him in the chest, stomach, and back. With each kick, a dull moan came from Little.

Finally, Kilbane cocked the hammer of his gun, pointed it at the helpless man on the ground, and fired.

The sudden roar of the gun startled the mules, and they bolted, throwing Jacob back against the cabin. He heard Kilbane shout, "Mack! Eldon! After him! Kill the peddler!"

Jacob looked back and saw Jarvis and Ray vaulting into their saddles. He pulled out the whip, cracked it over the mules' heads, and shouted, "Hee-y-a-a-h-h!"

The wagon was bouncing and fish-tailing, throwing up clouds of dust. Jacob could hear his merchandise falling and clattering around inside the cabin.

A wide river spanned by an ancient bridge came into view in the near distance. Jacob raised up and looked behind and saw the two riders coming at a full gallop, but he still had a good lead on them. He was speedily drawing closer to the river.

The mules were leaning hard into the harness at their top speed.

The afternoon sun reflected like gold off the wide river as the old bridge loomed up before him. Guiding the mules seemed impossible, but they had the presence of mind to see the bridge and were perfectly lined up to cross it. The ground grew rougher as it neared the river, causing the wagon to bounce worse than before.

As the wagon approached the bridge, it hit a deep rut, and the mules' hooves were suddenly pounding hollowly on wood. The wagon's right side struck the aged railing. It skidded sideways, then careened to the other side and struck the railing hard. The impact broke the wood with a loud crack, freeing the mules, who kept running, dragging harness and reins.

The wagon tipped dangerously to one side, with Jacob hanging on for dear life, and crashed through the railing. Jacob went flying from the seat. The wagon sailed toward the slow-moving current. Both Jacob and the wagon hit the water thirty feet below at almost the same time.

It took Jacob a while to surface, and when he came up, gasping for breath, he looked around and saw that the wagon was going down, and most of its contents, though some items were floating on the surface.

He looked past a floating wooden box and saw the two outlaws sitting their horses on the bank of the river by the bridge. He pulled his head back so they wouldn't see him and heard one of them say, "He's not gonna get far on foot."

"Maybe he went down and isn't comin' up," said the other.

"Maybe. But even if he's alive, he won't be for long. C'mon. Let's go get Wade and Dub."

CHAPTER FIFTEEN

As soon as Mack Jarvis and Eldon Ray were out of sight, Jacob paddled to the east bank of the river and crawled out. He lay on the grass, panting. His teeth were chattering uncontrollably.

The air was cold, and there was a breeze, which chilled him to the bone. Suddenly his line of sight fell on a rock overhang on the opposite bank of the river. Beneath it, brush had collected and clung to the bank. Though the water was cold, Jacob scooted down the bank and slipped into the river. Keeping a sharp eye on the east bank and the damaged bridge, he swam across the broad stream as fast as he could.

When he reached the rock overhang, he wriggled his way back underneath the brush, made a small opening so he could see the bridge and the other bank, and waited. His teeth continued to chatter. He wondered where the mules had gone. Even if he lived through this, he probably would never see them again.

His wagon was gone. His money was gone. Everything he owned in the world was gone. He wished he had never come west. He should have stayed in New York. He should have been able to stay in spite of the memories of Miriam, and work as his brother's partner for the rest of his life. He should have—

Suddenly he heard the rumble of galloping hooves. Moments later Wade Kilbane and his men drew rein on the east bank, at the edge of the bridge, and stared downstream. What was left of the wagon had sunk in the river, which was more than deep enough to cover it. The buoyant materials had long since floated out of sight.

"You can see where the bridge railing is broken, boss," said Eldon Ray. "The wagon went straight down, and stuff was all over the river. If you ask me, the peddler's down there, too, deader 'n a doornail."

"Yeah? And what if he's not down there? What if he's alive and goin' to some rancher for help so he can locate the nearest lawman? You two should've stayed here and made sure he was dead."

"Well, boss," said Mack Jarvis, "if he didn't drown, he sure can't have gone far."

Kilbane swore vehemently. "I don't like 'ifs,' Mack! I want that peddler dead, and I want to know he's dead! I sent you two to kill him, and all I get are 'ifs.' I want him found!"

"Since we know he went in the river, boss," said Dub Fielder, "he no doubt came out somewhere downstream."

"Good thinkin', Dub," Kilbane said.

The three men exchanged glances, unsure if their boss was being serious or sarcastic.

"Okay," Kilbane said, "let's cross the bridge and head downstream on the west bank."

As the outlaws rode the bank just above him, Jacob heard Kilbane say, "We've got to find that peddler. He could tell the law what we look like, and he definitely heard Clyde call me Wade."

"We'll find him, boss," Jarvis said. "Don't you worry. This country ain't that big. We'll track him down."

"You'd better, or you two are in deep trouble."

Jacob waited until he couldn't hear the men anymore, then pushed out from under the rock overhang. He couldn't stay in the icy water any longer. Shivering uncontrollably, he crawled up the bank and looked downstream. The outlaws were nowhere in sight. He climbed higher on the bank. After a careful panorama of the entire area, he climbed over the crest and limped as fast as he could, heading west.

As he made his way across the rough terrain, Jacob kept looking back to see if the outlaws were coming after him. Some twenty minutes after leaving the river, he paused once more to take a backward look and saw riders in the distance to the south. With his heart banging against his ribs, he made a dash to a thick stand of brush under some cottonwood trees and plunged in.

Peering between the leafless branches, Jacob watched the riders closely. When they came close enough, he counted four. They returned to the bridge and crossed it. When they passed from view, Jacob breathed a sigh of relief and moved on. He had lost his hat when he plunged into the river. His coat seemed twice as heavy as usual, since it was soaked with water. He stopped long enough to remove the coat and wring it out.

He decided to carry the coat for a while and give the rest of his clothing a chance to dry out. As the sun was setting, Jacob watched the shadows of the land shift and the colors change along the horizon. The southern part became purple against distant mountain peaks. Drawing from his memory of the map given to him by Manfred Collier, Jacob told himself those were the Uintahs.

He was still shivering when the last rays of the sun disappeared and a small ranch house and barn came into view. At first he planned to go to the door and ask for help. But after thinking on it, he decided it wasn't right to involve them. If Kilbane picked up his trail, he might kill the ranch people for helping Jacob.

He paused to study the homestead in the gathering twilight. He would take refuge in the barn and be gone in the morning before the rancher learned of his presence.

There was little light on the western horizon when Jacob arrived at the pole fence that surrounded the corral. There were a few horses in the corral, along with three milk cows. He could see beef cattle in a field on the other side of the house.

He waited outside the corral until darkness had fallen, then crawled through the pole fence and made his way to the back door of the barn. The latch snapped loudly when he pulled it down. He waited for any sounds from inside the barn or from the house.

All was silent.

The rusty hinges complained as he pulled the door open and peered into the dark maw of the barn's interior. The barn appeared unoccupied. He stepped inside and pulled the door shut, latching it. There was a faint light coming from the windows of the house. Jacob carefully made his way toward the two windows on that side of the barn to take a look. He stumbled against a grain barrel, righted himself before he fell, then took a few more steps and stumbled over a wooden crate of some kind.

He drew up to the closest window, which was dusty and fly-specked, and looked toward the house. He could see movement inside. To the right of the house, almost parallel with the barn, was a fruit cellar. His empty stomach growled at the thought of food.

Suddenly the back door of the house opened. Jacob could make out the form of a man as he stepped onto the porch, paused, and struck a match. The flare of the match showed Jacob a lantern in the rancher's hand. When the wick was burning, the rancher closed the back door, stepped off the porch, and headed for the barn. The lantern light also showed Jacob a gun belt on the man's waist.

Jacob stumbled back the way he had come, groping for the unidentified wooden crate. When he bumped into it, he shuffled to the grain barrel and felt around it with his hands to see if there was room enough to hide behind it. When he found ample room, he ducked down just as the latch on the door was thrown and the door swung open. Jacob prayed that the rancher wouldn't find him.

The barn filled with yellow light and the sound of heavy footsteps. At first it seemed the man was coming directly toward Jacob, but then an interior door opened, and Jacob heard the rancher step into some kind of room. The light in the open part of the barn dimmed.

There were metallic sounds, which Jacob took to be tools being shifted around on a wooden bench or table. Seconds later, the open area brightened again, and the door clicked shut. The light grew brighter around Jacob. A tremor rocked through him as he held his breath.

The footsteps halted, and the man placed the lantern on the floor of the barn. Trembling, Jacob peered around the barrel and saw the rancher open the lid of the wooden crate he had stumbled against. The rancher took something out of the crate, dropped the lid, then picked up the lantern and headed for the door.

Once again, Jacob was surrounded by darkness. He exhaled a sighing breath and limped to the window. He was just in time to see the rancher pass through the back door of the house. Then all was still.

Jacob's stomach growled, causing him to look back toward the fruit cellar. He had heard about fruit cellars in the West. He hated to take food from the rancher, but he had to eat.

He stepped to the door and opened the latch with as little noise as possible. A couple of horses followed his movement as he made his way to the pole fence. He noted a stock tank next to the gate and could tell it was full of water. He crawled between the poles and made his way to the fruit cellar.

When he fumbled for the latch to the cellar door, he

found that it opened easily. He swung the door wide, and the sweet aroma of dried fruit met his nostrils. He groped around in the pitch-black darkness and found small cloth sacks hanging on thin cords. He pulled one of the sacks to his nose and took a whiff. Apples. Dried Apples.

His mouth watered at the thought of eating the apple slices. He was able to free the sack from the cord. Then reaching out in the darkness, he took hold of another sack and smelled it. More apples. He took that sack also.

As he was moving past the house, he saw the light vanish in the rear windows. He hoped the family was going to bed. He was bone-tired and didn't want another visit from the rancher.

Jacob stopped at the stock tank, bent over, and scooped water into his mouth with one hand. When his thirst was satisfied, he went back into the barn, closed the door, and groped his way to the spot where he had hidden behind the grain barrel earlier. He sat on the floor, leaned against a roof support, and ate his fill.

The air inside the barn was not nearly as cold as outside. He was glad that his clothing was beginning to dry out. Even though his coat was still damp, it now helped to keep him warm. He lay down on his side, put his hands between his knees, and wished for a pillow. He pulled the coat collar up around his ears and soon fell asleep.

After a fitful night, Jacob rose up and looked toward the windows on the back side of the barn. He could make out a slight hint of gray in the eastern sky. He stuffed the apple sacks in his coat pockets, slipped out the barn's back door, and headed across the corral for the pole fence.

The little man limped his way westward, moving as fast as he could. By the time the sun came up, his bad leg was hurting him. He hid in a large stand of brush and allowed himself a few more apple slices. He rested for a while till the pain in his leg eased up, then was back at it, limping across the rolling hills, doing his best to stay out of the open areas.

Noon came with a heavy cloud bank covering the sun. This turned the air a bit colder. Jacob dropped into a dry, tree-lined gully and hid himself in some heavy brush while he ate some more apple slices.

While he was eating and watching for any movement along the ridges of the gully, he pondered just where he should go. He recalled Manfred Collier telling him that with the army there, as well as the townspeople, Fort Bridger was the most populated place between Rawlins and Evanston, unless maybe Rock Springs had grown some since Collier was last there.

Jacob would not turn around and head for Rock Springs. He might run into Kilbane and his bunch. The safest place was Fort Bridger.

The day passed slowly for Jacob. His game leg caused him to stop every half hour or so to rest. He had skirted several farms and ranches, not wanting to involve the people in his problem.

Finally, when the sun went down and darkness was descending on the land, Jacob spotted a ranch house and out-buildings. He had finished off the last of the apple slices in midafternoon. He was tired, his leg was throbbing with pain, and he was hungry.

He hauled up in a grove of cottonwoods about fifty yards from the ranch buildings and looked the place over. There were horses in the corral, and off to the south was a large herd of beef cattle. At the moment, no people were in sight.

Jacob decided he would again spend the night in the barn. Maybe these people had a fruit cellar, too. He waited till it was completely dark, then moved in. The clouds had left the sky in late afternoon, and now the stars were twinkling in the black canopy overhead. There was no moon. The wind picked up and moaned across the hills.

Jacob made a beeline for the corral and barn. When he drew near the corral fence, he saw light in two of the barn's windows at one end. Moving as quietly as possible, he crawled between the poles and threaded his way among the horses in the corral, touching them as he limped along.

As he came close to the barn, he could see tiny cracks in the wall where light seeped through. Then he heard someone whistling. Curious, he slipped up to the end wall by the windows and found a crack in the wall. Pressing his face to the rough wood, he saw the rancher milking a big Holstein cow by the light of two kerosene lanterns. One lantern was on the floor, and the other hung from a hook in a stanchion at the end of the feed trough.

When the rancher was done milking, he let the cow out of the barn and doused the lantern on the stanchion. He picked up the bucket of milk and stepped outside, setting the lantern down long enough to close the barn door, then headed for the house.

Jacob slipped up to the corner of the barn and waited till the man went inside. Then he hurried along the front of the barn to the opposite end, looking for a fruit cellar. There was enough light coming from the windows of the house to illuminate the immediate area, but there was no fruit cellar in sight.

Slowly, Jacob limped toward the back porch, hoping he might find something to eat there. Just as he drew near, the back door opened. The rancher's wife was saying something over her shoulder to someone. She then said, "Here you go, boy," and stepped back inside, closing the door.

Just then Jacob saw the big black dog by the light from the kitchen window. He froze in place. The dog began nibbling at something the rancher's wife had tossed outside for him. Jacob began to quietly back away.

Suddenly the dog's head came up. A deep-throated growl rumbled from him, and he looked in Jacob's direction, peering into the heavy gloom. Jacob froze in his tracks, his heart pulsing in his throat.

The big beast continued to growl for a few seconds, then went back to whatever he was eating.

Jacob's breathing was ragged as he eased slowly backward. His hunger was gone. In its place was the earnest desire to get away from the ranch. He was glad it was a moonless night and that dogs didn't have eyesight like cats.

Back he went, a careful step at a time. He bumped into something, and the dog's head came up again. He released a menacing growl, then sniffed the night wind. His teeth protruded from a lip-curling snarl. He laid his ears back and lowered his haunches.

Then the dog catapulted off the porch and charged straight for him. Jacob ran, almost as if he had no crippled leg. But it was of no use. The dog hit him from behind, snarling and snapping. Jacob went down face-first, tumbled a few feet, then started to get up. Sharp fangs ripped at his left pant leg, and Jacob felt pain. He kicked at the snapping fangs, then felt them bite and rip into the pant leg at his calf.

He kicked the dog in the mouth as hard as he could, making him yelp, then pulled his knees under him and rose to his feet. He started to run, but it took the dog only seconds to leap on him again and sink his teeth into the back of Jacob's coat at the neck. He heard cloth tear at the back of his neck at the same time he felt the hot breath of the dog.

The dog's weight kept Jacob on the ground, and the beast began shaking his head angrily, ripping the collar apart.

Jacob raised up on his knees. The dog let go of the collar and went for his face. Jacob raised his elbow in the nick of time. The fangs sank into the sleeve of his heavy coat instead.

The dog backed up and came for him again. Jacob fell on

his back, his heart pounding in terror, and used his arm to fend off the fangs once more. He rolled over, and his hand touched what felt like a length of tree limb. In desperation, he lashed out with a fist and was fortunate enough to strike the animal squarely on the nose. The dog yelped, backed off with a whine, then growled and sprang at Jacob, snapping and snarling.

Jacob struggled to gain his feet. He was on his knees when the black beast lunged at him again, cutting his left hand. Ignoring the pain, Jacob got to his feet and braced himself for another attack. He swung the heavy limb and caught the dog on the side of the head. The dog let out a yelp and fell to the ground, stunned.

The little man ran as fast as he could toward a wooded area north of the ranch house. He plunged into the woods and stopped behind a large tree, his ragged breathing sawing in and out.

Jacob looked back and saw the rancher, a lantern in one hand and a rifle in the other, approach the dog. He heard the man talking to the dog, and he suddenly became aware of the wounds on his face and his left hand. They were stinging like fire.

He watched the rancher, who rose to his feet and looked all around, holding the rifle in a ready position. "Who's out there?" the rancher called.

Jacob tried to keep his breathing subdued.

The rancher repeated his question and waited. When there was no response, he turned his attention back to the dog, who was barely moving.

Jacob limped through the dark patch of woods and soon was in an open field. By this time, the ranch was out of sight.

With only stars to light his way, he stumbled across the field toward a small stand of trees. Feeling safe when he reached them, he tossed the broken limb aside, dropped to the ground at the base of a huge oak, and touched the wound on his face. He was thankful to find that it was only a scratch, and the blood was already drying up.

The gash on his hand was worse. It burned like fire and was still bleeding. He reached under his coat, pulled the tail of his shirt out, and tore off a generous length of it. He wrapped it around his hand and used his teeth to tie a knot.

Further investigation told him one leg of his trousers was ripped, but he could find no blood. His coat collar was hanging loose, and the sleeves were torn to shreds.

Exhausted, Jacob peered through the darkness, trying to find a good place to lie down and sleep. Just a few feet the other side of the small stand of trees was a gully. He carefully eased down the gentle slope to its grassy bottom. There were bushes along the base of the slope, and soon he found a level spot at the foot of the bushes where he could lie down.

Though hunger pangs clawed at his stomach and his throat cried for water, Jacob was glad for the relative safety of the gully. He touched his face again, and his fingertips came away dry. The cloth wrapped around his hand was moist with blood, but the flow seemed to have slowed.

He considered removing his coat and rolling it up to make a pillow, but the night air was too cold. He sat up and felt around in the dark, trying to find the best way to lie down so his head could be elevated at least a little. His hand touched a large stone with a smooth surface. As he examined it with his fingers, he found that it was about three inches thick and flat on both sides. He lay down again, adjusted the stone until it felt just right under his head, then pulled his legs up in a fetal position. He tucked his hands between his knees for warmth and tried to go to sleep.

But sleep eluded him.

Jacob thought of his mules, wondering if they had found food. He thought of the wagon and everything he had lost. His Torah and Talmud were gone. He had no money. What would he do now to make a living? He dared not try to return to Cheyenne City and start over. The killers would have an easy time finding him if he stayed in the peddling business. Somehow he would have to earn enough money to send Mr. Collier what he owed him for the mules and wagon.

But how could he do that? Even if he was able to find a job at Fort Bridger, he would also live in fear of Wade Kilbane.

He thought of his brother Henry back in New York. No doubt Henry and his family were fast asleep in their nice warm beds.

"Jacob," he said to himself, "if you live through this horrible nightmare, you're going to find a way to return to New York and forget this wild, dangerous country."

Jacob adjusted his head on the stone. He thought of Jacob of old, the man who slept outdoors one night with his head on a pillow of stone and dreamed of God's angels going up and down a ladder between heaven and earth—the man who became Israel under the hand of almighty God.

And Jacob Kates wept. While tears coursed freely down his cheeks, he said, "O God of my fathers; God of Jacob, who slept with his head on a pillow of stone, I need You to send an angel to me. I am desperately in need of an angel's help."

CHAPTER SIXTEEN

The day had been an unusually warm one for late October. The sun was lowering in a sapphire sky and would soon touch the distant Uintah peaks to the southwest.

The valley shimmered in amber and gold light as Glenda Williams left her café next door to the hotel and walked the half block to her house.

At the Williams home, Abby Turner finished the homework assignment Miss Lindgren had given her that day, then picked up her jacket and left her room. Out on the back porch, she picked up an empty clothes basket and walked to the clothesline, humming a new song she'd learned at church. Glenda had done the washing that morning after Abby had gone to school and planned on bringing in the wash when she came home. But Abby was determined to do all the work she could around the house to show Gary and Glenda how much she appreciated their taking her in and giving her a place to live.

The wash still on the line gently flapped in the breeze as Abby took pieces down and dropped them into the basket. Suddenly the breeze flapped a towel against her, and she caught a hint of the fresh outdoor fragrance created by the breeze and the sunshine. She pressed the cloth to her face and inhaled the wonderful, clean aroma.

When the last piece was off the line, Abby hummed the new song again, and just as she stepped into the kitchen, Glenda came down the hall.

"Honey, you didn't have to bring the wash in," Glenda said, smiling at her. "You need to be doing your homework."

"Oh, I got it all done a few minutes ago, Miss Glenda, so I thought I'd go ahead and bring in the wash."

"Thank you, Abby. But don't think because we took you into our home that you have to do all the work."

"I'll do all I can. You and Mr. Gary have been so good to me. I want to show my appreciation."

"We love having you live with us, honey," Glenda said. "Well, now that the wash is in, I'll fold it and put everything away."

"No, *we* will fold it and put everything away," Abby said.

Glenda smiled and hugged her.

Working together, Glenda and Abby soon had everything folded and laid out on the kitchen table.

"That's strange," Glenda said.

"Hmm?"

"Gary's Levi's. I don't see them here."

"They weren't on the line."

"But they had to be, honey. I distinctly remember washing them and hanging them up."

"They sure weren't there."

"Maybe the clothespins came loose. The Levi's are probably lying out there on the ground somewhere."

"I didn't see them," Abby said, heading for the back door, "but I'll go check right now."

"Okay. I'll put these other things away."

Glenda was just returning to the kitchen when Abby came in and said, "No Levi's in the yard, Miss Glenda." She opened her hand and showed her two clothespins. "These were lying in the grass under the clothesline. I hadn't noticed them before."

Glenda nodded. "Well, they couldn't have blown off the

line. There's been no wind to speak of today. Just a gentle breeze."

Abby's face stiffened. "You don't suppose...you don't suppose somebody stole them?"

"I can't imagine such a thing. Why would somebody in this town steal Gary's Levi's?"

"What else could it be?"

"I don't know, honey."

Three blocks away, Julie Powell finished sweeping her house while five-year-old Casey and three-year-old Carrie were playing in the parlor. She went to the back porch with the happy laughter of children ringing in her ears and picked up a clothes basket.

As she was taking clothes off the line, she noticed an empty place between two of her dresses, where she had hung one of her husband's shirts. Two clothespins lay on the ground beneath the empty place on the line. Julie picked them up, deep furrows showing across her young brow.

On the other side of town, Mary Carter, wife of Judge William Carter, was sitting in her kitchen with Regina Samuels, whose husband was the town's barber and mayor. The two women had been enjoying coffee while chatting.

Mary scooted her chair back, saying, "Excuse me, Regina, I set an apple pie out on the back porch to cool just before you came. I need to bring it in."

"I really should be going," Regina said, lifting her cup for a final sip of coffee.

"Just a minute," said Mary, heading for the door. "I'll be right back."

Mary stepped out onto the back porch, and her head bobbed when she saw that her pie was missing. "What?"

"What's wrong, Mary?" Regina called.

Looking all around the porch, Mary called back, "My pie's gone!"

Regina moved out onto the porch. "You mean somebody's taken it?"

"Guess so. It's not here. I had it lying right there on the seat of that old rocking chair."

"Why, who would do a thing like that?"

"Nobody in this town that I know of. I can believe some drifter would come through town and steal it, but drifters who pass through Fort Bridger never come on this street."

Hannah Cooper and her helper of the day, Leah Morley, were waiting on customers at the general store when they saw Edie O'Brien come in.

Patty Ruth ran to greet her. "Hi, Mrs. O'Brien!"

Edie smiled down at the little girl and patted the stuffed bear's head. "How are you and Tony today, honey?"

"Jus' fine."

"That's good. Hello Hannah…Leah."

Both women greeted her warmly from behind the counter, and Edie went to the shelves to begin picking up the things she needed.

"So how's things at the O'Brien household, Edie?" Hannah said.

"All right, except for one thing," the physician's wife said.

"And what's that?"

"Someone got into our fruit cellar night before last and stole some bags of fruit."

Hannah looked surprised. "Really? I can't imagine that."

"Well, it happened. Must be some drifter came through town and decided to grab some free food."

The door opened, and Glenda Williams came in with Dora Thurman, wife of Fort Bridger's pharmacist. They picked up on the conversation as Carlene Bledsoe gave Edie O'Brien a strange look and said, "Well, isn't that something? We had some fruit taken out of our fruit cellar just last night. Dan went out to get some dried peaches for breakfast this morning and noticed that a couple of the peach bags were missing. Somebody's going around stealing in this town."

Glenda and Dora had been talking along the same lines before they came in the store. They drew up to the counter to listen.

Lois Dawson and Rebecca Kelly were also in the store and came together at the end of the same row of shelves, facing the counter. Lois spoke up first. "We must have some hungry thieves loose around here. I had a bushel basket of apples on my back porch, and someone took about half of them."

"Those hungry thieves must also need some socks and underwear," Rebecca said.

All eyes went to her.

"I hung up the wash yesterday morning, and when I went out in early afternoon to bring it in, someone had taken a pair of my husband's long johns and a pair of socks."

"Well," said Glenda, "I came home from the café a little while ago, and a pair of Gary's Levi's had been stolen off the clothesline."

"I don't know what to make of this," Hannah said, handing Edie her change from the sale.

Dora Thurman said, "Curious, these thefts…"

"What do you mean?" Edie asked.

"Everything reported stolen are food and clothing—the necessities of life."

"That is odd," said Glenda. "Usually if it's a drifter—or

drifters—they'll steal anything they can get their hands on."

"I don't think I've seen a strange face in town for at least a couple of weeks," Carlene Bledsoe said. "Of course, they can come and go without my seeing them."

"We need to report this to Marshal Mangum," Hannah said. "There may be others in town who have had things stolen, and it could get worse. The marshal can be on the alert and let everybody in town know to keep a sharp eye. If the thief is still in town, he must be caught and stopped."

"I'll be going right by the marshal's office on my way home," Lois said. "I'll stop and tell him about it."

That evening, the Coopers went to the Williams home for supper. While they were removing their coats, Glenda said, "Marshal Mangum was here about twenty minutes ago."

"Good," Hannah said. "So Lois found him and told him about the thefts?"

"Uh-huh. He told me that the Powells had one of Justin's shirts stolen off their clothesline. And that Mary Carter put an apple pie on her back porch to cool, and it was stolen. Add that to Gary's Levi's, along with all the other things we heard about at the store today, the marshal says we've got us a sharp cookie somewhere in this town. Whoever he is, he's slick. Nobody's seen a thing until they find their articles missing. The marshal is interviewing everyone who's missing something."

"I hope Marshal Mangum catches him soon," Gary said.

Glenda sighed. "Well, let's get to the table. Abby and I have supper ready."

Everyone found their places at the table. As usual, Chris made sure he was sitting next to Abby. Patty Ruth took note of it and started to say something, but she happened to look toward her mother, who gave the little girl one of her "Don't you say it, or you're in deep trouble" looks.

Patty Ruth avoided her mother's stern eyes, but kept her remark to herself.

Gary asked Chris to lead them in prayer as they thanked the Lord for the food. Chris did so, and added a special plea—that God would let the thief be caught.

At the amen, Glenda said, "Fair warning to all...I have black walnut cake for dessert, so save some room."

"Glenda, you know I can't resist your black walnut cake," Hannah said. "This baby and I are going to be too big if you don't quit baking that scrumptious stuff every time you have us over for supper."

Glenda smiled and said, "Can I help it if you find it irresistible?"

"Sure you can help it. Stop baking it when we're coming to supper." Hannah paused, then added, "But I'm glad you made one for tonight!"

Everybody laughed.

As the meal began, the subject went back to the Fort Bridger thief.

"Even with Justin's shirt and Mary's pie being taken," Hannah said, "it's still just the necessities of life—food and clothing."

B. J. said, "Maybe the thief's like Robin Hood of Sherwood Forest. Maybe he's stealing food and clothes and giving 'em to poor people who don't have much."

"I hope it's something like that," said Mary Beth. "Then at least he would be a good thief."

Chris chuckled. "How do you know the thief is a he, Mary Beth? Maybe it's a she."

Patty Ruth started to say something around a mouthful of mashed potatoes.

"Ah, ah, ahh, Miss P. R.," Hannah said. "We don't talk with our mouths full."

The five-year-old swallowed quickly, then said, "Chris, that's dumb."

"What's dumb?"

"Sayin' that the thief might be a her. Womans don't be thiefs. Jus' mens."

"Oh yeah? Females have been known to steal."

"Womans don' be bad like mens," Patty Ruth countered. "They don' rob banks, they don' be gunfighters, an' they don' scare little kids. But mens do. Sometimes I'm afraid there's a bogeyman under my bed or in my closet, but I'm never afraid it's a bogeywoman!"

There was laughter around the table. Though Chris tried not to join in, his sister's reasoning finally touched his funny bone, and he laughed harder than anyone else.

The air was briskly cold as the Coopers walked home along Main Street under a star-filled sky. About halfway home, Mary Beth looked up and said, "A falling star!"

Every eye in the family saw the "tail" of the falling star; then it disappeared.

"Where'd it go, Mama?" Patty Ruth asked.

"It just sailed off to another part of the universe, honey."

"Will it be back?"

"No. Once they fall like that, they never come by earth again."

B. J. looked up with awe and said, "Miss Lindgren says there are millions and millions of stars."

"Yes," said Mary Beth, "and just think of it...the Bible says God has given a name to every one of them."

"Is there one named Biggie?" Patty Ruth asked.

"No, honey," said Mary Beth. "There's no star named Biggie."

"How do you know?" challenged the five-year-old. "There might be. God loves Biggie. Maybe He named a star after him."

Hannah frowned at Mary Beth, who said, "Well, Patty Ruth, maybe there is a star up there named Biggie."

Patty Ruth grinned triumphantly. "See? I ain't never been to school, but I know lots of stuff."

Chris chuckled. "I pity poor Miss Lindgren when you do go to school, baby sister."

Patty Ruth put a hand to the side of her mouth so her mother couldn't see and stuck out her tongue.

When the Cooper children were ready for bed, Hannah gathered them together for family prayer time.

"I want us to pray tonight for the thief in our town," she told them.

B. J. cocked his head. "Yeah. We need to pray he'll get caught and Marshal Mangum will lock him up in jail."

"I didn't mean that," Hannah said. "I think whoever is doing this is in need. I think he's only stealing because he needs food and clothing. Let's pray for him."

The next morning, Chris left the upstairs apartment to feed and water Buster before he had his own breakfast. A cold breeze slapped his face as he descended the stairs, and when the breath plumed from his mouth in the cold air, the breeze quickly carried it away. He pulled his coat collar tight around his neck as he crossed the alley.

Buster came trotting up to the corral gate, whinnying his "good morning" to his master.

"Morning, big guy!" Chris said, opening the gate. He

stepped through, pulled the gate shut, then hugged Buster's long neck. "Hungry?"

Buster nickered.

"Well, come on, let's get your breakfast cooked!"

The barn felt warm in comparison to the cold air outside. Chris opened the grain barrel and breathed in the rich aroma of the oats-and-barley mixture. He scooped out a generous amount into the feed trough for the strawberry roan, and while he was pouring it in the trough, he heard a thumping noise overhead.

He looked up toward the hayloft and said, "Buster, did you hear that?"

Buster was interested in only one thing, and it wasn't thumping noises in the hayloft. He began to chomp on what grain was already in the trough.

Chris gave him the rest of his portion, tossed the scoop into the barrel, and dropped the lid. As he stepped to the ladder that led to the loft, he heard another thump and felt a cold sensation on the back of his neck. He stood there, listening, but the only sound in the barn was Buster's loud chomping.

Chris scurried up the ladder and picked up the pitchfork leaning against the wall. He ran his gaze over the hay that nearly filled the loft and quickly pitched the proper amount down to Buster.

As he turned to place the fork back against the wall, he thought he saw the hay move in the far corner. His heart quickened pace. He thought about Patty Ruth's bogeyman. Frozen in place, Chris studied the hay in the corner for a moment, but nothing moved.

Shrugging, he told himself it had only been his imagination.

He propped the pitchfork against the wall and turned around to climb down the ladder. Before he stepped on the first rung, he took another look at the suspicious corner and...the hay moved! Ever so slightly, but it moved!

A sudden chill penetrated his bones. He made a swift move to the pitchfork, grabbed it, moved to the corner, and holding it as a weapon, said loudly with a quaver in his voice, "All right, whoever's under that hay, come on out! I've got a pitchfork here! Come out real slow, or…or I'll stab you!"

"No, please!" came a fearful voice. "Don't stab me!"

Chris held the pitchfork poised as a large section of hay moved, and a small man with bald pate and a fringe of gray hair appeared. He was holding a tattered overcoat, which he had been using as a blanket. There was a thin gash on one cheek that had scabbed over, and Chris noticed a bloody cloth wrapped around the little man's left hand. Chris lowered the pitchfork.

"Please don't stab me, boy," Jacob said, adjusting his sitting position and lowering the coat. "I need a place to hide. I won't hurt your barn, I promise."

Chris turned and propped the pitchfork against the wall, then hunkered down in front of him. "What's your name, mister?"

"Jacob Kates."

"Why do you need a place to hide?"

"A gang of killers is out to get me. They've been tracking me for days."

"What did you do?"

"I saw them murder a man in cold blood. They want to kill me so I can't tell the law what I saw."

"Where'd this happen?"

"Several miles east of here. Can I tell you about myself so you'll understand?"

"Sure."

"Before I do, what's your name, son?"

"Chris Cooper. I live in the apartment upstairs above the general store right here. My mother owns the store."

"I see."

"Go ahead, Mr. Kates."

"Well, Chris, I'm Jewish...from New York." Jacob told his story about why he had come west. Chris listened intently as Jacob told him about the murder of Clyde Little and his wagon plunging into the river. Jacob explained his flight from the killers and how he had been bitten by the big black dog.

Genuine fear was in Jacob's eyes as he finished his story and said, "Please, Chris, don't tell anybody I'm hiding in here. Those killers are determined to find me and kill me. They'll no doubt track me to Fort Bridger. A slip of the lip could get me killed. You won't tell anyone, will you?"

"I'll only tell my mother," Chris said softly.

The fear in Jacob's eyes intensified and his hands trembled. "No! Please! Don't even tell your mother. If she doesn't know, there is no way for her to inadvertently let it slip."

The fourteen-year-old thought for a moment. "Okay, Mr. Kates. I won't tell my mother you're here. How long will you need to hide in our barn?"

Jacob bit down on his lower lip. "Well...I...I won't feel safe till spring. Then I'll try to find a way to go back to New York."

"Chris!" came Hannah's voice from across the alley.

"Oh-oh. That's Mama," Chris whispered. He cupped a hand to the side of his mouth and called back loudly, "Yes, Mama?"

"Are you all right?"

"Yes, ma'am!"

"What's holding you up? Your breakfast is getting cold! It's almost time to head for school!"

Chris swallowed hard, looked at Jacob, then called back, "Sorry, Mama! I'll be right there!"

"Well, you hurry!"

"Yes, Mama! I'll be right there!" Then to Jacob he said,

"I've got to go. But Mr. Kates, it's going to get plenty cold in here before long."

"I know, but I have to stay hidden."

"I'll try to find a way to bring you enough blankets to keep you warm...and food and water. And I'll figure out a way to bring you clean clothes and underwear as often as I can. Have you found the privy at that end of the barn?"

"Yes. Does your mother or anyone else in your family ever come out to the barn?"

"Not very often."

"Good."

"Whenever I come in, I'll call to you in a low voice, so you'll know it's me. If the door comes open and I don't call, then you be as still as you can. Okay?"

"Yes." Tears welled up in Jacob's eyes. "Thank you, Chris. Thank you."

The youth patted Jacob's shoulder. "I'm glad to help you." He looked at the blood-soaked cloth on Jacob's hand. "I'll bring you a clean bandage and some alcohol to clean that bite with."

The tears spilled down Jacob's cheeks. "Thank you so much."

"Be back later," Chris said, heading for the ladder. "After school. This afternoon." He started down the ladder, and when his eyes were level with the floor of the loft he paused, then was gone.

Jacob wiped the tears from his face and said, "You did what I asked, God. Indeed, Chris Cooper is Your angel to Jacob Kates!"

CHAPTER SEVENTEEN

Hannah Cooper and her other three children looked up from the breakfast table as Chris barged through the door. Biggie dashed to meet him, yapping a welcome.

"You'll have to hurry and eat so you won't be late to school, son," Hannah said as Chris peeled out of his coat.

Mary Beth giggled. "We thought you were eating oats and hay for breakfast with Buster, big brother."

"I just got busy doing some things in the barn, and let the time get away from me."

"What's there to do 'cept feedin' Buster?" Patty Ruth asked.

"Lots of things," Chris said, wishing the subject would be dropped. "Things little girls wouldn't understand."

"Like what?"

"Patty Ruth, eat your breakfast," said Hannah. "This is Tuesday, isn't it?"

"Yes, Mama."

"And what does that mean?"

"Means I'm goin' to Belinda's house to play all day."

"Well, if you don't hurry up and get your breakfast down, you'll still be up here eating when Mrs. Fordham and Belinda come to get you."

Chris looked at the clock on the wall and gobbled his food while Mary Beth and B. J. started putting on their coats.

He finished in time to get his own wraps on so he could head for school with them.

The three kissed their mother, and B. J. was first to the door. When he opened it, he gave his big sister a sly grin.

"Don't do it, B. J."

The eight-year-old rushed past her, halted at the top of the stairs, then made his thunderous descent. Chris brushed by Mary Beth as she turned and said, "Mother, why don't you tell Brett Jonathan to go down the stairs like a gentleman?"

Hannah smiled. "He just does that to get your goat, Mary Beth. If you don't let it get to you, it'll take all the fun out of it, and he'll quit."

Mary Beth shrugged her shoulders and sighed. "See you this afternoon, sweet mother."

As Mary Beth started to close the door, Patty Ruth called from the table, "How 'bout your sweet li'l sister?"

"I'll see you, too, sweet li'l sister."

Hannah opened the store with Julie Powell at her side. The Powell children stayed with a neighbor on the days when Julie worked at the store.

Patty Ruth and Tony the Bear were adjusting some items on a low shelf near the counter when Betsy Fordham and little Belinda came in.

Belinda ran to her friend. "Patty Ruth! Guess what!"

"What?"

"Mommy made peanut butter cookies, and we can have some, even before lunch!"

"Oh, boy! I like peanut butter cookies!"

"Are you and Tony ready to go, honey?" Betsy asked Patty Ruth after chatting for a moment with Hannah and Julie.

"Yes, ma'am. I'll get my coat and cap!"

Patty Ruth hugged and kissed Hannah, saying, "Bye, Mama," and skipped toward the door with Belinda.

Just as the little girls reached the door, Judy Charley Wesson came in, wearing her Colt .45 buckled up. She wore a short denim jacket, an old weathered hat, and high-top lace-up work shoes.

"Hi, Aunt Judy!" Patty Ruth reached up to give her a hug.

Judy bent over and hugged her, saying, "How's Aunt Judy's li'l punkin?"

"Jus' fine. I'm goin' to Belinda's house in the fort. We're gonna play all day."

"That's good, honey." She turned her attention to Belinda and noticed the child eyeing the gun on her waist. "Hi, Belinda," Judy said.

"Hello, Mrs. Wesson," she said, hardly taking her eyes off the gun.

"So you girls are a-gonna have yoreselves a big day playin', huh?"

"Yes, ma'am."

"Wal, I hope you have a mighty nice time of it."

Betsy greeted Judy, then took the girls outside. As they were walking down the boardwalk toward the fort gate, Belinda said to Patty Ruth, "Is your Aunt Judy a gunfighter?"

"Huh-uh. Only mans are gunfighters. Not womens. Aunt Judy jus' wears her gun in case some bad guys come into town and Marshal Mangum needs help."

At the Fort Bridger school, it was recess time following a lesson in world history. Just before dismissing the class, Sundi Lindgren said, "I want all of you to put on your coats and button them up good. It's pretty cold outside today. Chris, I need to see you immediately after we dismiss for recess."

"Yes, ma'am."

"Oh-oh, Chris," said one of his friends from the fort, "you're in trouble now!"

Laughter swept across the room.

Sundi made a mock scowl at the boy and said, "Edgar, if I hear any more speaking out like that, you're the one who will be in trouble!"

There was some subdued laughter, but it died quickly when the schoolmarm folded her arms across her chest, dipped her chin, and looked at them from the tops of her eyes.

Class was dismissed, and Chris waited till the room was almost empty before leaving his desk to approach the teacher. "Yes, ma'am?"

"When I asked for the book reports that were due today, you told me you left yours at home."

"Yes, ma'am."

"Chris, one of the things a person must learn as they grow up is to shoulder responsibility. You're planning to go to West Point when you graduate from high school?"

"Yes, ma'am."

"Graduates of West Point come out as officers—lieutenants—don't they?"

"That's right."

"What do you think your chances will be to graduate from West Point and become an army officer if you're assigned a book report there, and when it comes due, you tell your professor you forgot it…you left it in your dormitory room?"

Chris blushed. "My chances wouldn't be too good, would they?"

"No, they wouldn't. You knew the book reports were due today, didn't you?"

"Yes, ma'am."

Sundi looked her student square in the eyes. "Tell me, Chris. Is the book report finished?"

"Yes, ma'am. It is. I…I'm very sorry that I forgot it. But I don't want a failing grade. May I run home and get it?"

"So, if I let you go home and get it, you could come back real quick with it in hand and turn it in?"

"Yes, ma'am. It's done. I promise."

Sundi Lindgren smiled. "All right. Recess is over in twenty minutes. I believe if you run, you can be back here inside twenty minutes. Right?"

"Sure."

"All right. Don't stop for anything. If you're not back with the book report by the time recess is over, I will not give you an A on it, even if it deserves one."

"Yes, ma'am. May I be excused?"

Sundi nodded. "You are excused."

Jacob Kates was eating one of the apples he had taken from a back porch the day before when he heard the horse in the corral whinny. Then the barn door opened.

"Mr. Kates! It's me, Chris!"

Jacob rose to his feet and limped to the edge of the loft as Chris climbed the ladder.

Chris saw the limp and frowned. "Did you hurt your leg too, Mr. Kates?"

"Many years ago. I limp all the time."

"Oh. I'm sorry." Chris handed Jacob a paper bag. "I got to thinking about your hand, so I snuck in the storeroom at the store and got you some wood alcohol to kill the germs. Sure don't want you getting blood poisoning. And there's a bandage roll in there, too."

"Thank you."

"How are you on food?"

"I still have part of an apple pie, some apples, and some

dried fruit. I already went down and drank water at the pump by the stock tank."

"Okay. I have to get back to school. See you tonight."

The boy half slid down the ladder, picked up a small canvas knapsack, and darted out the door.

Jacob looked toward heaven. "Thank You, God, for sending me the angel I prayed for."

Chris ran hard down the alley, turned left, and made a beeline down Main Street toward the south end of town. He was sucking for air when the schoolhouse came into view, and his heart sank when he saw Miss Lindgren ushering the smaller children back inside. The older ones, he knew, had already gone in. And he was still more than a block away.

Chris hated to go in, but there was no alternative. He crossed the playground, still at a hard run, drew up to the door, and closed it behind him as every head turned his direction.

Miss Lindgren looked at him with a sober face and said, "Bring the book report to me, Chris. You're late, you know."

Chris swallowed with difficulty, feeling the eyes of all his schoolmates on him as he moved up the center aisle. When he reached the desk, Sundi stood up and extended her hand. It was obvious that she was perturbed.

Chris gave her the book report and started to turn away.

"Just a minute, young man. Stay right here."

He turned back to face his teacher.

"Chris, you said you would go home and return with the book report before recess was over."

"Yes, ma'am."

"Did you have some kind of problem that hindered your journey?"

He cleared his throat. "Ah…no, ma'am."

"Then you must have been playing around. Is that correct?"

"Well, no, ma'am. I wasn't playing around. I just…well, I

had something I had to do, which was very important."

Miss Lindgren arched her eyebrows. "And that was?"

Chris's features turned crimson. "Well, Miss Lindgren, it was...ah...something very personal, and I can't tell you."

Sundi stared at him for a long moment, then said, "I will read your book report tonight, and we'll talk about it in the morning."

"Yes, ma'am."

"You may go to your seat now."

Chris walked to his desk and sat down. He glanced at his sister, who gave him a look of compassion, then at his brother, who showed no emotion at all.

The next afternoon when the Cooper children came home from school, they took their books to the apartment, had a small snack that Hannah had left for them on the kitchen table, then went downstairs to the store. It was the custom to do whatever their mother needed done in the store—stock shelves, dust, sweep.

When Chris, Mary Beth, and B. J. entered by the back door, there were several customers in the store. Some were in line at the counter; others moved down the aisles, picking up items to purchase; and still others stood around chatting. Patty Ruth was at the checkers table with eight-year-old Joshua Patterson, whose mother was gathering a few items for purchase.

Behind the counter were Rebecca Kelly and Glenda Williams, who had doubled up that day so Hannah could rest. Hannah was seated on a stool, talking to Marshal Lance Mangum.

Patty Ruth greeted her siblings when they came in, and Hannah paused in her conversation with the marshal to assign jobs. Chris and Mary Beth were to stock shelves, and B. J. was to sweep out the storeroom.

Hannah turned back to the man with the badge and said, "Well, Marshal, I'm glad that no more thefts have been reported."

"Me too," he said. "Maybe the thievish drifter has moved on."

"I hope so. But I'm still puzzled about him."

"What do you mean?"

"Why, he only stole food and clothing."

"That's true. Not like your common drifter who steals whatever he can grab."

The door opened and both Hannah and Mangum looked up to see Heidi Lindgren. Heidi went directly to them. "Pardon me, Hannah," she said, "I need to speak to the marshal for just a moment."

"Certainly. If it's something private, you can go to the storeroom. B. J.'s back there, but—"

"No, no. I only need a minute. It's nothing private. I was passing by, and someone who came out mentioned the marshal was in here, and I needed to speak to him. Marshal, whenever you have a spare moment, would you stop by the dress shop?"

"Sure...will do."

Heidi thanked them for allowing her to intrude and headed for the door.

Hannah watched her go and found herself wishing the marshal were a Christian. For the sake of his own soul first, but also for the possibility that he and Heidi would find an interest in each other.

Mangum excused himself and left the store.

"Mother," Mary Beth said as she came out of the storeroom, "we seem low on dried fruit...apricots, figs, and apples. Is there more somewhere other than the regular place in the storeroom?"

"There should be plenty yet, Mary Beth. And they should be in the normal place. I'll check for you."

When Hannah and Mary Beth moved into the storeroom, Chris went in as if he were going after something else to put on the shelves. Acting busy, he watched his mother's search. Hannah was surprised at her low stock of dried fruit, saying she couldn't understand how she could have let the supply get so low.

"Mother, something else...we always keep five canteens on display out in the store, and the rest are kept right over here."

Hannah looked in the direction her daughter was pointing.

"One is missing, Mother. I just checked the inventory sheet, and we haven't sold any canteens since yesterday afternoon. Somebody's stolen one."

It wasn't long until Hannah and Mary Beth also discovered that three blankets were unaccounted for, along with a container of wood alcohol and a roll of bandage material.

"Mother," Chris heard Mary Beth say, "it looks like the thief is still in town, and somehow he's gotten into this storeroom."

"I'd say he's still around, honey, but how has he gotten past the counter without our seeing him?"

"Well, if he came through the back door to the storeroom, he could get in and out without being seen."

"But he wouldn't know that unless he'd already been back there. And he sure was taking a chance on getting caught. We're in and out of the storeroom many times a day."

Mary Beth shook her head in bewilderment. "He's a sharp one, all right."

"Chris?" Hannah said.

"Yes, Mama?"

"Would you run down to the marshal's office and tell Marshal Mangum we've had some things stolen here, and I need to see him about it?"

"Sure. I'll be right back."

Marshal Mangum returned to the store with Chris and listened as Hannah told him what had been stolen. Mangum agreed the thief was still around. He was determined to catch him.

That evening at the supper table, Hannah looked at her eldest and said, "Chris, I haven't heard how you did on your book report."

Chris felt a blush creep up his neck and bloom on his cheeks. "Well, I...I got a B on it."

"You got a B?"

"Yes, ma'am."

"Did Miss Lindgren tell you why?"

"Well, yes. It was because I was late turning it in."

"What? You...? I've never known you to be late getting your lessons done, even a book report. Why didn't you have it done?"

"I had it done, Mama. I just forgot to take it with me yesterday morning when I went to school. Remember? I was out in the barn a little too long and had to gulp down my breakfast. In my rush, I forgot to take the book report."

"I see. And this is why you didn't get an A on it?"

"Yes." Chris added that Miss Lindgren had sent him home to get the book report, giving him till recess was over to return. He had been a little late, and after Miss Lindgren had read the report, she said it was excellent, but because he was late turning it in, she would only give him a B.

"Chris," Hannah said, "I noticed something not quite right about you this afternoon when you came into the store from school. Was the B on the book report what was bothering you?"

Chris dropped his gaze and sat in silence.

Hannah reached across the table, squeezed his hand, and

said, "No more late schoolwork, son. Understand?"

Chris nodded.

"And while we're talking about being late, you were at the barn longer than necessary this morning, too. You almost had to wolf down your breakfast again. Is there a problem of some kind out there in the barn? Something you're doing that could wait till after school or Saturday?"

He looked up, meeting her gaze. "There's no problem, Mama. I'll get my work done out there as usual from now on."

That night in her bed, Hannah's thoughts were on Chris. Even at the supper table, he'd had a strange look in his eyes that only a mother could read. Something was awry. She prayed for guidance from the Lord to get to the bottom of Chris's strange behavior.

The next morning, Hannah watched Chris go outside to do his chores before she started breakfast. Mary Beth, B. J., and Patty Ruth were busy in their rooms, getting ready for the day. Ever since she had learned her mother was going to have a baby, Mary Beth had taken on the task of putting Patty Ruth's long red hair into pigtails each morning.

Hannah called to them and said she was leaving the apartment for a few minutes. If the girls were dressed and ready before she got back, Mary Beth was to start breakfast. Patty Ruth and B. J. could help her.

Hannah bundled up, then made her way down the stairs and headed for the barn. She quietly lifted the latch on the corral gate, stepped through, then latched the gate with barely a sound. As she walked softly toward the open barn door, she heard Chris's voice coming from within. She knew he talked to Buster a lot and thought nothing of it until she heard another voice. A mature male voice.

She inched her way inside the door. Buster was at the feed trough, munching grain. Above him, in the hayloft, Chris stood talking to a small, thin man. Hannah stepped forward so that both Chris and the man could see her and said, "Chris, who is this man?"

Chris's head whipped around, and his face showed a combination of fear and surprise. The little man's face showed the same.

Chris licked his lips nervously. "Mama, this is Jacob Kates. Mr. Kates is in trouble, and I've been helping him."

"You have a fine son here, Mrs. Cooper," Jacob said. "My life is in danger, and he's doing what he can to keep me from getting killed."

"All right. How about coming down here and telling me about it?"

Chris climbed down the ladder first and waited for Jacob to descend.

After Jacob told Hannah his story, her heart went out to him. She was also relieved to know what Chris's problem had been for the past couple of days.

Chris admitted taking the things from the storeroom, and that it was Mr. Kates who had stolen the food off porches and the clothing from clotheslines.

Hannah studied Jacob's fear-shadowed features as he said, "Mrs. Cooper, please don't tell anyone I'm here. The men who are after me probably already know I came to Fort Bridger. They're probably lurking about now, waiting for some clue to my whereabouts."

"I understand your fear, Mr. Kates," Hannah said, "but we have a very good marshal in this town. His name is Lance Mangum. I think we should let him in on this. If he knows about you and those men who are after you, he can be on the lookout for them. May I tell him? I promise, I'll tell no one else."

Jacob pondered her words briefly, then nodded. "All right, ma'am. Let's let the marshal in on it."

Hannah smiled. "Now, you're probably getting a bit tired of eating fruit. How about if I get Chris and his brother and sisters fed their breakfast and off to school, then I'll take you to the apartment and feed you a good hot breakfast?"

Tears misted the little man's eyes. "That is very kind of you, ma'am. It sure sounds good."

"All right. You stay here in the barn till I come for you. Chris and I won't tell his brother and sisters about you."

"Thank you, Mrs. Cooper."

Chris smiled at the little man and said, "See you after school."

Jacob raised his tear-dimmed eyes heavenward and said, "Looks like You sent me two angels."

CHAPTER EIGHTEEN

When Hannah Cooper and her oldest son emerged from the barn, Mary Beth was crossing the alley. B. J. and Patty Ruth were standing on the platform at the top of the stairs.

"Mother," Mary Beth said, hurrying toward them, "I thought you were in the store. Is something wrong at the barn?"

"No, honey. Everything's fine. Did you start breakfast?"

"Yes. It's about ready, and I didn't know whether to go ahead and feed B. J. and Patty Ruth or to wait till you and Chris came in."

"Well, we can all eat now. Let's hurry, so you won't be late to school."

It was Sylvia Bateman's day to help Hannah at the store. And since it was Thursday, Betsy Fordham would keep Patty Ruth all day.

Hannah waited in the store with Sylvia until Betsy and Belinda came for Patty Ruth. When they had gone, Hannah told Sylvia she had some things to do that would take a good part of the morning and said she would ask one of the other regulars to come in and help.

Sylvia assured her that she could handle the store by herself and told Hannah to go do whatever was needed.

Jacob Kates was sitting at the edge of the loft when Hannah returned to the barn. Hannah smiled up at him and said, "All right, Mr. Kates. Let's go get some breakfast in you."

She led the little man up the stairs to the apartment and sat him down in the kitchen while she prepared his breakfast. He filled her in on some of the details of his story, and Hannah's heart was stirred with compassion.

While working at the stove and cupboard, she said, "After you've eaten, Mr. Kates, I want to take a look at that dog bite on your hand. Are you having any trouble with the gash on your face?"

"No, ma'am. It seems to be healing up all right. And I think my hand is starting to heal."

"Good. I'll take a look at it anyhow and change the bandage. Now, if you'll come over here to the table and sit down where I've set your place, you can have yourself a hot breakfast."

The food smelled wonderful to the little man who had been living on fruit for several days. As he sat down, he looked up at Hannah and said, "I don't know how to thank you, Mrs. Cooper, for being so kind to me."

She picked up the coffeepot from the stove and poured him a cup of the black, steaming liquid. "The only thanks I'll need will be to see your ordeal ended, and to know you're not in danger from those killers anymore."

"You don't even know me and yet, like your son, you care. I was beginning to think people in this part of the country didn't want anyone else coming here to live."

"There are some hard hearts here in the West, Mr. Kates, but you'll find some very lovable people here, too."

"I know there are lovable hearts in the Cooper family," he said.

Hannah wanted to tell this Jewish man that behind the love she and Chris were showing him was the love of the Lord Jesus Christ, but she knew she needed much wisdom and guidance from the Holy Spirit.

Hannah dished up a big bowl of hot oatmeal, then put a large pat of butter in the center. As it began to melt, she pushed a sugar bowl and a cream pitcher close to him and said, "I'll let you put these on the way you like them."

Jacob looked up and gave her a slanted smile.

"That's it," she said. "You look better with a smile on your face."

"I haven't had anything to smile about in some time, Mrs. Cooper."

Hannah stepped to the stove and picked up a plate of hot biscuits, then set them before him and said, "Maybe these will help you to smile some more." She slid the bowl of butter within his reach and set a jar of strawberry jam on the table. "Now you just have yourself a feast, Mr. Kates."

Jacob spread butter and jam on a biscuit and said, "Chris told me about your husband's heroic death, ma'am. He must've been quite a man."

"He was, I assure you."

"And I hope I get to meet your other children. Chris told me about Mary Beth, B. J., and Patty Ruth. From what he said, your Patty Ruth must be some character."

Hannah smiled. "All four of my children are very special, Mr. Kates. They each have their distinct personalities and special traits. But Patty Ruth...you're right. She's a pistol!"

"When is your baby due, ma'am?"

"March."

"I see. Are you doing all right, carrying it?"

"I get a little tired and have some backaches now and then, but overall I'm doing fine, thank you."

Jacob continued to devour his food.

"Tell you what," Hannah said, "you go ahead and finish your breakfast, and I'll go get Marshal Mangum. There's plenty of coffee in the pot. Just help yourself."

"I'll be right here, ma'am. Sorry you have to do the walking."

"That's all right. Walking is good for expectant mothers. I'll be right back."

Marshal Mangum looked up from his desk when Hannah came into the office. "Good morning, Hannah," he said with a bright smile, and rose to his feet.

"Good morning, Marshal," she replied. "My, that's a handsome shirt!"

Mangum chuckled. "Remember the other day when Heidi came into the store and asked if I'd stop by her shop?"

"Mm-hmm."

"She'd made this shirt for me."

"Oh, really? She does beautiful work with women's clothing, but I didn't know she ever made men's clothing."

"I didn't either, but I'm convinced the lady is quite talented."

"Some special occasion?"

"No. She said she just thought I needed a new shirt, so she made it for me. Pretty good fit without being measured for it, wouldn't you say?"

"For sure," Hannah said.

"What can I do for you, dear lady?" the lawman asked.

"I have our thief in custody," she announced.

Mangum's brow wrinkled. "Pardon me?"

"I said I have the Fort Bridger thief in custody."

"You've captured him?"

"Well, Chris actually captured him. I'm the one who put him in custody."

"What—? How—? What are you holding him with?"

"Oatmeal, biscuits, strawberry jam, and hot coffee."

Lance shook his head. "Will you please explain this?"

"Yes, on the way to my apartment. Can we go now?"

"What are we waiting for?" Mangum said, taking his coat and hat from the rack behind his desk.

Jacob was just finishing the last of the biscuits and jam and was licking one final crumb from his mouth when he heard footsteps on the wooden staircase outside. He relaxed when he recognized Hannah's voice.

The door opened, and Hannah stepped inside with the tall, rugged marshal behind her. Jacob pushed his chair back and stood up. Hannah told him she had related his story to the marshal while they were walking from his office.

The two men shook hands, and Hannah had them sit down at the table. She poured coffee for everyone, then said, "I need to go down to the store and see how my helper is doing. You gentlemen feel free to drain the coffeepot." Pausing at the door, she said, "I'll work on that hand when you and Marshal Mangum are finished, Mr. Kates."

When the door closed, they sat down and Mangum said, "Now, tell me every detail about the murder you witnessed. What Hannah gave me was pretty sketchy. I want to know everything I can about the killers. Can you give me a description of them?"

"I can, but I can also tell you the victim's first and last name. He was definitely a member of the gang. And I can tell you the first names of the rest of them."

"Well, good. Hannah didn't say you knew their names."

"I didn't tell her. I only wanted her to understand what I've been through these last several days."

"Sure. Now, tell me more."

"Well, sir, the boss of the outfit is a huge man. His name is Wade something. The others were called Mack, Eldon, and Dub. And the gang member who ran off with the gold was

Clyde Little. As I told Mrs. Cooper, I saw the leader shoot Little, and when my mules bolted, Wade told Mack and Eldon to catch me and kill me."

Even as he spoke, Jacob saw a change come over Marshal Mangum's countenance. Mangum leaned back in the chair and smiled.

"What are you smiling for?" Jacob asked, cocking his head. "I didn't say anything funny."

"No, but I can happily inform you that your worries about being tracked down and killed by Wade Kilbane and his bunch are over."

Jacob's eyes widened. "What do you mean, my worries are over?"

"Clyde Little was definitely one of the gang, Mr. Kates," Mangum said. "This bunch has terrorized people all over eastern and central Wyoming. They've been robbing and killing for a long time. The others were Mack Jarvis, Eldon Ray, and Dub Fielder. Every one of them had a price on his head."

"Had? Is the good news that they're dead?"

Mangum smiled again. "That's it. I received word from the Sweetwater County sheriff in Green River yesterday that Kilbane and his three henchmen were caught a couple of days ago and hanged."

Jacob felt a great weight slip from his shoulders. "Marshal," he said with a wide smile, "that's the best news these ears of mine have ever heard! I've got to go down to the store and tell Mrs. Cooper!"

At that very instant they heard slow footsteps on the stairs outside.

Mangum left his chair and headed for the door, saying, "I think she's back."

Hannah was just topping the stairs when the marshal opened the door. "We were about to come down to see you," he said.

"We? Mr. Kates was going to come down to the store?"

"Yes'm. With good news. I'll let him tell you."

Jacob had slipped up behind the tall man. When Hannah stepped through the door and saw his beaming face, she said, "Well, Mr. Kates, by the look on your face, I'd say you must have some very good news!"

"Yes, ma'am! When I told Marshal Mangum the names of the killers, he knew of them right away. He said they were caught in Green River and hanged a couple days ago...every one of them!"

"Then you have nothing else to fear!" Hannah said.

"That's right! I don't have to hide anymore."

"Oh, I'm so glad," she said.

Jacob scratched an ear. "Now, if I can find a job, I'll put enough money together as fast as I can and head back to New York."

Mangum cleared his throat. When both Hannah and Jacob turned to look at him, he said, "Mr. Kates, there's another matter to deal with. You stole food and clothing from citizens of my town."

Jacob's face colored. "Yes, sir. If I can talk to the people I stole from, I'll make my apologies...and if I can get a job, I'll pay every one of them back. That is, unless you're going to lock me up in jail."

The marshal winked at Hannah and said, "Stealing food and clothing is a pretty serious offense here in the West, Mr. Kates. As much as you took, you'll probably have to do two years in jail."

"T-two years?"

"Maybe three. I'll have to talk to Judge Carter."

The little man blinked. "Maybe three, Marshal?"

"Well, I'll tell you what, Mr. Kates," Mangum said, a smile working its way across his face, "since you've said you'd face the people you stole from, and that you'll try to find a job so you can pay them back, I won't bother to talk to the judge."

Relief brought color back to Jacob's face. "Oh, thank you, Marshal. Believe me, I wouldn't have stolen those things if I hadn't been in dire need. And—"

"I understand, Mr. Kates. And I'm glad to see you feel bad about it. That's what I was looking for. I know every person you stole from quite well, and I can already tell you that your attitude about it will make them feel good toward you. They're not going to press charges."

"You don't think so?"

"No. Especially when they understand why you did it and that you're willing to work and pay them for what you stole."

"There's a verse in the Bible about that," Hannah said. "Proverbs 6:30. 'Men do not despise a thief, if he steal to satisfy his soul when he is hungry.'"

Jacob's face lit up. "Oh, yes! I remember reading that."

Mangum rubbed his jaw. "I didn't know the Bible said anything like that. It sure makes sense."

Hannah smiled. "God's Word always makes sense, Marshal."

Mangum nodded, then said, "Well, I've got to get back to the street. Might be some bad guys down there." Then to Jacob he said, "Mr. Kates, I'll make arrangements for you to meet each of the people you stole from."

"That's fine, Marshal. Let me know when you're ready."

"Where will I find you? Are you going to make Mrs. Cooper's barn your permanent home?"

"I'll make arrangements for his lodging," Hannah said. "You can find him right here with us."

"All right," Mangum said, and left.

Jacob wiped a hand over his face. "Whew! He had me scared there for a minute. I thought sure I was going to jail."

Hannah eyed the bandaged hand. "Let's take a look at that hand, Mr. Kates."

She examined the wound and said that it seemed to be healing. While she was applying alcohol to it, she said, "Mr. Kates, I've been praying the Lord would send me someone to hire for the store. I have a few of the ladies from the fort and the town who come in and help me on a volunteer basis, and they won't let me pay them. But none of them want a full-time job."

Hannah laid the cotton swab aside and corked the bottle. As she started to wrap a fresh bandage around his hand, she said, "You said you've been in the mercantile business for years."

"Yes, ma'am."

"You've sold goods over the counter?"

"Yes, ma'am."

"You could sell goods over the counter in Cooper's General Store."

A spark came into the little man's eyes. "Of course!"

"Would you like a job?"

"You mean you would hire a thief and trust him with your money?"

Hannah tilted her head and gave him a tender look. "You're no thief. You're a man who has gone through a horrible ordeal because you were kind enough to pick up someone who needed a ride. You're in need of some friends. I want to be one of those friends, Mr. Kates. You need a job, and I need someone with your experience. You're an answer to prayer."

"So are you," he said with a smile. Then a frown etched itself on his brow.

"What's the matter?" she asked.

"You may not want me since I don't work on the Sabbath. I know Saturday is your busiest day."

"I've already thought of that, Mr. Kates. I'll use my volunteer help on Saturdays."

"Then you know something about my Jewish faith."

"Yes. I've learned much about it ever since I became a Christian as a girl."

"And you still want me as your employee?"

"Yes, of course. If you still want to go back to New York, you can work for me as long as you're here."

Tears filmed Jacob's eyes. "Mrs. Cooper, if you want to hire me, I'll forget about going back to New York. And ma'am, you don't have to pay me very much. I can get along on—"

"Mr. Kates, the store is doing quite well. I can afford to pay you a living wage. And I will. Now, something else…we've got to find you a place to live."

"I'll find something. If in the meantime, I could still sleep in your hayloft—"

"You've had enough sleeping in the barn," she said, tying off the bandage. "The storeroom downstairs is at the north end of the store. It's a large room. I can use the empty building that used to be the sutler's store inside the fort to store things. We'll empty out half of the storeroom and have a wall built in. One end already has a small stove to help keep things warm back there when winter comes. I can have a door built in the wall. The stove will be in your room. If you don't mind leaving the door open during the coldest part of the winter, it'll keep the storeroom from getting too cold."

"Certainly I don't mind."

"I sell pretty nice cots in the store. You can have one of them, and I'll buy you whatever furniture you need, unless we have some pieces that will suffice. Until we get this all set up, you can sleep on a cot in the storeroom. All right?"

Jacob scrubbed a tear from his cheek. "Yes, ma'am. You are so kind to me. Thank you." He paused, then said, "Mrs. Cooper, you know about Jacob in the Bible—the son of Isaac and Rebekah?"

"Yes."

"And you remember how one night when he was on his

journey from Beersheba to Haran, he slept with his head on a pillow of stone?"

"I remember it well."

"One night, when those killers were after *this* Jacob, I slept in a gully with my head on a stone for a pillow. I thought of Jacob of old, and how in his dream he saw God's angels going up and down the ladder from heaven. And I prayed for an angel to help me in my time of trouble."

"Bless your heart."

"God sent that wonderful boy of yours to provide for me when I was hiding in the hayloft. Chris was that angel. But God didn't stop there. He also gave you to me. You're my second angel."

Hannah smiled. "I'm always glad when the Lord chooses to use me as one of His servants, Mr. Kates. Now, let's talk about your wages. And let me explain about your working hours, what is expected of you, and that kind of thing..."

While Hannah and her new employee discussed his pay and his new job, Marshal Lance Mangum walked about town, talking to each person who had reported stolen items. When they heard that the thief was now at Hannah Cooper's place and Mangum told Jacob's story, not one person wanted to be reimbursed. They were eager to meet the "Fort Bridger thief."

When Mangum appeared at the apartment and told Jacob the good news, the little man wept again and asked if he could go and talk to each person right then. Mangum gladly volunteered to escort him.

Hannah's back was giving her some pain, and she went downstairs to tell Sylvia she would rest in the apartment until the children came home from school.

When Mangum and Kates returned to the apartment, they

found Chris, Mary Beth, and B. J. with their mother. Chris was thrilled that things had turned out so well, and Mary Beth and B. J. were intrigued by Jacob's story. They took to Jacob just like their mother and Chris had.

While Mary Beth worked with Sylvia behind the counter and B. J. did his sweeping job, Hannah, Chris, and Jacob went to the storeroom to see what needed to be done—other than having a wall put up—to turn the room into comfortable quarters.

The woodstove stood in a corner, and there were small windows in each of the outside walls. While they were making plans, Gary Williams came in, having already spoken to Jacob, and offered to let him stay at the hotel for free until he could come up with a place to live. Hannah explained to Gary about the conversion of half the storeroom into Jacob's apartment, and Gary said he could stay in the hotel until the apartment was ready.

Jacob was overwhelmed at the kindness shown to him by the people of Fort Bridger.

Soon Betsy Fordham brought Patty Ruth home, and she was introduced to Jacob Kates. They hit it off immediately, and Jacob found himself captivated by the precocious five-year-old.

That night, Jacob gladly slept in the storeroom, close to the stove.

Friday was Leah Morley's day to work the counter with Hannah. With just a little bit of instruction, the two women had Jacob selling goods. He took to it as if he'd worked there all his life. Hannah left Jacob with Leah and walked to the residential section a block east of the store, where a house was under construction. She talked to contractor Clayton Farley, who said he would bring a small crew on Monday and have the wall up in the storeroom in a few hours.

When Hannah returned to the store, she saw Pastor Andy Kelly and Rebecca, who had beard about the "Fort Bridger thief" from Marshal Mangum.

"Quite a story," said the pastor as he stepped ahead of the ladies, pausing with his hand on the knob. "So this Jacob Kates is an Orthodox Jew, and you've hired him on a full-time basis?"

"That's right. We struck a deal. He'll work the counter and stock shelves Monday through Friday, and he'll even do what handyman work is needed, and the janitorial work. But he gets Saturdays off to observe his Sabbath."

"That's very kind of you, Hannah," Rebecca said. "Saturday is your biggest day of the week."

"I want to see him come to know the true Messiah," Hannah said. "If I'm going to reach him, I must first show respect for his faith. After all, God used the people of Israel to give us His Word, and to give us the Lion of the tribe of Judah."

"You are right," said Kelly. "That makes it even easier for me to at least invite him to church, knowing you've shown him this kind of respect."

"So you'll still need some volunteer help on Saturdays, won't you?" Rebecca asked.

"Yes."

"Well, put me down. I'll be glad to help."

When they entered, Leah Morley was waiting on the store's only customer, and Jacob was putting some items on the shelves from a large box.

"Mr. Kates," Hannah said, approaching him with the Kellys behind her, "I want you to meet my pastor and his wife. Pastor and Mrs. Kelly, this is Mr. Jacob Kates."

Jacob smiled warmly, shook hands with Kelly, and bowed slightly to Rebecca, saying, "I am very happy to meet you, Pastor and Mrs. Kelly."

"We heard about your situation from Marshal Mangum, sir," said the pastor, "and wanted to come by and meet you."

"That is very thoughtful, sir."

"Hannah has explained that you are Jewish, Mr. Kates, and that you'll be observing your Sabbath each week."

Jacob smiled at Hannah, then replied to Kelly, "Yes, sir."

"As pastor of the church, I'd like to invite you to attend our services on Sunday, Mr. Kates. I want you to know that we'd love to have you and that you're more than welcome to visit us."

"That is very kind of you, Pastor," Kates said, "but I adhere strictly to my Jewish faith. I lost my Torah and my Talmud when my wagon crashed into a river on my way here, but I have much of both memorized."

"I understand," Kelly said, "but I want you to know, if there's ever anything I can do for you, I'd consider it a pleasure."

"Thank you, Pastor," Jacob said. "You are very kind. In fact, I've been treated kindly by everyone I've met in this town."

The door opened, and a huge form filled the doorway. When Andy Kelly saw who it was, he murmured, "That may be about to change."

CHAPTER NINETEEN

There was fire in Buford Wynn's eyes as the lumbering bear of a man swaggered into the store, looking back and forth between Hannah Cooper and Jacob Kates. Andy Kelly gently pushed Rebecca behind him and moved close to Hannah, edging a little in front of her.

Wynn scowled at Jacob, then at Hannah, saying, "My missus and me was about to come in and give you some business, lady, but we heard a bunch of people out front talkin' about the new man you just hired." His eyes flicked to Jacob, who looked like a midget compared to him. "This him?"

"Yes," Hannah said. "You have some objection to my hiring Mr. Kates?"

"Yeah. Folks out there said he's a no-good Jew."

Kelly's back arched. "Is that 'no-good' part yours or theirs, Wynn?"

The big man glowered at Kelly. "The 'no-good' part's mine. You got a problem with that?"

Andy Kelly gave Wynn a level, unblinking stare. "Yes, I do have a problem with it, Mr. Wynn. It was bad enough the attitude you showed toward Negro people the last time you were in this town. Now you show that same attitude toward Jewish people. You're dead wrong to feel that way, and I resent it."

"Ain't no sissy preacher gonna talk to me that way!" Wynn blurted. Even as he spoke, he swung a meaty fist at Kelly's jaw.

Kelly ducked the blow as Hannah and Jacob moved back. The missed punch infuriated Wynn, and he set himself to swing again.

"Don't do it, mister!" Kelly said.

Wynn threw the punch. Kelly dodged it, and with lightning speed he grasped Wynn's wrist, spun him around, and put his arm in a hammerlock, shoving it up till Wynn howled.

"You're going outside!" the preacher said, pushing him toward the door.

Wynn stiffened in resistance, and Kelly rammed the arm higher. Wynn howled again and allowed Kelly to push him out the door. People on the street turned to look as Wynn appeared on the boardwalk with Pastor Andy Kelly in full control of him.

Hannah, Rebecca, Jacob, and Leah all gathered at the door to look on.

"You just cool off, Mr. Wynn," Kelly said.

Buford breathed hard through clenched teeth. "Don't tell me what to do!"

Kelly shoved the arm higher, and Buford howled in agony.

"I said cool off! Resisting me isn't going to get you anything but more pain. Now, when you're ready to act like a civil human being, I'll let go of your arm. Until then, we stay just like this."

"Okay, okay, okay," Wynn said. "I've had enough."

"You're sure?"

"Yes. Let go of me."

"Before you let go of him," Hannah said, stepping up close, "I want to say something. Mr. Wynn, we have a nice town here, and everybody gets along well…everyone, that is, except you. Until you apologize to the Carvers and to Mr. Kates, you are not welcome in my store."

Wynn did not respond.

"I'll let go when you say you're going to behave yourself, Mr. Wynn," said the preacher.

Through gritted teeth, Wynn said, "All right! All right! I don't want any more trouble."

"Promise?"

"Yeah, yeah."

Kelly released him and took a step back.

The voice of an older man in the crowd cut through the air. "Best thing for you to do, Wynn, is straighten up or get out of town!"

Others joined in, voicing their agreement.

"We don't need your kind around here, Wynn!" a woman called.

As Wynn began rubbing his arm and shoulder, Pastor Kelly looked back toward Rebecca. "Look out, preacher!" somebody shouted.

Kelly caught the movement in his peripheral vision and ducked. Wynn's fist hissed over his head.

"The thing for you to do, Mr. Wynn, is get in your wagon and go," Kelly said, his fists poised to defend himself. "If you keep swinging at me, I'll have to cut you down. And I don't want to have to do that. Just go…now!"

Buford let out a maniacal roar and came in swinging. Kelly unleashed a hard punch that sent the big man reeling off the boardwalk. He stumbled and fell facedown in the dust of the street.

The crowd cheered.

Nelda Wynn sat in the family wagon a couple of doors down the street. Her attention was fixed on her fallen husband, but she showed no emotion. Kelly crouched by the unconscious man, then hoisted him onto his back and carried him toward the wagon where Nelda sat.

Kelly caught a glimpse of Marshal Lance Mangum riding into town from the south. Mangum drew up on his horse, and people started telling him what had happened.

Kelly dumped Buford Wynn in the bed of the wagon. "I'm

sorry, Mrs. Wynn," he said, looking up at Nelda, "but he didn't give me a choice."

"I understand, Reverend," she said, taking up the reins. "We'll have to do our business in Green River." She put the horses in motion and drove away without looking back.

That evening, Hannah invited Jacob to the apartment for supper. The children welcomed him, and he enjoyed their warmth and friendliness. It made him feel good that Patty Ruth wanted him to sit beside her at the table. Hannah asked Chris to pray over the food, and Jacob bowed his head with the others.

After the meal, Jacob helped Hannah and Mary Beth with the dishes, while Chris and B. J., Patty Ruth and Biggie played in the parlor.

During the light conversation that went on in the kitchen, Hannah spoke carefully but openly of her faith, and soon Jacob was asking her questions about her beliefs. Some of the things Hannah told him Jacob had never heard before, and he showed mild interest.

When the dishes were done and the kitchen cleaned up, Hannah said, "Mr. Kates, would you like to hear why I believe these things we've been talking about?"

Jacob was a little cautious but said, "Yes, I would."

Hannah sent the children to bed, telling Chris and Mary Beth to pray and read the Bible to the younger ones. Hannah invited Jacob to sit down at the kitchen table, then excused herself while she went to her room for her Bible.

At first she stayed with the Old Testament, taking Jacob to passages about the promised Messiah such as Psalm 22, Isaiah 7 and 53, and portions of the book of Zechariah. She then asked if he would allow her to show him some things Jesus said about Himself and what the New Testament said about His being the fulfillment of those Old Testament passages. Jacob was on edge, but because Hannah had been so kind and generous to him, he allowed it.

When Hannah was done, Jacob said, "Thank you for what you've shown me, Mrs. Cooper, but you understand, this goes against what I've been taught all my life."

"I know, Jacob. But I want you to know Jesus as I know Him."

"I appreciate that, ma'am, but I must hold to my Jewish faith."

"I understand how you feel, Mr. Kates," she said. "You mentioned that you lost your Torah and your Talmud in the river...I don't have a Talmud, but I do have a new Bible I haven't even used. You can have it if you like. You could read your Old Testament Scriptures that way."

The little man smiled. "You are so kind to me. I would love to have it."

"I'll go get it for you."

When Hannah returned, she gave Jacob a key to the store's back door and sent blankets and pillow so he could sleep on a cot in the storeroom. He thanked her, told her good night, and headed out the door. Hannah invited him for breakfast and said she would see him in the morning.

As the young widow lay in bed that night, she prayed earnestly that the Holy Spirit would take the Word and remove the blinders from Jacob's eyes that he might see Jesus as the Messiah.

The following Monday morning, Clayton Farley was at the general store early with three other men. First they hauled many boxes of goods to the vacant sutler's store inside the fort, then they went to work on the wall. By early afternoon it was finished.

Jacob was busy all day working the counter, and Hannah found him quite efficient. She knew the two of them could handle the workload together until the time of her baby's arrival drew near. She would then call on her volunteer help to work with Jacob.

The little man found Patty Ruth a sweet delight to be around. Her misuse of a few words had him laughing at times, and she quickly claimed his heart.

When the other Cooper children came home from school, they were glad to see the wall up and to know that Mr. Kates would have comfortable quarters. When the store closed at its regular time, they all went to work to help Jacob get settled.

Hannah had a spare chest of drawers, which Jacob and Chris carried down from the apartment to the storeroom quarters. A small washstand with water pitcher and bowl were provided, along with a chair and small table. Dishes, pots, pans, towels, and washcloths were taken from the shelves in the store.

Hannah knew Jacob would want his privacy, but she also told him he was welcome to take as many meals with them as he wanted. He would be able to cook what meals he desired for himself on his stove. He could take whatever foodstuffs he would need from the shelves in the store.

By six-thirty, Jacob's room was all set up, and a cozy, cheerful fire was burning in the small stove. Since the evening was upon them, Hannah took her new employee and her children to Glenda's Café for supper.

The sun was reaching its apex in the azure sky as the Wells Fargo stage drew near Fort Bridger. Wintry air whistled around the leather covers on the windows, and the passengers huddled under the buffalo robes the Fargo people provided.

Julianna LeCroix had talked the agent in Rawlins into providing another small blanket to wrap Larissa in, but in spite of it, the baby was coughing with a nasty rattle in her throat and had a fever. Julianna was sure the drafty stagecoach was to blame. The baby had been well when they left Rawlins after more than a week in a warm room.

Chester and Tess Downes and Jean Morden looked on with concern as the young mother tried to make the baby comfortable.

Julianna had told Jack they would have to ask the agent in Fort Bridger to delay the departure of the stage for Evanston long enough to take Larissa to the town doctor. Jack could almost feel the breath of Tack Lombard's hired killers on the back of his neck, but he knew the baby needed a doctor's attention. Usually Larissa was a happy baby, but now her eyes were dull and glazed, and she was fretful. She continually whimpered and rubbed at her left ear.

Tess Downes looked at Larissa with pity and said, "You folks are going to take her to the doctor in Fort Bridger, aren't you?"

"Oh, yes," said Julianna. "We're hoping the agent will delay the stage's departure long enough for us to let the doctor look at her. I hope you won't mind the wait."

"Of course not," Chester said. "What's a little more time when we're already better than a week late?"

When the stage pulled up in front of the Wells Fargo office, a skinny little man stepped out the door. Behind him was a rail-thin woman who wore a Colt .45 on her hip.

"Howdy, Biff...Ollie," said the skinny man. "Seems like ages since I seen ya!"

"Was a long delay," said the driver.

The little man opened the door of the stage, gave the passengers a lopsided grin, and said, "Howdy, folks! Name's Curly Wesson. I'm the Fargo agent here, and this cute thang with me is my wife and assistant, Judy."

Judy gave them a wide smile and said, "Welcome to Fort Bridger, folks. Y'all climb out and stretch your laigs. We're sure sorry ya had to stay all that time in Rawlins. But at least you're on your way now."

Chester stepped out, then helped his wife and sister-in-law down. As they headed inside, Jack took the baby and held her with one arm while helping Julianna out of the coach.

Larissa's blanket covered her, but when she coughed and her throat rattled, both Judy and Curly looked on with concern.

"Sounds like thet thar baby's sick," Judy said.

"Yes, ma'am," said Jack. "Our little girl needs to see a doctor. I assume this town has one?"

"Shore does," said Curly. "Dr. Frank O'Brien, an' he's the best."

"We need to talk to you," Jack said. "Could we step inside out of the cold?"

Curly nodded. "Shore. C'mon in."

"I'll see to he'pin' Biff 'n' Ollie hitch up the fresh team," Judy said.

Curly led the young couple inside the office. The other passengers were in the little buildings out back.

"Now, whut can I do fer ya, sir?" Curly asked.

"Could you hold the stage until we can take the baby to the doctor, sir?"

Curly lifted his hat and scratched his bald head. "Wal, mister, I cain't hardly do thet. Your fellow passengers are already many days late gittin' to Evanston, an' we got passengers waitin' in Evanston who've been there a long time. An' on top o' thet, thar's people a-waitin' over here at the Uintah Hotel who've been there a long time, an' they gotta wait till the stage gets all the way to Evanston, turns around, an' comes back. I cain't hardly hold it up no longer than to change horses."

The door opened, and Judy came in. "Them fellas said

they'd hitch up the horses by theirselves, honeypot."

Julianna had pulled the blanket away from the baby's face, and when Judy stepped close, she said, "Thet sounds like croup to me. Ya gonna take 'er to Doc O'Brien?"

"They was a-wantin' us to hold up the stage while they do thet," said Curly, "but this here stage has gotta keep movin'. Couldn't you folks stay over for a few days for the baby's sake? I think I could even git Wells Fargo to pay the hotel bill."

Julianna looked into Jack's eyes and saw his fear and desperation. "Private conversation?" she said.

Jack set his gaze on Curly. "Is there a room where—"

"Shore." Curly gestured over his shoulder. "Ya can use the office back there."

When they were in the office with the door closed, Julianna said, "This baby's life is at stake, Jack. You could go on alone now and probably make it."

Jack shook his head. "No. As long as we appear as husband and wife, and you're with me, the killers won't think I'm the guy they're after. I'd rather be delayed here with you than to try it on my own. Larissa's welfare is the most important thing right now. Let's get her to that doctor."

"Thank you," Julianna said as the baby coughed again.

"Mr. Wesson," Jack said as they stepped back into the outer office, "we've decided to stay over so our baby can have the proper care. Where do we find Dr.— What did you say his name is?"

"O'Brien. Frank O'Brien."

Hannah Cooper sat in Dr. O'Brien's office while he examined the big toe on B. J.'s right foot. He had dropped a heavy box on it at school while carrying the box from a back room for Miss Lindgren.

O'Brien looked through his half-moon glasses and said, "Well, B. J., I can't say for sure right now, but you may lose that toenail. I—"

The door to the outer office opened, and Edie's plump face appeared. "Frank, we've got an emergency out here. A couple who were on the stage to Evanston have a very sick baby. Could you look at her right away?"

Doc looked at Hannah. "Would you and B. J. mind waiting?"

"Of course not. We'll wait out in the office."

"That won't be necessary. Just take yourselves seats over there by the cabinet."

Edie ushered Jack and Julianna into the examining room. "Mr. and Mrs. LeCroix, this is my husband, Dr. Frank O'Brien. Doctor, this is Jack and Julianna. The baby's name is Larissa."

"Glad to meet you folks," said the short, stout physician. "Let's put Larissa over here on the examining table so I can get a look at her. And this nice lady who's going to wait while I work on the baby is Hannah Cooper. The boy is B. J."

"Happy to make your acquaintance," Jack said.

Jack stood close to Julianna and took her hand as the doctor unwrapped Larissa. She looked up at him with a weak smile.

Larissa coughed while the doctor was warming the stethoscope with his hand. Before he listened to her lungs, he said, "I can tell you right now, she's got a bad case of the croup. Edie, honey, get the teakettles steaming. We'll use camphor." He touched the little brow. "She's got a fever. We'll need some cool water to place her in after the camphor steam treatment."

Edie nodded and hurried away.

"Can I help you, Edie?" Hannah asked.

"No need, honey. You just rest yourself."

After listening to the baby's lungs, Dr. O'Brien checked her nose, throat, and both ears. "Heavy mucus in her throat," he said without looking up. "And she's got infection in her left ear. Edie, dear, warm up some peppermint oil for this little ear too, will you please?"

Soon the doctor was using a medicine dropper to place warm oil in the baby's infected ear. He inserted a tiny piece of cotton afterward to keep the oil from running back out.

While waiting for the water to reach the boiling point, Dr. O'Brien explained that they would use a bath towel to make a "tent" over a steaming teakettle, which would be placed on a nearby table. When the water began to cool, they would switch teakettles in order to make the treatment last a full ten minutes. The peppermint camphor in the teakettles combined with the steam would help break up the congestion in the baby's lungs, and it would soothe her little throat.

The doctor told Julianna to hold Larissa on her lap at the table, and both would be under the "tent" during the treatment.

When the treatment was over, baby Larissa was definitely breathing easier, and when she coughed, it rattled loosely. Larissa was then placed in a small tub of cool water for several minutes until the doctor found her fever coming down. He wanted to watch her for a while, so he had Julianna hold her while he finished working on B. J.'s toe.

When the toe was wrapped and B. J. had gingerly put on his shoe, Dr. O'Brien told Hannah he wanted to look at the toe again in three days. He then turned to Jack and Julianna and asked, "Are they holding the stage for you?"

"No, sir," Jack replied. "They had to go on."

"Actually, that's good, because I'm going to need to see the baby every day for at least a week. And if you could work out a way to do it, Mrs. LeCroix, she needs this same kind of steam and camphor treatment four times a day. We can do it here, but it would be better if you could do it wherever you're staying."

"We'll have to stay at the hotel, Doctor," Julianna said. "Do you know if they have stoves in the rooms?"

"They have fireplaces," Hannah said. "But I'll tell you what. I own the general store here in town, and my four children and I live in the apartment above the store. You folks could use my bedroom, and I can sleep on the couch in the parlor. The bedroom has a small stove. You can use it to heat the water, and I have two teakettles you can use."

Julianna was shaking her head. "Oh, no. We can't impose on you like that, Mrs. Cooper."

"It's no imposition, believe me. My children and I will be glad to have you."

Dr. O'Brien gave Julianna a sufficient supply of peppermint camphor to last a week, and Edie set an appointment for the doctor to see Larissa the next day.

Hannah and a limping B. J. took the LeCroixs to the apartment. Chris, Mary Beth, and Patty Ruth welcomed them warmly.

Hannah made supper for the LeCroixs and Jacob Kates, who had been invited earlier in the day. As the evening progressed, she had a strange feeling as she watched Jack and Julianna together. She thought back to the moment at the doctor's office when Jack had taken Julianna's hand and she'd given him that empty smile. Something was not right, yet she couldn't put her finger on it.

Chris made sure there was plenty of wood and water in his mother's room, and Julianna gave Larissa her steam treatment before bedtime while Hannah sat nearby and looked on. When the treatment was finished, Hannah told Jack and Julianna to awaken her in the parlor if they needed anything. They thanked her for her kindness and told her good night.

As soon as the door closed and Hannah's footsteps faded away down the hall, Jack said, "I'll feed the fire during the night so we can have steam quickly if we need it."

"Then you won't get any sleep," Julianna said.

"Sure I will. I can make myself wake up when I know I

have to. As usual, I'll be sleeping on the floor in front of the door. I'll try not to disturb you when I put the logs in the stove."

"I appreciate it, Jack," she said, almost smiling. "Thank you for caring about my baby."

"She's a sweetheart," he said softly. *And so are you*, he thought.

CHAPTER TWENTY

Julianna LeCroix awakened from a troubled sleep to the sound of little Larissa's wheezing. She had left a lantern burning low on the dresser, and when she sat up, she saw Jack lying on the floor in front of the door. He had a pillow from the bed and was using a couple of blankets he'd found in the closet. He was beginning to stir.

Julianna went to the crib Hannah had provided. The fire in the stove was crackling. Julianna guessed that it was probably three or four o'clock in the morning.

She picked up Larissa and went to the stove to put a teakettle on to boil. The peppermint camphor was already in the water.

Jack stood up, rubbing his eyes, and said in a whisper, "Is she worse?"

"Her cough is looser, but she's wheezing. I'm going to give her another treatment."

Jack opened the stove and stuffed in another log.

Julianna walked the floor with the crying baby, and after a few minutes, she stepped to the stove and placed the second teakettle on to boil. When the first teakettle began to steam, Julianna and Larissa got under the tent. Jack switched teakettles for Julianna after about five minutes, and by the time the treatment was over, the baby was breathing better again.

Jack stood close by while Julianna sat on the edge of the

bed and rocked the baby, humming softly to her. Soon Larissa was drowsy. She took a couple of deep breaths, stuck a thumb in her mouth, and fell asleep.

Julianna laid her in the crib, covered her, then looked at Jack in the soft light and said, "Thank you for your help."

He smiled. "You're welcome."

Julianna slid back in bed. Jack waited till she was under the covers and comfortable, then returned to his bed on the floor.

The next morning while Hannah was preparing breakfast, a messenger came from the fort to inform her that Captain John Fordham was taking Betsy and Belinda to Green River for the day, and Betsy would not be able to keep Patty Ruth for her usual Tuesday stay. Hannah thanked the corporal who had brought the message and sent a message back, saying she hoped the Fordham family enjoyed their day together.

After breakfast, Hannah helped Julianna give the steam treatment to Larissa while the three oldest children prepared for school. Patty Ruth looked on with interest. When Hannah had told her she wouldn't be going to the Fordhams', she said, "That's all right, Mama. I'll help Uncle Jacob in the store."

Hannah had shown surprise at hearing "Uncle Jacob," and Patty Ruth told her that Mr. Kates had asked her to call him that.

When it was time for the three older children to leave for school, B. J. limped to the door and opened it for his big sister. Mary Beth stepped out ahead of the boys and said, "B. J., be sure to taunt me this morning by doing your thunderation down the stairs."

The eight-year-old gave her a pained look. "You know I can't do it with this sore toe."

"Yes," she said with a smile, "I know."

When the door closed behind them, Hannah looked at the clock on the kitchen wall and saw that she was behind schedule. Jacob had chosen to prepare his own breakfast in his quarters and would be expecting Hannah down a few minutes before eight. It was already four minutes before the hour, and she didn't even have the kitchen cleaned up yet.

Jack was sitting at the table, having a second cup of coffee. Julianna had just returned to the kitchen from feeding Larissa in Hannah's bedroom and sat down with him.

"Larissa asleep?" he asked.

"Like a log," replied the weary mother.

Hannah stood over Jack and said, "Mr. LeCroix, I'm running a little behind schedule. Could I get you to run downstairs and tell Jacob to go ahead and open the store? Tell him I'll be there shortly."

Jack looked up at Hannah and stammered, "Ah...Mrs. Cooper, I ah...just can't bring myself to leave Julianna and the baby, even for a few minutes. I'm sorry, I—"

"I understand," Hannah said, perturbed at Jack's lame excuse. "Then would you do me a different favor?"

"Why...ah...sure."

"Would you finish cleaning up the kitchen for me? Jacob is quite new in the store, and it's best that I be with him as soon as possible."

"Oh, sure. Be glad to."

"We'll both clean up the kitchen, Mrs. Cooper," Julianna said.

"All right. Thank you. Come on, Patty Ruth."

The little girl picked up her stuffed bear, then said to the couple, "You don't have to be afraid of Biggie. He won't bite you."

Julianna smiled and said, "That's good to know."

While Hannah was helping Patty Ruth put on her coat,

she said to the LeCroixs, "I know you're taking Larissa for her appointment with Dr. O'Brien this morning, so just come and go as you please. Chris brought in more wood earlier, so there's plenty for the stoves. Take care of that precious baby."

"We will, Mrs. Cooper," Julianna said. "Thank you for your kindness."

When Hannah and Patty Ruth entered the store, customers were coming and going as usual. After the initial rush was over, Hannah asked Jacob to put up a new display in the front window while she handled the counter. Patty Ruth was at the window with Jacob. The child kept up a string of chatter, asking her new friend questions about his days as a peddler.

Patty Ruth was still chattering—to Jacob's delight—when she noticed Curly Wesson pass the window and head for the door. When the bell jingled and Curly entered, he found the five-year-old standing there with a big smile, holding Tony in her arms.

Curly and Judy had met Jacob in the store the day before. Curly acted as though he didn't see Patty Ruth. "Good mornin', Mr. Kates," he said. "How ya doin' today?"

"Just fine, Mr. Wesson. And you?"

"Finer 'n frog fuzz, thank ya." He looked back toward the counter and greeted Hannah and what customers he could see. Then he acted as though he'd just spotted the little girl.

"Why, lookee here!" he exclaimed. "I have a purty li'l gal right smack-dab in front o' me!" Bending low, he asked, "Whut's your name, li'l girl?"

She giggled. "Patty Ruth."

"An' how old are you?"

"Five," she said, keeping her feet planted, but swiveling herself back and forth at the waist.

"Five! You're five years old?"

"Uh-huh."

"Wal, do ya know whut I do when I meet a li'l girl, an' her name is Patty Ruth, an' she's five years old? Do ya know whut I do?"

"Huh-uh."

A big grin spread over Curly's mouth. "I hug 'er!" He took her in his arms, and she hugged him back.

Patty Ruth stepped back, looked up at Curly, and said, "What's your name, mister?"

"Patty Ruth!" Hannah called. "Not now, honey. I'm sure Uncle Curly needs to make his purchases and be on his way. You can do the other part later."

"Okay, Mama."

"Judy'll be here in a li'l while to do some shoppin', Hannah," Curly said. "I jus' wanted to stop in an' ask about the LeCroixs. Somebody said they're stayin' with you. How's the baby?"

"She's better, Curly. They're taking her back to Dr. O'Brien in a couple of hours so he can check her."

"Wal, I'm glad to hear she's better. Gotta go. See ya later."

Nearly two hours had passed when Hannah heard the back door of the store open. From where she stood behind the counter, she saw Jack and Julianna come in. Julianna was carrying the warmly wrapped baby.

There were a few customers in the store, and Patty Ruth was still with Jacob at the front window, where he was creating an eye-catching display.

The young couple drew up to the counter, and Julianna said, "We're off to Dr. O'Brien's office, Mrs. Cooper. We just gave Larissa another steam treatment. She's sounding better each time."

"Wonderful," Hannah said, then turned to introduce the LeCroixs to an elderly couple who stood at the counter. At the same time, Jacob was slipping on his coat at the front of the store.

"Where you goin', Uncle Jacob?" Patty Ruth asked.

"There are some smudges on the glass out there. I'm going to clean them off."

"Could I go outside with you?"

"Sure, if your mother says it's all right."

Patty Ruth ran back to the counter. "Mama, can I go outside with Uncle Jacob an' help him clean the window?"

"Sure, honey. Put your coat and cap on."

Jack and Julianna followed Patty Ruth as she headed out the door. They met Judy Charley Wesson coming in and paused when they recognized the Fargo agent's wife.

"Mornin', folks," Judy said, looking first at the parents, then at the bundle in Julianna's arms. "How's that li'l baby doin'?"

"Better, ma'am," said Jack. "We're taking her to see Dr. O'Brien right now."

"Wal, I'm shore glad to hear she's better. Doc'll fix 'er up right good. You c'n bank on that. So you're gonna stay here in town for a while while the baby's gittin' better, eh?"

"Yes'm."

"Wal, jis' let us know when ya wanna book your ride on to Evanston."

"We sure will, ma'am," Jack said, touching his hat brim.

Outside, Patty Ruth watched Aunt Judy disappear through the door, then turned back to see Jacob rubbing on the glass with a large white cloth. She let her gaze drift to the street. Traffic was light at the moment.

Suddenly she heard a dog bark. She looked across the

street and saw Clem Cooper's wagon parked in front of the barber shop. Clem was not in sight, but Lucky was on the wagon seat, looking at her and wagging his broken tail. He barked again, greeting his little friend.

The child was so glad to see the dog that she forgot her mother's warning about never going into the street. Jacob's back was toward Patty Ruth, and he didn't see her dart off the boardwalk toward Lucky.

Across the wide street from the general store, just in front of Clem Cooper's wagon, four rough-looking riders had reined to a halt and were looking around. At the same time, Jack and Julianna came out of the store with Larissa in her mother's arms.

Patty Ruth was almost to the middle of the street when one of the riders shouted, "Hey! There he is!" and clawed for his gun.

Jack saw the four men go for their guns, and he gently shoved Julianna back through the open door, saying, "Get inside, quick!" Even as he spoke, he whipped out his Colt .45 and fired, hitting one of the men. The man peeled out of the saddle, but not before his gun went off, sending a bullet chewing into the dust directly in front of Patty Ruth. She stopped as a cloud of dirt stung her face.

Guns barked as the riders fired back at Jack, who dropped flat on his belly behind a rain barrel and blasted away at them.

Jacob Kates had just turned around at the window to see what was happening when a bullet hit the glass, shattering it. There were shouts coming from the street, and a woman screamed.

Jacob was about to dash for the store when he saw Patty Ruth in the middle of the street. She was caught in the crossfire, frozen in terror. Bullets buzzed like angry hornets all around her.

Jacob charged off the boardwalk and ran toward Patty Ruth, his gimp hindering his speed. He was within a few feet of Patty Ruth when he felt a bullet bite his side. The impact made him twist to the left. He staggered but maintained his balance long enough to grab the little girl and scramble under Clem Cooper's wagon.

Patty Ruth was still too frightened to cry out, but she recognized who had delivered her. She wrapped her arms around Jacob's neck and clung to him for all she was worth.

Judy Charley Wesson drew her Colt .45 and dashed toward the door. Hannah ran past her shocked customers toward the terrified young mother and baby. The door stood wide open, and admid clouds of gun smoke, Hannah saw her little daughter and Jacob in relative safety beneath a wagon in front of the barber shop. Hannah breathed a quick prayer and pulled Julianna and the baby farther away from the spot where bullets were chewing the front of the store.

The three remaining riders had taken refuge behind rain barrels and wagons and were unleashing all the firepower they could on Jack. He was stunned when the skinny woman with the snaggletooth hunkered down beside him and started firing. She dropped one of the killers with her first shot.

Judy noticed a rip in the upper sleeve of Jack's coat and saw that it was ringed with blood. "You're hit!" she cried as she sent another shot at one of the remaining riders, causing him to duck without firing.

"Yeah," Jack said, firing another round. "No time to look at it! Thanks for your help!"

"My pleasure." Judy took careful aim at the spot where one of the gunmen kept raising up behind a wagon in order to fire. When he came up, she dropped the hammer, and the man ducked as her bullet buzzed past his ear.

Just outside of Fort Bridger to the east, Major Bart Slone was leading his patrol unit of a dozen troopers toward the fort when

Captain Don Harris, who rode next to him, said, "Major, do you hear that? Sounds like gunfire in town!"

Slone stiffened in the saddle, having just heard the gunfire, and thrust an arm forward, shouting, "Into the town, men! Guns ready!"

In an instant, the patrol was at a gallop. Less than a minute had passed when they thundered into town, took a turn onto Main Street, and made a beeline for the clouds of smoke. A middle-aged man rushed off the boardwalk and pointed toward the men who were firing toward the general store, crying, "Those are the ones you're after, Major!"

The two hired killers who were still alive threw their guns down at Major Slone's command and stepped into the street, hands held high. At the same time, Marshal Lance Mangum galloped into town from the opposite side, having just returned from delivering a subpoena from Judge Carter to a rancher a few miles west of Fort Bridger.

The townspeople looked on as the troopers made a circle around the two hired killers who stood with their hands above their heads. Mangum dismounted and threaded his way through the soldiers. Several people were speaking at once, telling Mangum what had happened.

Hannah moved as fast as she could across the street toward her daughter and Jacob, who were coming out from under the wagon. Jack and Judy were on their feet, and Julianna was just coming out of the store. Curly hurried down the street toward his wife.

Hannah trembled as she pulled Patty Ruth into her sheltering embrace and looked at Jacob, whose coat was crimson with blood on his left side. "You saved her life, Mr. Kates," Hannah said. "You could've been killed yourself, but you ignored your own safety to keep my baby girl from being killed. Thank you. Oh, thank you! And you've been shot, too."

"It's just a scratch, ma'am," Jacob said.

"I want Dr. O'Brien to see your wound." She looked around. "Could someone help Mr. Kates down to the doctor's office?"

"I'll take him, Hannah," said Cade Samuels, who had come out of his barber shop when the shooting started.

"Thank you, Cade. I need to go over here and see about my houseguests."

As Samuels ushered Jacob away, Hannah bent over her little daughter and said, "I'm so thankful Jesus took care of you, honey, and that He sent Jacob to get you out of the line of fire."

Patty Ruth had put on a brave front up to this point, but now the tears began to spill down her cheeks. Hannah held her close and kissed her forehead.

Jack holstered his Colt .45 and stepped into the street as Marshal Mangum and Major Slone were talking to the hired killers, trying to get them to tell who they were and why they had started shooting.

Suddenly Jack found Julianna by his side. She had left Larissa inside the store with one of Hannah's customers so she wouldn't be out in the cold air. Julianna looked at the blood soaking his arm. "Jack, you've been shot!"

"It's not too bad," he said without breaking stride. "I've got to talk to the marshal and the major. Larissa all right?"

"Yes. She's fine."

"Good."

Julianna stayed by Jack's side as he weaved past the soldiers who surrounded the two men with their hands in the air. The killers were refusing to say a word.

"I'll find out who you are sooner or later," Mangum was saying as Jack and Julianna appeared. "You might as well tell me now."

"I can't tell you their names, Marshal," said Jack, "but I can tell you who they work for. They're professional killers, and they were hired to kill me. The man who hired them is a

Colorado range bull by the name of Tack Lombard."

"I know about Lombard," said Mangum. "Why were they after you, sir? And what is your name?"

Hannah Cooper had made her way through the circle of soldiers, leading Patty Ruth by the hand, and before Jack could reply to the marshal's questions, Hannah spoke up. "This man, his wife, and baby daughter are guests in my home, Marshal. This is Jack and Julianna LeCroix."

"LeCroix," repeated Mangum. "Well, Mr. LeCroix, I think we'd better get you to the doctor. Looks like you took a bullet. I'll put these hired killers in jail and come over to Doc O'Brien's office. You and your wife can tell me the whole story then."

"He ain't no Jack LeCroix," said one of the killers. "His name's Bower. Jack Bower. He caused Mr. Lombard's grandson to be killed when he got in a gunfight with another gunhawk down in Colorado. And that woman ain't his wife, neither. He abducted her at Cheyenne, we found out. Made her travel on the stage with him as his wife. When we were trackin' him, we put two and two together and figured him out. That's how we knew to come to Fort Bridger lookin' for him."

Mangum handed Major Slone the keys to his office, told him where the cell keys were, and asked him to take the prisoners and lock them up, saying he needed to go with Bower to the doctor's office.

Mangum turned to Julianna. "Ma'am, I take it your name really is LeCroix?"

"Yes, Marshal, it is."

"If you'll wait at Hannah's place, I'll come and talk to you later."

"Marshal," she said, "we ah…I have an appointment to take my baby to see Dr. O'Brien. She's a very sick little girl."

"All right. Maybe I can talk to both of you at the same time."

"Larissa's in the store," Julianna said. "I'll get her."

Curly Wesson had joined his wife, and they were standing close to Jack while he and the marshal waited for Julianna to return with the baby.

Jack excused himself to the marshal and stepped up to Judy. "Mrs. Wesson, I don't know how to thank you for siding me in that gunfight."

"Wal, I was glad to do it, Mr. LeCr—I mean, Mr. Bower. You...uh...ain't really no gunfighter, are ya? You don't seem like one."

"No, ma'am. I'm not a gunfighter. I've had to defend myself against the like a few times, like happened in Colorado a couple weeks ago. That's what caused all this trouble. I might be dead now if you hadn't joined me in the fight." Then to Curly he said, "Mr. Wesson, this wife of yours is quite a woman."

Curly lifted his hat, scratched his bald head, and said, "Don't I jist know it!"

As the marshal, Jack, Julianna, and Larissa headed for the doctor's office, Hannah turned to Glenda Williams and asked her if she would mind the store. Then Hannah took Patty Ruth by the hand and said, "Let's go see about Mr. Kates, honey."

Suddenly there was a loud bark, and Lucky was coming toward Patty Ruth, hopping on his three legs. Clem was right behind him.

"Lucky!" cried the little redhead, dropping to her knees to hug him while he showered her with kisses.

"Mrs. Cooper," Clem said. "I was in the barber shop when all of this started. I hope Lucky's not in trouble for luring Patty Ruth across the street." As he spoke, he picked the dog up, allowing him one last lick across Patty Ruth's cheek.

Hannah smiled. "No, Clem. Lucky's not in trouble."

Clem's brow furrowed. "And how about—"

"I'll have a talk with Patty Ruth later."

Clem told the child how glad he was that she was all

right, then carried the dog back to the wagon.

Again, Hannah was about to head for the doctor's office, but Clayton Farley came out of the crowd and said, "Hannah, I wasn't here when the shooting was going on, but someone pointed out that your big front window was shot out."

"Oh, yes," she said, touching her forehead. "I haven't had time to think about it."

"Well, I'll board it up right away for you, and I'll donate a new glass. I have some that size in storage here in town. I'll take care of it within the next day or so."

"Thank you, Clayton," she said. "I appreciate it, but really, I can pay you for the glass."

"No, you can't," he said, shaking his head.

"Why not?"

"Because I said so," came his reply as he walked away.

"Lord, You're so good to me," she breathed. "Okay, Patty Ruth, let's go see about your Uncle Jacob."

CHAPTER TWENTY-ONE

When Hannah and Patty Ruth Cooper arrived at Dr. O'Brien's office, the door to the clinic stood open. They entered and looked around.

Edie was working on little Larissa at a small table while Doc was bent over Jacob at the examining table. Julianna was standing beside her baby, and Jack was seated on one of four chairs by the medicine cabinet, gripping his wounded arm. Marshal Lance Mangum stood in front of Jack, listening to the details of his story.

Edie looked up. "Come on in, Hannah...Patty Ruth. You can sit down over there by Mr. Bower at the cabinet."

Hannah sat Patty Ruth next to Jack, then moved to the examining table and looked down at Jacob. Dr. O'Brien was putting finishing touches on the bandage covering the wound on his side.

Hannah waited till he finished, then said, "Doc, is it bad?"

"No, honey. It only took four stitches to close it up. He'll be fine."

Hannah's eyes were misty as she looked down at Jacob and said, "I want to thank you again, Mr. Kates, for saving Patty Ruth. There's no doubt in my mind she would've been killed if you hadn't taken her to safety."

Jacob smiled, sent a glance across the room to Patty Ruth, then said, "Mrs. Cooper, that little girl has so endeared herself to me, I'd do it again in a heartbeat."

"I don't doubt it," Hannah said, squeezing his hand.

Hannah moved up beside Julianna and looked down at the baby as Edie was swabbing her throat to remove mucus. "How's Larissa doing?"

"Mrs. O'Brien says the steam treatments are definitely having a good effect. Her temperature is lower, and she's breathing better."

"Wonderful," said Hannah, putting an arm around Julianna's shoulder and giving her a squeeze.

She heard Marshal Mangum say, "Well, Jack, next time you want to collect a debt somebody owes you, it'd be best if you collected it somewhere private, rather than in public."

"You've got that right, Marshal."

"I'm going to the office now," Mangum said. "I'll wire the authorities in Fort Collins and tell them what's happened here, and that you believe it was Tack Lombard who sent these men after you. I'm sure nothing can be done as far as pinning it on Lombard, but at least the law in Fort Collins will know about it."

Jack nodded.

"I'll let you know when I find out the identity of the four who tried to kill you. A quick check on the 'wanted' list will probably tell me."

"There we are, little darlin'," Edie said to Larissa. "You can go back to Mommy now."

Julianna pressed the baby to her chest and took a seat beside Hannah, who was now sitting beside Jack and Patty Ruth.

Dr. O'Brien helped Jacob to a sitting position on the examining table, and while Jacob buttoned up his shirt, Doc said, "I want to see you tomorrow so I can check on the wound and change the bandage." Doc helped him down from the table and guided him toward the chairs by the cabinet. "You need to sit down for a while, Mr. Kates. Mr. Bower, let's get you on the table."

Julianna turned to Hannah. "Would you mind holding Larissa for me?"

"Of course not," Hannah said, taking the baby.

Julianna moved up close to the examining table as Dr. O'Brien was carefully checking the wound. "How bad is it, Doctor?" she asked.

"Didn't hit the bone. It'll take some stitches, but he'll be fine."

Julianna sighed. "Oh, I'm glad for that." She went back to her chair and sat down. Hannah gave Julianna a knowing smile.

Edie assisted her husband as he stitched up Jack's wound then began bandaging it.

When they finished, Doc said, "Mr. Bower, you shouldn't travel for a few days. I'll want to check the wound and put a new bandage on it every day for at least a week."

"Okay, Doctor. I guess I can stay here that long."

"Now, you just lie there and rest for a while before you try getting up."

While the O'Briens were cleaning up and putting things away, Julianna went to the examining table, looked down at Jack with tender eyes, and said, "I want to thank you for what you did at the store when those killers showed up."

Jack's brow furrowed. "What do you mean?"

"You know…moving Larissa and me out of the line of fire even though it meant putting your own safety at risk."

Jack managed a smile. "Just something I had to do." He studied her for a moment, then said, "Julianna, there's something else I have to do."

"What's that?"

"I must apologize to you."

"For what?"

"For making you and Larissa captives just to save my own hide. I was wrong, Julianna. I should never have put the two of you in danger as I did. I…I'm asking you to forgive me. I need to know I have your forgiveness."

Julianna swallowed hard, took a short breath, and said, "I forgive you, Jack."

He sighed with relief. "Thank you."

"I need forgiveness, too," she said.

"What on earth for?"

"I should have believed you when you told me a gang of killers was after you. I never accepted that. I thought you were running from the law."

"Who could blame you, Julianna? I certainly don't."

Just then Lance Mangum came in. Glancing at Jack on the table, he said, "How's this patient doing, Doc?"

"He's a little weak at the moment. I had to put in ten stitches to close up the wound. But he'll survive."

"Good." He walked to the examining table and stood beside Julianna. "Well, Jack, I found all four of those men on the 'wanted' list. Murder, every one of them. The two I've got in jail will be picked up by federal marshals in a couple days and taken to Cheyenne City. They'll hang."

Jack nodded. "Too bad something can't be done about Tack Lombard."

"Well, there's an old saying: 'Give a bad man enough rope, he'll hang himself.' One of these days…"

"I sure hope so."

Mangum rubbed his chin thoughtfully. "Speaking of something being done about Lombard, Jack…I've also got a problem about *you.*"

"Me? What kind of problem about me, Marshal?" Jack asked.

"You heard one of those killers I just jailed say that you abducted Julianna at Cheyenne City and made her travel on the stage as your wife. The law carries a pretty stiff penalty for kidnapping. How about it? Is that what you did?"

Jack's faced paled. He licked his lips nervously and nodded. "Yes, sir. I can't deny it."

Mangum's features were hard. "Then I must arrest you for kidnapping Julianna and her baby. You put their lives in grave danger."

"Marshal, Jack was desperate," Julianna said. "Those killers were breathing down his neck. I know he put Larissa and me in danger by forcing us to travel with him, but it was the only thing he could think to do under the circumstances."

"Still, I shouldn't have done it, Julianna," Jack said. "It was selfish and foolish of me. I would never have forgiven myself if any harm had come to you."

"You've already admitted that, Jack," she said. "Marshal, only moments before you came in, Jack and I talked this thing out. He asked me to forgive him for what he did…and I forgave him."

"Well, that's all fine and good, ma'am, but the law hasn't forgiven him. I've got to arrest him for kidnapping you and your daughter and—"

"Marshal, Jack risked his life to save Larissa and me when the shooting broke out in front of the store. Doesn't that count for something?"

"How did he do that?"

Julianna explained the incident at the general store in every detail, making sure Mangum understood that Jack had hazarded himself to protect Larissa and her from being shot. When she finished, she could see a slight softening on the marshal's countenance.

"Marshal Mangum, you *are* the law in Fort Bridger, are you not?" Julianna said.

"Yes, ma'am."

"Then I'm asking the law to forgive Jack for abducting Larissa and me, even as I have. Please…do not charge him with kidnapping."

Mangum rubbed his chin again and took a deep breath.

"Marshal," Jack said, "if you feel you have to arrest me and press charges, I certainly have it coming."

Mangum looked at the pleading in Julianna's eyes. His features softened even more. He smiled at her, then said to Jack, "I'm going to forget what happened, Jack."

"Oh, thank you, Marshal!" Julianna cried. "Thank you!"

"Yes, Marshal, thank you," Jack said.

Doc winked at Mangum. "You're doing right, son."

Mangum gave him a lopsided grin, then turned to Jack and asked, "So, you plan on leaving Fort Bridger soon?"

"He can't travel for at least a week, Marshal," Doc said. "He needs some rest so that wound will get a good start at healing."

"Then I guess I'll be around for at least a week, Marshal," Jack said. "Some reason you need to know?"

"Oh, I would just like a little time with you before you go."

"Sure," said Jack, looking puzzled. "We'll get together."

When Mangum had gone, Jacob said, "Mr. Bower, if it's all right with Mrs. Cooper, you can stay in my room with me while you're here. You can have the cot, and I can sleep on the floor."

"I'm the one who'll sleep on the floor if she approves my staying with you," said Jack. "I'm used to it. Ever since I picked up Julianna and Larissa, I've slept on the floor of every place we've stayed."

"That's right," said Julianna. "On the floor at the door, so we couldn't escape during the night. Even in Hannah's bedroom."

"I'll be glad for you to stay with Mr. Kates, Jack," Hannah said, "but neither one of you will be sleeping on the floor. We'll simply move another cot in there."

"I'll go along with that," Jack said, grinning. "Thank you, ma'am…and thank you, Mr. Kates."

"And Julianna," said Hannah, "you and the baby can continue to sleep in my room while you're here."

"That should be at least another week, Mrs. LeCroix," spoke up Dr. O'Brien. "We need to get Larissa over her croup completely before she travels in another drafty stagecoach. Is Evanston your final destination?"

"No, Doctor. Larissa and I are taking another stage to Boise. We're going to live there with my husband's parents. My husband died several weeks ago."

O'Brien turned to Jack. "And where will you be going from here, Mr. Bower?"

Jack thought on it a few seconds. "I'm not sure, Doctor. Probably back to Colorado. I do ranch work all over the territory when needed. I move around a lot but manage to make a living."

"I guess you're what they call a drifter, eh?" said Doc.

Jack glanced at Julianna, then looked back at the doctor. "Yeah. That's what I am. A drifter."

By the time Hannah and her group arrived back at the store, word had spread all over town and the fort about the shoot-out. Sundi Lindgren allowed the Cooper children to go home since their mother and her store were involved.

Chris, Mary Beth, and a limping B. J. rushed into the store, spotted their mother behind the counter with Glenda Williams, and began asking questions all at once.

Julianna, Jack, and Jacob were sitting by the checkers table near the potbellied stove. Larissa was on Julianna's lap, and Patty Ruth was standing next to mother and baby.

While many customers listened, Hannah filled in the details for her three oldest, making sure they understood Jacob's valor in saving Patty Ruth's life.

Hannah was about to tell Jack's story, but Patty Ruth stepped up to her three siblings, laid the back of her hand on her forehead, and said with a slight quaver in her voice, "Yes,

Chris, Mary Beth, and B. J., you almost lost your precious little sister today."

The trio exchanged glances then told Patty Ruth how glad they were she was all right. Each gave her a hug, and the little actress wallowed in the attention. An afterthought gripped her, though she didn't let on. What if one of them had brought up that she shouldn't have gone into the street to see Lucky? Patty Ruth was hoping her mother would forget to have a talk with her about it. Sometimes their talks developed into spankings.

Hannah went on to tell her three oldest children about the men who had tracked Jack down, wanting to kill him. "Jack, I'll let you explain the rest."

Chris, Mary Beth, and B. J. gathered in front of Jack. He jolted them by saying he was not really Julianna's husband, then told them the whole story, including his real name.

Chris was fascinated by the story. "Mr. Bower, I've heard of Howie Spence! He was really fast! And you outdrew him! Wow! How long have you been a gunfighter?"

"Chris, I'm not a gunfighter. Gunfighters go around looking for someone to provoke into drawing against them so they can boast about how good they are. That's a foolish thing to do. I've been forced to draw against a few, and in order to stay alive, I've had to outdraw them. That's all. I'm not looking for trouble. I'm a peaceful man. All I want to do is find the right woman, get married, settle down, and enjoy life."

Patty Ruth said, "How come you don't marry Miss Julianna? She's really pretty! An' she's nice, too."

Julianna's features tinted.

"Well, honey, I can't marry Miss Julianna until she asks me to marry her."

Patty Ruth put her hands on her hips. "Mr. Jack! Womans don' ask mans to marry 'em! Mans ask womans!"

"Patty Ruth," Hannah said, "have you thanked Uncle Jacob for saving your life?"

"Uh-huh."

"Well, I think you should thank him again. Right now."

"Okay."

The five-year-old went to Jacob, opened her arms, and said, "Thank you for savin' me from those bullets, Uncle Jacob."

Jacob hugged her and kissed her cheek. "You're welcome, sweetheart."

Mary Beth led the way, and the other three Cooper children hugged Jacob and thanked him for keeping their little sister safe.

Tears welled up in the little man's eyes and began to spill down his leathered cheeks. As he looked around at the faces of the Cooper family, he said, "Let me tell all of you a story."

Jacob told them about the night he was hiding from the men who were after him, and how, with a pillow of stone under his head, he thought of Jacob in the book of Genesis. "That night I prayed for an angel to help me. God has been so good. He gave me five angels...the whole Cooper family!"

All of the Coopers went to Jacob and hugged him, telling him they loved him. It was the happiest moment Jacob Kates had known since arriving in the West.

Julianna watched the tender scene and thought of the time she had told Sapphire about her pillow being made of stone. She recalled how Sapphire had alluded to Jacob of old, and of the angels.

When a quiet moment came, Julianna told them about her own pillow of stone, then said, "Mr. Kates, it looks like God gave both of us the same five angels!"

That night, after all the Cooper children were in bed, Hannah had teakettles boiling on the kitchen stove and helped Julianna give Larissa the steam treatment. When the baby had been fed, she was placed in her crib in Hannah's bedroom and soon was fast asleep.

The women sat down at the kitchen table with cups of hot tea before them and began to talk. Hannah asked about Julianna's life before she got on the stagecoach as Jack's hostage in Cheyenne City.

Julianna told Hannah all about her arranged marriage to Jean-Claude LeCroix, about losing her estate to the crooked men after Jean-Claude's death, and why she was going to Boise to live with his parents.

Hannah poured them both another cup of tea and asked, "So even though your marriage to Jean-Claude was arranged, did you fall in love with him after you were married?"

"No. There was a fondness that grew between us, but I was never in love with him. He knew that. And I knew he was not in love with me. I've never been in love, Hannah, but from what I know about it, Jean-Claude and I never had that."

Hannah nodded, took a sip of tea, and said, "Are you having a problem about going on to Idaho and saying good-bye to Jack?"

Julianna's hand trembled slightly, and she set her cup down. "Hannah, you're a tenderhearted woman. And you've been in love. Tell me what you think. I...well, something strange is going on in my heart about Jack. This started not too long after Larissa and I found ourselves traveling as his wife and daughter. There's something about being with him. Something...well, I love being close to him. And especially now, since everything has come out in the open. I find myself dreading that awful moment when I have to tell him good-bye. I need him, Hannah. I find myself wishing we could be alone, now that the hostage thing is over. I want to be in his arms—to have him hold me and whisper tender words in my ear. Would you say this is love?"

Hannah smiled. "Sounds like the love bug has bitten you deeply. So what now?"

Julianna shrugged. "It takes two to be in love for anything to work out. Jack hasn't shown any sign of having this kind of feeling for me."

Hannah chuckled. "Oh, no? Well, I've seen it!"

"What?"

"Julianna, I know what love light in the eyes looks like. I've seen it every time Jack looks at you."

"You have?"

"I have." Hannah smiled. "Of course when I saw it before the truth came out, I thought nothing of it. That's the way it should be when a man loves his wife. And of course, I thought you were his wife."

Julianna was shaking her head back and forth slowly. "And you really saw this, Hannah?"

"Yes, I did. The real thing. No doubt about it."

Julianna took another sip of tea, leaned her head back, and closed her eyes for a few seconds.

Hannah figured she had said enough and turned the subject to the pillow of stone story. She talked about Jacob in the Bible, how he had been renamed Israel by the Lord, and how God had established the nation of Israel through him. From there, Hannah prayerfully pointed out that God's Son had come to earth through that nation.

Julianna was listening, yet her thoughts went back to what Hannah had told her about Jack. However, when Hannah referred to Calvary and the need for sinners to repent and receive the Lord Jesus for salvation, she had Julianna's full attention.

The young woman's thoughts went back to Charles Finney and Kathleen Lindley and how they had shown concern for her. Now, here was Hannah Cooper showing the same concern. But this time it was different. The Spirit of God had fertilized the Seed of the Word in Julianna's heart.

Before Julianna knew it, Hannah had her Bible open and

the Holy Spirit was doing His work. Julianna began to cry. While wiping tears, she said, "Hannah, are you acquainted with the name Charles Finney?"

"Oh my, yes. A wonderful man of God, and a great preacher. I've never had the privilege of hearing him, but I've heard much about him, and I've read many of his sermons. Why do you ask?"

"On this trip from New Orleans, I had a layover between trains in Chicago. Mr. and Mrs. Finney saw me crying and asked if they could help. One thing led to another, and Mr. Finney ended up showing me the same things from the Bible that you just did."

Hannah's face lit up. "Well, what do you know? The great Charles Finney!"

"And then, on the train from Chicago, a young woman named Kathleen Lindley tried to show it to me again. I wouldn't let her, but she got in some words anyhow."

"Well, God bless Kathleen Lindley," Hannah said. "Can you see, dear, that God had His hand in sending both Mr. Finney and Kathleen to you?"

Julianna sniffed. "Sort of looks that way."

"You've thought a lot about it, haven't you, dear?"

Julianna wiped more tears and looked up at the ceiling, then said, "Oh, yes. Every day."

"Jesus loves you, Julianna," Hannah said softly. "He's looking down at you this very minute from heaven, yearning to save you."

"Hannah, would you help me? I want to be saved."

After Julianna had received the Lord into her heart, Hannah said, "Julianna, what happened today is just what Paul talks about in 1 Corinthians 3—Charles Finney planted the seed of the Word in your heart, Kathleen Lindley watered it, and God gave the increase and allowed me the joy of leading you to Jesus."

Julianna left her chair, threw her arms around Hannah's neck, and thanked her for caring about her. Now Hannah was wiping tears.

"You probably won't ever see Mr. Finney or Kathleen again here on earth," Hannah said, "but one day in heaven you can hug them and thank them for caring too."

"Oh, I will! And there's someone else I want to thank. The precious Lord Jesus…for saving a sinner like me!"

The next day while Jacob ran the store, Hannah went to the parsonage and talked to the Kellys. They, of course, knew about the shoot-out and had learned some of the information about Hannah's guests. Hannah filled them in completely, then told them of leading Julianna to the Lord. The Kellys were thrilled to learn of Julianna's conversion and gladly accepted Hannah's invitation to come and meet her and to talk with her about being baptized.

That evening the Kellys arrived at the Cooper apartment just after the store closed. The pastor went over the Scriptures about baptism and explained the process to Julianna. They agreed that during the Sunday morning service she would come forward to be baptized.

"Now, Hannah," Pastor Kelly said, "you said this Jack Bower is staying down in the storeroom with Jacob?"

"Yes."

"I'd like to talk to him. You said he won't be in town long, right?"

"Only a week or so."

Kelly nodded, then said to Julianna, "You've been with this man for several days. Have you heard him say anything about God or the Bible, or anything along this line?"

"No, sir. We didn't discuss anything like that."

Kelly picked up his Bible. "Rebecca, honey, I'll be back in a little while. You ladies pray for Jack Bower, and for Jacob Kates too."

"We will," said Rebecca.

"Let me go get my children from their rooms," Hannah said. "I want them to learn everything they can about praying for lost souls."

CHAPTER TWENTY-TWO

Andy Kelly prayed as he descended the stairs toward the alley. He knocked on Jacob's door, and Jacob greeted him and introduced him to Jack, then invited him to sit on the room's single chair while they sat on their cots.

The preacher talked about the shoot-out and commended both men for their heroism. He asked about their wounds, and after they had told him the details and explained that Dr. O'Brien said they would heal up fine, Kelly looked at Jack and said, "Mr. Bower, that bullet that hit your arm...another eight or nine inches to the right would have put it through your heart."

"Yeah, and don't I know it," Jack said.

"I'd like to ask you something, if I may."

Jack smiled. "Sure."

"Let's say that slug had gone through your heart. Where would you be right now?"

"Lying on a slab at the undertaker's," he said with a chuckle.

"I don't mean your body. I mean you. Your soul. Where would you be?"

"You mean heaven or hell?"

"Yes."

Jack adjusted himself nervously on the cot. "I...I don't know. Fella can't really know where he's going, can he? I mean, since he can't be sure if he's lived good enough to go to heaven."

"This will no doubt come as a surprise to you, Mr. Bower," said Kelly, "but a person doesn't go to heaven by living good enough."

"Really?"

"Really." Kelly raised his Bible chest high. "Mr. Bower, do you believe this Book in my hand is the Word of God?"

"Sure."

"If I could show you in here that salvation is not by man's works, but by the grace of God, would you believe it?"

"Sure."

"All right," said Kelly, opening the Bible and going over to sit beside Bower. "Let's take a look in here."

Kelly was aware that he had Jacob's attention, too, as he started reading Scriptures that pertained to salvation. He showed Jack the gospel, then read passages that declared that salvation was found only in the grace of God, not in man's accomplishments.

After nearly half an hour of reading and discussing Scripture, the preacher looked at Bower and said, "Now, from what you've seen here, if you had been killed in that shoot-out, where would you be right now?"

Jack glanced at Jacob, then met Kelly's gaze and said, "I'd be in hell, sir."

"Is that where you'd like to be?"

"Of course not."

"There's only one way to miss it. And that way is through a Person—the Lord Jesus Christ. Do you understand that, Mr. Bower?"

"Yes, sir. I've heard all of this before, but I never really paid it any mind. I just figured as long as a person did the best he could, he'd probably get into heaven when he died."

"But if that were true, there wouldn't have been any need for Jesus to die on the cross. Would there?"

Jack blinked. "Well, ah…no. I see your point."

"Good. So, what are you going to do with Jesus Christ?"

Jack's brow furrowed. "What do you mean?"

"Are you going to receive Him or reject Him?"

Jack glanced at Jacob again, then hunched his shoulders. "Reverend, I'm just not ready to make that decision right now."

Kelly looked him straight in the eye. "Are you ready to die right now?"

"No, sir. But I'm not ready to be saved, either. I need some time to think on it. I appreciate your concern. I really do. I just need to think on it."

"Will you come to church Sunday and hear me preach?"

"I just might do that."

"I hope you will."

Kelly closed the Bible and rose to his feet. He shook Jack's hand, then turned to Jacob and said, "Mr. Kates, what do you think about what I just showed Mr. Bower?"

"Pastor Kelly, I am sure Jesus was a good man. But He was not the promised Messiah. My Jewish faith is sufficient for me."

Kelly shook his hand and said, "I want you to know that you have a sincere invitation to attend our services on Sunday. We would love to have you."

"Thank you," said Jacob as he walked Kelly to the door.

Pausing for a moment, Kelly looked back and said, "I appreciate your letting me talk to you, Mr. Bower."

Jack smiled, and the preacher left.

On Sunday morning, Jack Bower and Julianna LeCroix were sitting in church with the Coopers, the O'Briens, the Wessons, and the Williamses. Pastor Andrew Kelly preached a powerful sermon on heaven and hell, pleading with the unsaved to come to Jesus for salvation.

Jack was seated on the aisle with Julianna next to him. He

was unaware of Julianna's conversion and that she was going to be baptized that day. Hannah was in the pew just behind them, holding Larissa.

During the sermon, Julianna could tell that Jack was miserable. She knew the feeling. She had felt the same way when Charles Finney and Kathleen Lindley had talked to her.

By the end of the sermon, Jack Bower was visibly shaken. The preacher had made heaven and hell so real, Jack could almost feel the flames under his feet. When the congregation stood for the invitation and the song was just beginning, Julianna was about to excuse herself to Jack so that she could step into the aisle, when suddenly he was on his way forward.

The pastor was there to greet Jack. Smiling, he took his hand and said, "Mr. Bower, why have you come?"

"Preacher," Jack said, his face pale, "I want to be saved."

Kelly turned him over to one of the male counselors, and Julianna was next to approach him. A female counselor took her to a front pew.

Others had come for various reasons, and soon the man counseling Jack brought him to the pastor. Jack was wiping away tears as Kelly asked, "Did you get it settled, Mr. Bower?"

"I did! And this man showed me that I should be baptized. I want to do that right now."

Elated, Kelly shook his hand. "Well, you just take a seat here on the front row, sir, and we'll take care of it in a few minutes."

When Jack moved toward the pew, he was surprised to see Julianna there. She smiled at him and patted the spot next to her.

The invitation song was still going on.

Jack leaned close to her and said, "Julianna...are you— did you—"

"Yes," she said, smiling at him through misty eyes. "You'll hear about it in a moment."

At the close of the invitation, Pastor Kelly prepared to read the cards that the counselors had filled out for each person who had come forward. When he read Julianna's card, he told of Hannah Cooper's leading her to the Lord, and that Julianna was making public her profession of faith in Christ and presenting herself for baptism.

When Kelly read Jack's name from the card, he told in brief why Jack was in Fort Bridger, and the people's hearts were touched. Moments later, Jack and Julianna were baptized, along with three others.

After the service people came by to shake hands with the new converts and speak words of encouragement. The Coopers, the Williamses, and Abby Turner waited till the line had dwindled, then offered their own words of joy and encouragement, especially to Jack and Julianna.

Gary and Glenda Williams had invited the Coopers, along with Jack, Julianna, and Jacob for Sunday dinner. During the meal, Jacob looked on in puzzlement as the conversation centered on Jack and Julianna being saved. He wondered about the joy everybody seemed to have and why his religion seldom made him feel that way.

When they were eating dessert, Gary looked across the table at Jack and said, "So where will you be going when Doc O'Brien tells you it's all right to travel?"

"Back to Colorado. I've worked off and on for a number of ranchers back there, and that's probably what I'll do again. Stay one place for a while, and when I get tired of that, move on to the next. Maybe one of these days I'll settle down...once I find me a wife."

"Might be good," said Gary, "if you'd just settle down to one job right here in the valley. You do like it here, don't you?"

"Oh, sure. I really do. With a little incentive, I'd seriously consider it. Are there ranchers around who might hire an experienced hand like me?"

"Just might be. That way, with the town growing and new people moving in, you'd stand a pretty good chance of that right woman walking into your life. By 'a little incentive,' do you mean if you had an offer for a full-time job you'd stay?"

"I'd give it serious consideration, Gary," Jack said, nodding. "I sure would."

It was midafternoon. Jack and Jacob were stretched out on their cots in Jacob's quarters. Jack had talked about his newfound faith for a while, then Jacob asked him about his years of drifting from ranch to ranch, picking up work. Jack had just started to tell him about it when he was interrupted by a knock on the door.

Jacob started to get up, but Jack was quickly on his feet. "You just stay there, my friend. It's harder to get up with stitches in your side than in your arm."

When he opened the door, Jack was surprised to see Marshal Lance Mangum, along with Gary Williams and four men he didn't know.

"Jack," said Mangum, "these men make up the town council. We'd like to talk to you."

"Well, sure. Come on in."

The councilmen grabbed chairs from the area by the potbellied stove inside the store and placed them in a half circle in Jacob's room. Before they sat down, Jack was introduced to Mayor Cade Samuels, chairman of the council, and councilmen Lloyd Dawson, Abe Carver, and Justin Powell.

"Jack," said Mangum, "Gary came to me about an hour ago with an idea. You're planning on going back to Colorado as soon as Doc O'Brien says you can travel, right?"

"That's what I've had in mind."

"Gary told me that if you had the proper incentive, job-wise, you'd stay here."

"I said that, yes."

"Good. Now, let me explain something. I went to these men about two months ago and told them that with the growth of the town, I was being stretched too thin in my job. Of late I've been out of town when things happened here and a lawman was needed. Would you agree that's not a good thing?"

"Certainly. I would think you ought to have a deputy marshal to help you."

Mangum grinned, glanced at Gary, and said, "Exactly. I checked with the sheriff of Larimer County, Colorado, to see for sure if a man of your description had actually outdrawn Howie Spence. He confirmed that he had. Even said that it appeared you purposely put him down without killing him."

Jack nodded.

"You mean Spence is still alive, Marshal?" asked banker Lloyd Dawson.

"No. He was murdered by some unknown person or persons while in the clinic in Fort Collins." Turning back to Bower, Mangum said, "I need a deputy who can handle himself, Jack, both with his gun and his fists. Since you outdrew Spence, that settles the gun question. And by the looks of you, I've got a feeling you can use your dukes."

Jack grinned. "I get by."

"We already have the authority from the town to hire a deputy marshal, Mr. Bower," said Cade Samuels. "Job pays sixty a month, and there's a small house coming open you can rent for three dollars a month right here in town. Interested?"

A slow grin crept over Jack Bower's face. "You gentlemen are willing to hire me on what you know about me, then?"

All of them nodded.

Jack looked at Lance Mangum. "Well, Marshal, if you can wait till Dr. O'Brien says it's okay, you've got yourself a new deputy marshal!"

Word spread fast, and in the church service that evening, people told Jack they were glad he was going to be the new deputy marshal.

Hannah and her children were thrilled to know Jack would be staying in Fort Bridger. After church that night, Hannah prepared a snack for Jack, Julianna, Jacob, and her children. Baby Larissa had already been fed, given her steam treatment, and was fast asleep in her crib, snug in a nest of blankets.

When all were seated around the oval table in Hannah's warm, fragrant kitchen, Jacob bowed his head with the others as B. J. prayed over the food.

Hannah had put together cold roast beef and cheese sandwiches with the thick, dark bread Mary Beth had baked on Saturday. For dessert she served dried-peach cobbler with fresh cream, along with coffee for the adults and hot cocoa for the children.

"How soon will you put on a badge, Mr. Bower?" Chris asked.

"I talked to Dr. O'Brien about it at church tonight. He said that since it's my left arm and not my gun arm, I could go to work by Wednesday."

Jacob spoke up. "I'll miss you, Jack. It's been kinda nice having a roommate." He grinned, then said, "Of course, I'll sleep better without all that snoring!"

Everybody laughed.

Mary Beth looked at the young widow and said, "Miss Julianna, I wish you and Larissa didn't have to leave. How many more days can you stay?"

"About a week. Dr. O'Brien wants to be sure Larissa is well before she's subjected to more drafty stagecoaches."

"Couldn't you just stay here till spring?"

Julianna smiled. "Believe me, I would like to. I'm not really looking forward to living in Boise. But I have no choice. My husband's parents are quite wealthy, and they're going to provide for us. I hope to get a job of some kind, just to get out of the house. But that will mean I'll have to find someone to take care of Larissa while I'm working."

"If you were living here, there'd be plenty of people who would be willing to do that," said Chris.

Julianna smiled. "I'm afraid there's a lot more to it than that, Chris. There'd be housing costs and things like that. I simply don't have the money. So Larissa and I must go and live with her grandparents."

On Wednesday morning, Mayor Cade Samuels and the rest of the town council, with Marshal Lance Mangum, gathered in the town hall. Everyone in town knew that Jack Bower was going to be sworn in as Fort Bridger's deputy marshal at nine o'clock and that the public was invited.

Dr. Frank O'Brien was there to assure everyone that Jack was fully capable of handling the job. In attendance, along with about a hundred others, were Hannah Cooper, Julianna LeCroix, and Glenda Williams. Jacob was running the store for Hannah so she could attend. Mary Beth had stayed home from school to watch over Larissa in the Cooper apartment.

The mayor, the marshal, members of the council, and Jack Bower were on the platform. At precisely nine o'clock, Mayor Samuels stood before the council, stating the purpose of the meeting, then called for Marshal Mangum and Jack Bower to stand with him. He called for Dr. O'Brien to give his professional opinion about Bower's wound and his capability of functioning as a lawman. When that was done, O'Brien took a seat in the audience.

Samuels administered the oath while Bower raised his right hand and repeated the words. When the oath had been taken, Samuels shook hands with Bower, welcomed him as deputy marshal of the town of Fort Bridger, then asked Marshal Mangum to pin the badge on him.

There was applause as Marshal Mangum pinned the badge on Jack Bower.

When the meeting was dismissed, people gathered around Jack, wishing him well. Hannah, Glenda, and Julianna waited till last.

That evening, Jack moved into the small furnished house.

Within three more days, little Larissa was doing quite well. Dr. O'Brien told Julianna she could travel by the following Wednesday.

Hannah planned a nice meal for Julianna's final night in the Cooper home and invited Jack and Jacob to join them. Mary Beth had baked a chocolate cake after coming home from school that day, and while everyone was enjoying it, Patty Ruth looked at the young widow across the table and said, "Miss Julianna, can you come back and see us someday? I would like to see what Larissa looks like when she's older."

"I hope we can do that, honey. Larissa and I would love to see all of you again."

Patty Ruth smiled and slipped Biggie a piece of her cake.

"Julianna, could I...could I talk to you in private yet this evening?" Jack asked.

Hannah's heart leaped in her breast.

Julianna smiled. "Of course. Where would you like to talk?"

"You can go down to my room if you want," Jacob said.

"Thank you, Jacob," said Jack. "Would that be all right, Julianna?"

"Certainly."

"Don't worry about Larissa," said Hannah. "Take all the time you need."

Jacob had left a lantern burning in his room. As Jack and Julianna entered, Jack motioned for her to take the chair. When she was seated, he eased onto the cot, facing her.

"Julianna, I—"

"Yes, Jack?" Her heart was pounding.

"I...I can't let you go without telling you something. I know you'll be gone out of my life by nine o'clock tomorrow morning, but I have to tell you that...well, that I'm in love with you."

Julianna bit down on her lower lip. "Jack, I...I have very strong feelings toward you. I found them in my heart even when I thought you were an outlaw."

"Really?"

"Yes."

Jack cleared his throat gingerly. "I know this probably surprises you, Julianna, but I just had to tell you. I know I'm not good enough for you. You're from a wealthy background and are used to a different type of life than I could ever give you. It's only right that you go on to Boise. No doubt you'll find some wealthy Christian man you can marry. I hope you're not angry at me for telling you that I love you."

Julianna was speechless.

"It's only right that you give Larissa a home of luxury to grow up in. I want the best for both of you. Your husband's parents can provide that. I...I'm sorry if I've upset you."

Julianna blinked nervously. "Jack, please don't say you're not good enough for me. That's not true. You're a good man. You've got a good heart. I—"

Julianna was interrupted by a loud knock on the door. Jack opened it and found Lance Mangum with a serious look on his face.

"Jack, I'm sorry to bother you, but there are some trouble-makers at the edge of town. I need you to go with me. Sometimes this kind of thing turns violent."

"Of course." Jack turned to Julianna and said, "Thank you for talking to me. I'll walk you back upstairs and—"

"There's no need for that. The marshal needs you."

Julianna watched the two lawmen dash out the back door of the store; then she closed Jacob's door behind her and headed for the apartment upstairs.

When the children were all in bed asleep, Hannah and her new friend sat down at the kitchen table with some hot tea. Julianna shared with Hannah what had happened between Jack and her in Jacob's room.

"I wish Jack didn't have such a low opinion of himself, Hannah, but there's nothing I can do to change that. He's convinced that I should marry in the social circles I used to move in."

"Julianna, you mentioned that you told Jack you have strong feelings for him."

"Yes, I did."

"But did you tell him you are in love with him?"

"Well, no. We got cut off so quickly."

"But he did tell you he's in love with you?"

"Yes."

"He needs to know that you feel the same way toward him, Julianna."

Julianna brushed away a tear. "There's no way I can see him anymore tonight. But I will tell him at the stage station in the morning."

"You see that you do," said Hannah. "From what you've told me, I think it'll make a big difference."

"I don't know. I'm not sure he can be convinced that he's good enough for me."

Early the next morning, Julianna packed her bags and prepared to resume her journey to an uncertain future. She felt heavy-hearted about it, but she could see no other choice. Maybe once she settled in Boise she could find a good job, and eventually she and Larissa could make it on their own.

If only Jack would ask her to stay in Fort Bridger! She shook her head and set herself to finish packing. The stage would be leaving at nine o'clock. She and Larissa must be on it.

At 8:45, Hannah, Patty Ruth, and Glenda were at the Wells Fargo office to tell Julianna and Larissa good-bye. Hannah was praying in her heart that when Julianna told Jack she was in love with him, he would not let her get on that stage.

Two businessmen had stayed all night at the Uintah Hotel and were set to continue their trip to Evanston. Curly Wesson introduced them to Julianna, then introduced her to driver Cal Springer and shotgunner Red Tipton. He then announced that the stage would be leaving in ten minutes.

Judy came out of the office and hugged Julianna. "Wal, honey, we're gonna miss you an' this sweet li'l thang aroun' here. You come back an' see us."

"We'll sure try, Judy."

"God bless ya, honey."

"You too," said Julianna, letting her gaze drift down the street. She caught a glimpse of Marshal Mangum riding his horse the other direction, but there was no Jack Bower.

Judy returned to the office.

The minutes passed swiftly as Glenda talked to Julianna about finding a good church in Boise. Soon Springer and Tipton were climbing into the box.

"Okay, folks," Curly said to the passengers. "Time to board!"

Julianna hugged Glenda, then Patty Ruth, then Hannah. She was thanking Hannah for all her kindness when Curly stepped up and said, "I'll hold the baby fer ya, Miss Julianna, while ya climb in."

Julianna let him take Larissa, gave a sigh of resignation, and moved toward the coach, even then scanning the street, hoping against hope to see Jack coming her way.

There was no sign of him.

She gave Hannah a despairing look and allowed Curly to use his free hand to assist her aboard. When she was seated, Curly handed her the tiny bundle and said, "Good-bye, Miss Julianna. May the Lord bless ya!"

The businessmen climbed in and sat across from Julianna, and Curly closed the door.

Tears were on Julianna's cheeks as she looked through the window and said, "Good-bye...I love you all."

Cal Springer snapped the reins, and the stage rolled out.

Hannah's tears spilled down her cheeks. *Where was Jack?*

Patty Ruth took hold of her mama's hand and said, "She's such a nice lady, Mama."

"Yes, she is, honey."

"Mama...little Larissa will grow up and be as big as me someday, won' she?"

"That's right."

"An' maybe when Larissa's as big as me, she'll have a frien' like Lucky who'll be across the street, callin' for her to come an' see him. An' if she does, her mama prob'ly won' spank her for that, don' you s'pose?"

Hannah bent over and hugged her little daughter and said, "Not if she'd promise never to do it again."

"Oh, I'm sure Larissa would make that promise, Mama!"

CHAPTER TWENTY-THREE

Julianna LeCroix felt as though her heart would break in two as the stagecoach rolled westward out of Fort Bridger. Why hadn't Jack come to tell her good-bye? He said he was in love with her, and she had read the truth of it in his eyes. Was it because he felt he wasn't good enough for her that he found it too painful to watch the stagecoach carry her out of his life forever?

Julianna had so hoped that when he came to tell her good-bye, and she told him she was in love with him, he would ask her to stay. But now, all hope of that was gone. *Dear Lord,* she said in her heart, *help me! Help me!*

She took out an embroidered handkerchief and dabbed at the tears welling up in her eyes. The two businessmen were looking at her. She gave them a shaky smile.

"Difficult time saying good-bye to someone special?" asked passenger Wiley Stamm.

Julianna sniffed and nodded. "You might say that, Mr. Stamm."

"Is Evanston your final destination, Mrs. LeCroix?" the other man, Darrold Conister, asked.

"No, sir. Larissa and I are going on to Boise, Idaho."

"Oh, I see. Still quite a ways to go yet."

"Yes," she said, lifting the baby from her lap to hold her in an upright position. She sniffed again, letting the tears stream down her face. Larissa put a chubby hand up to Julianna's wet cheek.

Julianna drew the baby close and kissed the top of her head, resolving as she had before that somehow—with the Lord's help now—she would make the best of their life in Boise.

The morning was relatively warm, and the leather curtains were rolled up, giving a full view of the rugged country around them. Julianna held Larissa tight and let her gaze drift past the rolling hills of sagebrush and tumbleweeds to the rugged Uintah Mountains in the southwest. After a few minutes she laid Larissa on her lap once more, and the rocking and swaying of the stage soon lulled the baby to sleep.

Julianna laid her head back against the seat and closed her eyes. She prayed silently, asking the Lord to give her strength for the rest of the journey. *Help me to meet whatever lies ahead of me in Idaho, Lord,* she prayed. *I'm so glad I'm saved and have You to lean on.*

They were about ten miles out of Fort Bridger when above the rumble of pounding hooves and the whir of wheels came the sound of more rumbling hooves and the rattle of a wagon.

Wiley Stamm looked out his window and said, "Wagon coming up behind us. The driver seems to be in a hurry. Looks like he's going to pass us."

Julianna turned and looked out the window to her right, but the approaching wagon was not yet where she could see it.

Darrold Conister was leaning close to Stamm, trying to see the wagon. They heard a shout. Conister blinked and said, "Looks like the man in the wagon is trying to get the driver to stop the stage."

"What on earth for?" remarked Stamm.

"I don't know, but he's wearing a badge! Some kind of lawman!"

Julianna caught sight of the two-horse team that was pulling alongside the stage; then she saw the driver and the sunlight glinting off his badge. Her breaking heart skipped a beat.

"Hey, driver!" Jack shouted a second time, waving his hat.

This time he got the attention of both Cal Springer and Red Tipton.

"Stop, please!" Jack shouted. "I need to talk to one of your passengers!"

"Which one?" came Springer's loud query.

"The lady with the baby!"

The stage was still going full speed. "Mrs. LeCroix!" called the driver, leaning from the box. "Lawman in the wagon wants to talk to you! Okay?"

Fresh tears were filling Julianna's eyes as she called back as loud as she could, "Yes! Yes! Please stop!"

Springer pulled rein, and the stagecoach began to slow down.

"This man wearing the badge must be a very special someone," Darrold Conister said.

"More than I could ever tell you, Mr. Conister," Julianna said.

Jack swung the wagon onto Julianna's side of the coach as it drew to a halt, the morning breeze carrying the dust clouds away. While the team snorted, breathing hard, he jumped out of the wagon and opened the door. "Julianna, would you step out of the coach so I can talk to you, please?"

"Of course, Jack."

Larissa had awakened but was not fussing.

"Here, ma'am," said Wiley Stamm. "I'll hold the baby for you. I'm a grandfather. I can handle it."

Driver and shotgunner looked on from the box as Jack helped Julianna step down and then gripped her by the shoulders. "Julianna, my love for you is too strong," he said, looking into her tear-dimmed eyes. "I can't let you go."

Julianna was trying to find her voice.

Jack went on. "I couldn't bring myself to come and tell you good-bye at the stage office. I couldn't stand the thought of watching you ride out of my life on this stage. I finally told myself that I couldn't let it happen. You told me that you had strong feelings toward me. I figured if there's that much, I really had something to go on. If I could get you to stay in Fort Bridger, I'd have a chance to turn strong feelings into love—the marrying kind of love. I—"

"Jack," she cut in, tears running down her cheeks, "I should have worded it differently. What I meant was that I am in love with you! I don't want the style of life I used to have. I want the kind I can have with you."

Tears now surfaced in Jack's eyes. "You mean it?"

"Yes, with all my heart!"

"Then will you marry me and let me adopt Larissa—after a proper courtship, of course?"

"Yes, I will! And I know Larissa would love to be your little girl."

"Oh, Julianna, you've made me the happiest man in all the world!"

With that, Jack folded Julianna into his strong but gentle arms and kissed her.

As he held on to Julianna's hand, Jack looked up at the crew and said, "Gentlemen, I'm relieving you of two of your passengers. I'll need the lady's luggage."

Red Tipton turned around in his seat and climbed onto the rack. He handed Julianna's luggage to Jack, who placed them in the back of the borrowed wagon. Julianna reached inside the coach, picked up her overnight bag, and handed it to the man she loved.

"I'll get Larissa in a minute," Jack said. "Let me help you into the wagon first."

Jack laid the overnight bag in the wagon bed with the other luggage, folded Julianna in his arms and kissed her again, then helped her climb up to the seat.

He returned to the stage, took the baby from Stamm, thanked him, and closed the door. "You've been very kind, sirs," Jack said to the crew. "Thank you!"

Cal Springer clucked to the six-up team, snapped the reins, and put the stage in motion. He and Tipton waved over their shoulders.

Holding Larissa, Jack moved to the side of the wagon. He tickled her under the chin as he had done many times before and said, "I love you, sweet little girl. Pretty soon you can call me Da-da."

Larissa smiled at him as if to say, "That's all right with me."

Jack handed the baby to her mother, rounded the wagon, and climbed up into the seat. He bent over, kissed the baby again, and said, "I love you, Larissa."

Larissa smiled at him again, stuck her thumb in her mouth, and snuggled against her mother's wildly beating heart.

Jack placed a tender hand on Julianna's cheek, kissed the tip of her nose, and said, "I love Larissa's mommy too. Very, very much."

Julianna smiled. "And Larissa's mommy loves you very, very much, Deputy Marshal Jack Bower."

Jack snapped the reins and swung the wagon around to head back toward Fort Bridger. "Let's go announce our engagement!"

OTHER COMPELLING STORIES BY
AL LACY

Books in the Battles of Destiny series:

☞ *A Promise Unbroken*

Two couples battle jealousy and racial hatred amidst a war that would cripple America. From a prosperous Virginia plantation to a grim jail cell outside Lynchburg, follow the dramatic story of a love that could not be destroyed.

☞ *A Heart Divided*

Ryan McGraw—leader of the Confederate Sharpshooters—is nursed back to health by beautiful army nurse Dixie Quade. Their romance would survive the perils of war, but can it withstand the reappearance of a past love?

☞ *Beloved Enemy*

Young Jenny Jordan covers for her father's Confederate spy missions. But as she grows closer to Union soldier Buck Brownell, Jenny finds herself torn between devotion to the South and her feelings for the man she is forbidden to love.

☞ *Shadowed Memories*

Critically wounded on the field of battle and haunted by amnesia, one man struggles to regain his strength and the memories that have slipped away from him.

☞ *Joy from Ashes*

Major Layne Dalton made it through the horrors of the battle of Fredericksburg, but can he rise above his hatred toward the Heglund brothers who brutalized his wife and killed his unborn son?

☞ *Season of Valor*

Captain Shane Donovan was heroic in battle. Can he summon the courage to face the dark tragedy unfolding back home in Maine?

Books in the Battles of Destiny series (cont.):

☞ *Wings of the Wind*

God brings a young doctor and a nursing student together in this story of the Battle of Antietam.

☞ *Turn of Glory*

Four confederate soldiers lauded for bravery mistakenly shoot General Stonewall Jackson. Driven from the army in shame, they become outlaws…and their friend must bring them to justice.

Books in the Journeys of the Stranger series:

☞ *Legacy*

Can John Stranger bring Clay Austin back to the right side of the law…and restore the code of honor shared by the woman he loves?

☞ *Silent Abduction*

The mysterious man in black fights to defend a small town targeted by cattle rustlers and to rescue a young woman and child held captive by a local Indian tribe.

☞ *Blizzard*

When three murderers slated for hanging escape from the Colorado Territorial Prison, young U.S. Marshal Ridge Holloway and the mysterious John Stranger join together to track down the infamous convicts.

☞ *Tears of the Sun*

When John Stranger arrives in Apache Junction, Arizona, he finds himself caught up in a bitter war between sworn enemies: the Tonto Apaches and the Arizona Zunis.

☞ *Circle of Fire*

John Stranger must clear his name of the crimes committed by another mysterious—and murderous—"stranger" who has adopted his identity.

☞ *Quiet Thunder*

A Sioux warrior and a white army captain have been blood brothers since childhood. But when the two meet on the battlefield, which will win out—love or duty?

☞ *Snow Ghost*

John Stranger must unravel the mystery of a murderer who appears to have come back from the grave to avenge his execution.

Books in the Angel of Mercy series:

☞ *A Promise for Breanna*

The man who broke Breanna's heart is back. But this time, he's after her life.

☞ *Faithful Heart*

Breanna and her sister Dottie find themselves in a desperate struggle to save a man they love, but can no longer trust.

☞ *Captive Set Free*

No one leaves Morgan's labor camp alive. Not even Breanna Baylor.

☞ *A Dream Fulfilled*

A tender story about one woman's healing from heartbreak and the fulfillment of her dreams.

☞ *Suffer the Little Children*

Breanna Baylor develops a special bond with the children headed west on an orphan train.

☞ *Whither Thou Goest*

As they begin their lives together, John Stranger and Breanna Baylor place themselves in danger to help a friend.

☞ *Final Justice*

After Silver Moon's Cheyenne village is destroyed, she lives for revenge. Can Breanna's compassion bring about a change of heart in time to prevent further tragedy?

Books in the Hannah of Fort Bridger series (coauthored with JoAnna Lacy):

☞ *Under the Distant Sky*

Follow the Cooper family as they travel West from Missouri in pursuit of their dream of a new life on the Wyoming frontier.

☞ *Consider the Lilies*

Will Hannah Cooper and her children learn to trust God to provide when tragedy threatens to destroy their dream?

☞ *No Place for Fear*

A widow rejects the gospel until the disappearance of her sons and their rescue by Indians opens her heart to God's love.

Books in the Mail Order Bride series (coauthored with JoAnna Lacy):

☞ *Secrets of the Heart*

Kathleen O'Malley Stallworth is a young widow, and now her wealthy in-laws have taken her daughter from her, claiming she's not fit to be a mother. Can Kathleen find faith and forgiveness as a mail order bride?

☞ *A Time to Love*

After her fiancé deserts her on their wedding day, Linda Forrest travels west to find the life—and the love—God has chosen.

Available at your local Christian bookstore